P9-DTP-736

# THE
# ULTIMATE
# INTERIOR
# DESIGNER

# THE
# ULTIMATE
# INTERIOR
# DESIGNER

*Ruth Pretty*

WARD LOCK

*To my dear husband Bill – for swapping adventures on the high seas*
*for the company of a rather crotchety author*

## ACKNOWLEDGEMENTS

I am deeply indebted to David Hicks for being so extraordinarily generous
with his time and amazing talent and for allowing pictures of his work
to appear in this book.
My heartfelt thanks also to interior designer Stephen Ryan, photographer
John Spragg and everyone at Cassell for their unstinting help.

First published in the UK 1997 by Ward Lock
Wellington House, 125 Strand, London WC2R OBB
A Cassell Imprint

Reprinted 1997
© Text Ruth Pretty 1997
© Illustrations Ward Lock 1997
First paperback edition 1998
Reprinted 1999

Designed by Andrew Shoolbred, Richard Carr and Nick Evans
Illustrations by Nicola Gregory and Valerie Hill
Room plans by Amanda Patton

*Front cover photograph*: Malcom Robertson / Ideal Home /
Robert Harding Syndication

All rights reserved. No part of this publication may be reproduced in any material form (including
photocopying or storing it in any medium by electronic means and whether or not transiently or
incidentally to some other use of this publication) without the written permission of the copyright
owner, except in accordance with the provisions of the Copyright, Designs and Patents Act 1988 or
under the terms of a licence issued by the Copyright Licensing Agency, 90 Tottenham Court Road,
London W1P 9HE. Applications for the copyright owner's written permission to reproduce any part
of this publication should be addressed to the publisher.

Distributed in the United States by Sterling Publishing Co., Inc.
387 Park Avenue South, New York, NY 10016-8810

A British Library Cataloguing in Publication Data block for this book
may be obtained from the British Library

ISBN 0-7063-7463-0 (hbk)
ISBN 0-7063-7736-2 (pbk)

Printed and bound in Spain by
Bookprint S.L., Barcelona

Reprographics by Jade Reprographics Braintree, Essex.

# CONTENTS

# FOREWORD

I am delighted to preface Ruth Pretty's book as, having had her work with me for a considerable time, I know how accomplished an authority she is on the subject of Interior Design and Decoration. With her staunch professionalism she has written and illustrated a very succinct manual of Interior Design. The designs in Ruth's book range from grand to simple, from small to spacious and from disciplined to homely, showing examples which will enable the discerning reader to recognize the styles of various schools of thought.

I have been involved in Interior Design since 1954 and I have seen the whole field of professional Interior Design emerge in such a way that would have been unimaginable forty-two years ago. I am told that I have been a taste-maker, an innovator and that I have changed the taste of my period, but all I have done is to look back to traditional solutions and look forward to new ways of solving a problem or creating a style.

I feel very proud of my profession now that it has become recognized and I rejoice in the number of young, gifted designers who are contributing to the development of style and establishing Great Britain as a centre for the best of Interior Design.

What will come after is impossible to hazard, but I am certain that the limitless invention of the artistic, creative mind will produce exciting new ideas. I shall, no doubt, be looked upon as very demodé any minute now, but I am happy to have been able to enjoy creating rooms, hotels, restaurants, gardens, furniture, carpets and fabrics that seemed right for four decades. I will never lose my critical eye for the work of contemporaries or the young and I shall follow the next movements and trends with the greatest interest.

To see is to understand, but alas! – too few are visually aware.

David Hicks

*Chairs covered in a brilliant parma violet fashion leather from France bring an exciting and unusual colour accent into a predominantly neutral interior, as designed by David Hicks.*

# INTRODUCTION

'Every design decision is an opportunity, not a problem!' – not an easy dictate to follow when your house is in chaos, your partner is asking for the umpteenth time when it will all be over and when every item of clothing you own is covered in a thick layer of dust. However, if you can keep this phrase at the forefront of your thinking, decorating will once again become the pleasurable process it should be.

It is so easy to lose sight of the purpose of interior design and for the whole process to become a major worry. Will the new carpet wear well? Does it go with the sofa? How deep should the curtain pelmet be and what sort of lighting is needed in a dining room? Mistakes are likely to be expensive or at the very least embarrassing and, rather than failing, many people opt for a less-than-exciting choice or for making no decision at all.

It is with just such questions in mind that this book has been written and it is hoped that the contents will tempt even the most timid to 'jump in' and have a go. Perhaps the most comforting aspect is that very often there is no wrong or right way of doing things – just degrees of appropriateness, and so long as the results are pleasing to you, the decision can be deemed to have been successful.

I grew up in an age when interior design as a profession was in its infancy and the consensus seemed to be that it should be practised only by those with something called flair. True, a creative talent is of great benefit to the designer, but, like riding a bicycle, design is a skill that can be learned and, with practise, performed successfully – with or without flair!

*The shape of the spiral stairway is reflected in the cabinet at its base and the walls are given interest by means of a painted rustication finish.*

The actual process of decorating can become a thoroughly enjoyable one too. Once the method of arriving at decisions has been simplified and the design process has been divided into 'bite-sized' portions which follow a logical pattern, the whole thing becomes more manageable and, with everything under control, it is possible to have the most enormous amount of fun.

Decorating is also a great adventure. No designer, however experienced, knows in advance precisely how a room will take to its new dressing – and there is always that tantalizing moment when the last few components are put into place before the exact result is known. Because no two rooms are entirely the same, even the professional designer is sometimes surprised by the results, and what works in one room may not in another. But experimentation is part of the thrill of decorating and few errors of judgement are beyond reprieve, often requiring little more than the juggling of furnishings or an additional coat of paint to put right.

Style is an area of great debate and choosing one for your home can cause dreadful dilemmas. Ideally it should be formed from a combination of the innate style of the building and a reflection of the owner's taste rather than from the current opinion of the interior design press or what a previous owner has thought fit. Several style ideas have been included in this book to inspire you and to set you off on your journey of discovery.

Interior design is not important in the scheme of life. We can surely get by without it and there are unquestionably much weightier subjects to involve us. Yet it can be the source of immeasurable pleasure and satisfies that very vital force of nest building that is in all of us.

Enjoy!

# How to Use This Book

To help you find your way around this book, the various aspects of interior design have been divided into three main sections, **Part I: The Designer's Approach**, **Part II: Room-by-Room Decorating** and **Part III: Style**, each of which is meant to be referred to in conjunction with the other parts of the book.

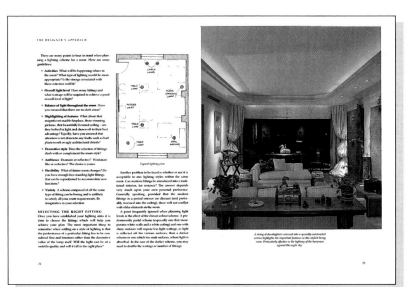

**The Designer's Approach** covers the main principles of design and how to apply them to any decorating project that you may be contemplating – whether you are attempting to refurbish a whole house or simply want to give one room a face-lift. You are also taken through the various stages, in sequence, that a designer follows when undertaking an interior design contract. Professional tips on the treatment of space, light, colour, pattern and texture are all dealt with and practical hints are given on how to draw room plans, assemble a scheme and mount materials on a sample board.

For help on how to approach the decoration of a particular room, turn to **Room-by-Room Decorating**, where you will find suggestions on how to meet special requirements of each room in a typical home. You will find here advice on such general topics as lighting, storage and furniture arrangements as well as hints on the selection of suitable wall and floor finishes.

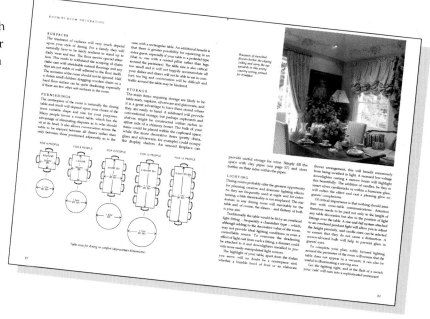

The section on **Room-by-Room Decorating** also features three variations of each room type, for example 'Dedicated Dining', 'Family Dining' and 'Occasional Dining'. In each case a photograph of an actual room is shown and, with the help of a coloured visual, the room is analysed and conclusions are drawn as to the design principles employed by the creator of the room. A plan demonstrating how the furnishings in the rest of the room could be arranged is also suggested.

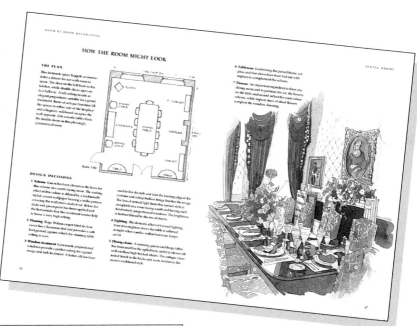

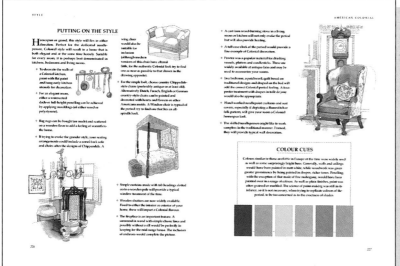

Settling on a suitable style for your home can pose quite a problem. The section entitled **Style** is included for inspiration. The first part deals with period pieces – styles with more than a hint of history (or a peek into the future) – and the second with styles possessing an international flavour. The background to each style is discussed and this is followed by a breakdown of materials that might be incorporated in such a scheme. The last part of each chapter is taken up with practical tips on how the style might be easily introduced into your own home today and a colour swatch is featured to inspire your colour schemes.

**EXAMPLE**

You are seeking advice on how to decorate a traditionally-styled formal dining room and are particularly concerned about lighting:

1. Look up **Dining Rooms** in Part II (Room-by-Room Decorating)

2. Read the section on **Dedicated Dining** – also in Part II

3. Consult the chapter on **Lighting** in Part I (The Designer's Approach)

4. Turn to **Period Pieces** in Part III for style inspiration

# THE DESIGNER'S APPROACH

# Space

One of the questions a professional designer is most often asked is: 'Just where do I start?' Without a doubt, you start here – with the space. It is not until you have organized the structure enclosing the space that you can begin to decide upon the finishes – the wallpapers, fabrics and furnishings.

Internationally renowned interior designer David Hicks defines an interior *decorator* as 'someone who specializes in creating new decorative schemes using existing furniture, objects and interior spaces'. He describes an interior *designer* as 'a professional who creates entirely new interiors by remodelling, commissioning new furniture and adding architectural detail'.

What makes many of us shy away from becoming designers is probably a combination of the regard in which we hold what someone else has deemed to be appropriate in the past and a fear of the irreversibility of structural changes. The dent in the decorating budget that structural works are likely to inflict also acts as a deterrent. But to dismiss all aspirations to mould an interior to our own needs for such misguided reasons would be to limit the opportunities offered by a given space. By reshaping an interior we are taking creativity to its logical conclusion and, in many cases, it is by adjusting the three-dimensional qualities that we can produce a space that is both aesthetically pleasing and that works for us. Structural alterations are something that held few fears for our ancestors – you have only to examine one of our finer old houses to discover any number of amendments and extensions which, because they happened so many years ago (when preservation orders were unknown) and are weathered in, are now considered admirable.

When you purchase a new house, there is little chance that your lifestyle or household coincides with that of the previous owners. Much better, then, to divert a portion of the decorating budget towards adapting the structure of the property to meet your needs and your taste and rather less towards surface treatments and furnishings which can always be gradually be built up in the years to come. Although not possible in every case, it is a great idea to live in a new house for some months before finalizing any decisions on radical changes. In that time you will experience the house's shortcomings and can judge just what you can and cannot live with.

It is just so tempting to dive in and start looking at fabrics and paint charts before any of the planning has taken place – I even know of some professionals who simply can't resist the temptation to finger fabric samples at the mere mention of a new commission – but it really does pay dividends to do things the right way around.

When designers are planning a project, they follow a very specific sequence:

1  They examine and change, if necessary, the *structure*.
2  They plan the arrangement of the *furniture*.
3  They plan the *lighting*.
4  They select the *scheme*.

The order of these stages is quite specific, each operation logically following on from the completion of the previous one. For example, it is not possible to arrange the positioning of light fittings before you have planned where the furniture is going to be sited and it would be quite illogical to choose upholstery textiles when you are not sure how many seats your room will accommodate.

There are many reasons why you might want to change the structure of your house in some way:

◆ **New room use** You may wish to convert an existing guest bedroom to a dressing room.

◆ **Change of lifestyle** Perhaps your new job requires you to entertain a lot at home, so you decide to join up a sitting room and a study to form a spacious dining room.

◆ **Additions to the household** A new baby is expected, so you determine to build an extension to accommodate a playroom.

◆ **Proportions need correction** Would the removal of a picture rail improve the division of space within your drawing room?

◆ **You wish to give character** The addition of a cornice may make your dining room more interesting.

◆ **Natural light is insufficient** By enlarging a window you might make a dark corridor more inviting.

The problem may require major surgery or could possibly be solved by doing something as simple as rehanging a door on the opposite axis.

Before deciding upon individual room treatments, it is a good idea to make sure that you have the rooms you need, that they are of the right size and that they are in the right place. A sketch (roughly to scale) of a floor plan for each floor together with the overall measurements of each room should help to throw up any fundamental problems – such as the dining room being too remote from the kitchen or there being too little space for a decent-sized living room for the family. It might also suggest some solutions – like how a small bedroom might be joined to an adjacent larger bedroom to form an en-suite bathroom. Once you have allocated each room to its purpose, it is time to deal with the rooms individually.

Drawing up room plans is where most designers start in their quest to achieve a workable space. This allows them to explore the possibilities of the space and to come to terms with its limitations. Professional plans are expertly drafted and tend to look highly technical – beyond the scope of most amateurs – but are, in their most basic form, simply a way of communicating ideas in a graphic medium. In other words, they don't have to be works of art so long as they say what you want to say.

Much rests on your ability to draw and understand simple plans. You can indicate to your builder any amendments you wish to make to the structure,

you can calculate where to place items of furniture and you can also work out the ideal lighting plan for your electrician to interpret. The comforting fact is that it is extremely easy to learn how to draw simple room plans – and, after the first one, they get easier!

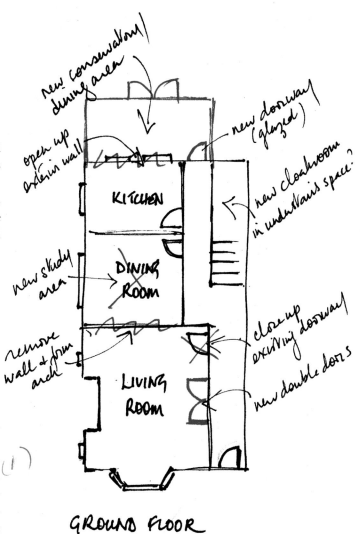

*Sketch floor plan showing proposed extension.*

## ROOM PLANS MADE EASY
The first stage involves drawing a rough sketch of the outline of the room. Try mentally to strip the room of all its embellishments and concentrate on the

structure itself. Next measure the lengths of walls, projections and recesses and mark these on your drawing where appropriate. To double-check that you have the correct measurements, add together the individual lengths of features and see if they equate to the total wall length.

To complete your survey record, note details of the following:

- ceiling height;

- height, width and position of windows;

- height, width and swing of doors;

- services (gas point, radiators, plumbing, light switches and so on);

- room orientation (does it face north, south, east or west?);

- architectural features (dado, niche, arch, floor-level change, sloping ceiling and so on);

- existing finishes (type, material, colour and condition).

Now it is time to start the finished drawing. To be of any use this needs to be to scale – that is, an exact replica of the room's shape, but in miniature. The easiest way to do this is to use finely squared graph paper, which is available from most stationers. The conversion ratio of your larger measurements into this small-scale drawing will depend upon the gauge of the squared paper. A useful size has large squares of 2cm and smaller ones of 2mm. Based on this example, you can calculate that one small square equals 10cm/4in, which should allow you to fit the average-sized room com-

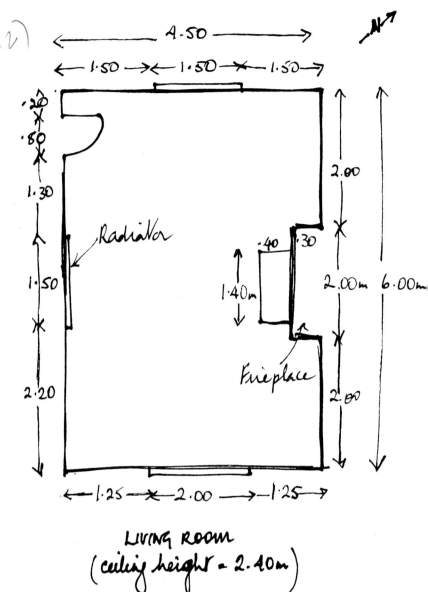

*Survey sketch for room plan.*

fortably on a sheet of A4 paper and will be equal to a scale of 1:50 – that is, your drawing is one-fiftieth of the actual size of your room. On this basis, if your measurement is 30cm/12in, you will draw a line three small squares long, and so on.

On the finished to-scale outline you can now add the positions of radiators and other services, the ceiling height measurement and an arrow to indicate which way faces north. Write in the room title and a note of the scale you have used (just as you might find on a map) and the plan is finished. Other details of your survey record can be written on an attached sheet.

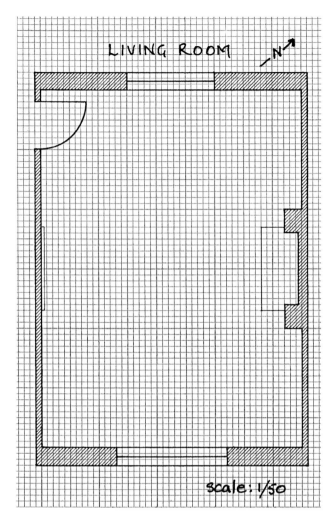

*Finished drawing of room plan to scale (here shown reduced).*

## MAKING THE BEST OF A ROOM ③

Now that you have an accurate record of the structure of your room, you can see, in a very graphic way, just what the problems are and how you can improve its proportions and features. Make these adjustments now and decorating the room will simply be a matter of dressing the surfaces.

It is very helpful at this stage if you take a good hard look at each room you are attempting to refurbish. What are the room's qualities – a classic cornice, a stunning period fireplace or perhaps a beautifully shaped window? List these and then go on to consider and list any unattractive characteristics the room possesses. Is the ceiling too low? Do you need more

space for the activities you have planned? And is the window positioned too near the corner of the room? The two lists will provide you with the starting point for your plans. It is from these lists that you will be able to decide what to highlight and what to change or disguise.

Here are a few problem-solving ideas you might like to adopt:

◆ A cupboard door opening out into a limited area – say, a corridor – can be split and made into double doors so that, when opened, they take up half the space.

◆ Storage that is built in can be disguised by treating cupboard fronts (and sides, if any) in exactly the same way as the surrounding walls and by continuing any architectural details (skirting/base board, cornice and so on) along their length and sides (see below).

◆ The appropriate use of mirror can visually double the size of a room. Sheet mirror above a fireplace can be a cheap alternative to a framed one. Ensure that the verticals coincide with the uprights of the fire surround, not the mantle shelf ends.

◆ In an asymmetrical room, box out wall recesses to match existing features (these can form useful storage areas too).

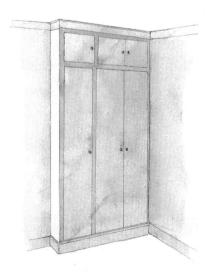

*Fitted cupboard details that follow those of the structure.*

- Doors are frequently swung on an inconvenient side. To ease the flow of human traffic and to get the best view on entering a room, it is preferable for the door to swing back against a nearby wall rather than into the room space.

- A disused fireplace can be brought back to life to give a room character and to form a focal point. Where no fireplace exists, a faux chimney breast can be created by forming a projection and attaching a fire surround.

- Make an aesthetically inconvenient door 'disappear' by converting it into a jib door – that is, by treating it in exactly the same way as the adjacent walls, skirting/base board and all.

- To give a bathroom a less clinical look, install a concealed built-in cistern to the WC. The disguise can be completed by placing a commode chair over the pan.

- When applying mirror to walls to create the illusion that the room is double in size, remember to exclude skirtings/ base boards and cornices or the effect will be negated. A checker-board flooring should end on half a square for the same reason. Equally, furnishings (tables, light fittings and so on) should be only half-size too, so that when reflected in the mirror they appear whole (see below).

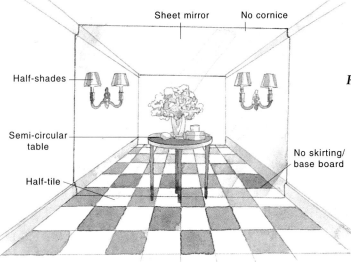

Half-shades

Semi-circular table

Half-tile

Sheet mirror   No cornice

No skirting/ base board

Always remember, if you are proposing to make any major structural changes, it is important that you consult a professional (architect/surveyor/builder) to ensure that your ideas are feasible, within building regulations and safe to undertake.

## VISUALLY CHANGING SPACE

Up to this point the discussion has been about how to improve rooms by physical means. In some cases, however, it may be possible to change the appearance of the structure by visual means – a preferable option if it involves less disruption and can be achieved at a smaller cost. Many problems can be overcome by the clever use of architectural details, colours and lighting. Alternatively the eye can be diverted from less attractive features simply by drawing attention to other highlighted details – for instance, by hanging prominent paintings on a badly plastered wall. Some suggestions are given below and on pages 20–1 on visually correcting proportions in unsatisfactory areas.

### Room Too Small

- Use light, cool, 'receding' colours on all surfaces.

- Incorporate mirrors wherever appropriate.

- Select furnishings that blend in with the background colours of the room.

- Scaling down the size of furniture will not necessarily help, but using less of it will.

### Room Too Big

- Select large-scale furniture.

- Treat the room as having separate areas by arranging the furniture and lighting in several 'conversation' groupings.

- Use dark, warm, 'advancing' colours on the walls and/or ceiling.

*Mirror used to increase the feeling of space in a small room.*

*High-gloss corn-coloured walls and a ceiling in the same finish provide surfaces that,
together with a full-height mirror, enhance the feeling of space in this city bathroom.*

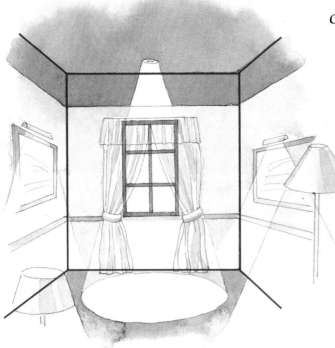

*Room proportions widened by the clever use of colour and light.*

*Dark, vertically striped wallpaper gives the illusion of height in this low-ceilinged room.*

### Ceiling Too High

◆ Emphasize the horizontals by installing picture rails, dados, Venetian blinds, wall trims and so on.

◆ Draw attention to the lower portion of the room by concentrating features there and by directing light to that part of the room.

◆ Use darker colours in the upper areas of the room. The ceiling colour, for instance, could be brought down to picture-rail height.

◆ Use light cool colours on the walls to allow the room to open out.

### Ceiling Too Low

◆ Emphasize the verticals with striped wallpaper, full-length curtains and so on.

◆ Disguise the horizontals – paint out or remove dado and picture rails.

◆ Use light colours on the floor and ceiling and darker shades on the walls.

◆ Use a reflective finish on the ceiling (for example, gloss paint) to give the room height.

### Long Corridor

◆ Break up the length of the corridor with a structural arch.

◆ Visually shorten the length with flooring in a horizontal or trellis pattern.

◆ Create 'pools' of light (perhaps from down-lighters) at intervals along the corridor length to add interest.

◆ Install a focal point at the end of the corridor to 'stop the eye'.

◆ Apply 'advancing' colours at either end of the corridor.

◆ Select 'receding' colours for the side walls to expand the width.

◆ Add plenty of mirror to 'push out' the walls and bring light to the area.

◆ Break up wall expanses with paintings, mirrors, console tables, chairs and so on. In a very narrow corridor where there is insufficient space for full-sized furniture, a shelf supported by two corbels might be formed with a mirror above.

## ARRANGING THE FURNITURE

Have you ever ordered a sofa that looked fine in the shop, only to get it home to discover that it swamped your room? It is a very easy mistake to make: the sofa was originally seen as small, relative to the large space of the store, but when placed in the relatively smaller space of your living room it appeared pro-portionally bigger. Now that you have your room plan, however, you will be able to place the sofa to scale on the drawing to gauge its impact before you make your purchase.

Mistakes are also easy to make when arranging furniture – mainly because of the lack of planning. You may find the following check list helpful:

◆ What activities will take place in the room (for example, dining, watching television, letter writing, bathing)?

*Pale floor, walls and ceiling, a half-mirrored jib door and vertically striped wallpaper all help to bring space, light and a sense of order to this 'impossible' corridor.*

◆ What furniture will each activity require (for instance, desk, side table, arm chair)?

◆ How much space will each function require?

◆ What are the associated storage requirements (for example, bookcase, dressing table, record rack, desk)?

◆ How will the human traffic circulate through the room?

Listing all of the above will help you to finalize your arrangements.

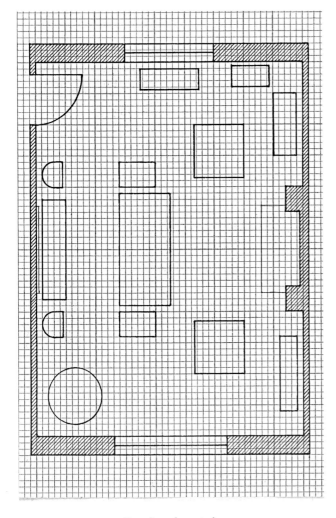

*Furniture layout plan.*

Physically moving your furniture around the room is one way to decide upon the most suitable arrangement, but it can be a little tiring and, in any case, the furniture may not be to hand at the time of making your plans. A much better way to configure where items are best placed is to draw them to scale on your room plan. Useful in this regard are stencils which feature common interior furnishings. These are available from most drawing office suppliers – but do remember to buy one that is compatible with the scale of your drawing. An alternative way of planning your furniture layout is to make card cutouts of the items you intend including (also to scale) and moving them around until you have a happy arrangement.

### Ten Tips on Arranging Furniture

1 A three-seater sofa rarely accommodates three people happily. Instead consider ordering a three-seater, but have it made up with two seat cushions.

2 If you choose furnishings with colours that closely match their intended background, the items will effectively disappear, leaving the room with a much less cluttered appearance: for instance, a beige sofa against a beige carpet and beige walls. If you wish a piece of furniture to stand out, this effect can be acheived by choosing furnishings in a contrasting colour.

3 In a dining room don't forget to allow enough space around the table, taking into account the need to pass behind a chair that is in use. A minimum space of approximately 90cm/3ft between a table and a wall will be required for comfort.

4 In a kitchen, wall units that extend all the way up to the ceiling will eliminate an obvious dust trap – an arrangement that will also provide extra long-term storage.

5 Stools and poufs are useful for occasional seating in a living room. They take up little space and can sometimes incorporate storage space in their base.

6 When designing wardrobes, be careful to allow sufficient depth for coat hangers – 60cm/2ft should accommodate most. Also, ensure that rails are at an accessible height.

7 Try to arrange furnishings so that people entering the room are greeted by a pleasant view.

8 Kitchen units and vanity units should have recessed plinths to make it possible to stand close to the work surface/basin.

9 When ordering furniture, consider access to the house. Calculate in advance just how various items can be moved into position (this may involve removal of a window or hiring a crane for cumbersome pieces).

10 Storage! Storage! Storage!

# Lighting

For far too long lighting has been bracketed with accessories in the overall scheme of decorating – an afterthought to pretty-up a room once all the real business of designing has been completed. But lighting is far too precious an asset to misuse in this way. If it is given too little thought, all the effort put into selecting expensive fabrics, stylish furniture and radiant colours is wasted. Utilized properly, it can double the value of all those elements – the colours, shapes, patterns and textures – that you have included in your scheme.

In the past it was considered extremely daring to rely upon any fittings beyond that wonderful thing which dangled from a rose in the centre of the ceiling; that most ugly and in-the-way of lights, the standard lamp; and the odd table lamp the size of (and frequently the shape of) a melon. The result too often was that the room took on a flat one-dimensional quality, it felt unwelcoming and even a simple task such as sewing was impossible in anything other than daylight.

These days we have no excuses. The range and sophistication of fittings available, principally as a result of developments in the commercial world of shopfitting, gallery illumination and stage lighting, allow us to recreate in our own homes the most magical of effects. We should think of lighting as a wonderful tool that can bring our rooms to life; a magic pot of light into which we are going to dip our brush – only to drop it in pools around the room.

## THE PURPOSE OF LIGHTING

Not only will a well-planned lighting scheme make rooms appear more generally pleasing but, more importantly, the correct lighting will facilitate the various activities carried out in any given room. Whether we want to write letters, cook or apply make-up – all these tasks will be helped if undertaken in appropriate lighting conditions.

Judicious use of light will also dictate exactly what our eyes will alight upon in a room (and, as a consequence, direct our eyes away from any less well-lit areas). This is where your list of all the best and least attractive features of the room (see page 17) will prove useful. With light you will be able to pinpoint and highlight all that is most appealing in the room and distract attention away from any faults.

An aspect of lighting frequently overlooked is its ability to help engender a certain mood. Whether your desire is to create drama at a dinner party or a restful ambience in a bedroom, it is by the careful selection of bulbs, shades and fittings that this can be achieved.

Only after considering these points is it advisable to select the actual fittings for the scheme. They will form part of the overall design and therefore offer an opportunity to reaffirm your chosen room style. A brass lantern in a Georgian hallway (see 'Georgian Style', page 186), a streamlined wall uplighter in an Art Deco living room (see 'Art Deco Style', page 204), or a tiffany lamp in a Victorian bedroom (see 'Art Nouveau Style', page 198) are all embellishments to evoke a special time and place.

## PLANNING A LIGHTING SCHEME

One of the snags, when it comes to planning a lighting scheme, is that so often we are faced with decisions on the supply of electrical lighting circuits and the positioning of sockets and switches long before we have even decided on the allocation of the room space, never mind selection of the schemes. This is where the room plan (see page 15) comes into play. Once the furniture is shown on the plan (without so much as a sofa side table being moved), we can see exactly how many light points, circuits and sockets will be needed and their best positions. Nothing is more aesthetically displeasing or as dangerous as an electric socket with multiple adapters and cables trailing spaghetti-like across the floor, so it clearly pays to think ahead.

There are many points to bear in mind when planning a lighting scheme for a room. Here are some guidelines:

◆ **Activities** What will be happening where in the room? What type of lighting would be most appropriate? Is the storage associated with these activities well lit?

◆ **Overall light level** How many fittings and what wattage will be required to achieve a good overall level of light?

◆ **Balance of light throughout the room** Have you ensured that there are no dark areas?

◆ **Highlighting of features** What about that magnificent marble fireplace, those stunning pictures, that beautifully beamed ceiling – are they bathed in light and shown off to their best advantage? Equally, have you ensured that attention is not drawn to any faults such as bad plasterwork or ugly architectural details?

◆ **Decorative style** Does the selection of fittings clash with or complement the room style?

◆ **Ambience** Dramatic or reflective? Workman-like or seductive? The choice is yours.

◆ **Flexibility** What of future room changes? Do you have enough free-standing light fittings that can be repositioned to accommodate new functions?

◆ **Variety** A scheme composed of all the same type of fitting can be boring and is unlikely to satisfy all your room requirements. Be imaginative in your selection.

## SELECTING THE RIGHT FITTING

Once you have established your lighting aims it is time to choose the fittings which will help you achieve your plan. The most important thing to remember when settling on a style of lighting is that the performance of a particular fitting has to be considered first and foremost rather than the decorative value of the lamp itself. Will the light cast be of a suitable quality and will it fall in the right place?

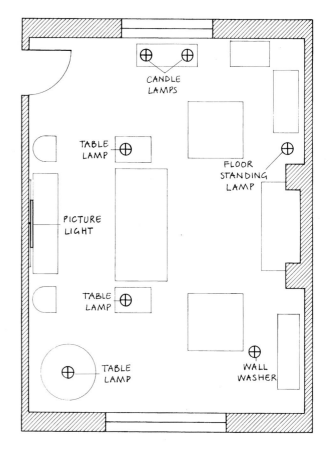

*Typical lighting plan.*

Another problem to be faced is whether or not it is acceptable to mix lighting styles within the same room. Can modern fittings be introduced into a traditional interior, for instance? The answer depends very much upon your own personal preference. Generally speaking, provided that the modern fittings in a period interior are discreet (and preferably recessed into the ceiling), these will not conflict with older elements in the room.

A point frequently ignored when planning light levels is the effect of the chosen colour scheme. A predominantly pastel scheme (especially one that incorporates white walls and a white ceiling) and one with shiny surfaces will require less light wattage, as light is reflected off the various surfaces, than a darker scheme or one which has matt surfaces, where light is absorbed. In the case of the darker scheme, you may need to double the wattage or number of fittings.

*A string of downlighters recessed into a specially constructed cornice highlights the important features in this stylish living room. Particularly effective is the lighting of the horseman against the night sky.*

## TYPES OF FITTINGS

There are many types of fittings available, and these are categorized below.

### Ceiling Lights

Ceiling lights can be classified as: traditional pendant, chandelier, fluorescent strip, lantern, spot, downlighter and wall washer, the last three of which may be recessed, surface-mounted or track-mounted.

A useful source of 'overall' lighting, the pendant is probably the most common of all fittings. It tends to cast a rather 'deadening' light, but this can be overcome by installing a dimmer switch so that your scheme does not rely so entirely on this one source but on others dotted around the room. Spotlights, downlighters and wall washers can provide a wonderfully focused beam to highlight precious pieces, but care must be taken to avoid glare from the bulb (especially in low-ceilinged rooms). The selection of bulb is critical – the colour of light produced and width of beam vary enormously.

### Wall Lights

Wall lights may take the form of: traditional bracket, uplighter, downlighter, picture light, striplight or angle-arm.

Modern or traditional, they can be chosen to throw light up, down or out. There are various theories about what is the best height for positioning wall fittings, but as a rule eye-level (say, around 1.5m/5ft) is a good starting point. Because of their prominent positioning, care should be taken to select fittings that are attractive in themselves. Picture lights, on the other hand, should be as unobtrusive as possible, blending with the picture frame. By attaching the picture light to the frame itself (rather than to the wall) and running a cable behind the picture to a small wall socket, you will have greater flexibility should you decide to substitute the current picture for one of a different size.

*The performance of different ceiling light fittings.*

*The performance of different wall light fittings.*

*The performance of different floor and table fittings.*

### Floor/Table Lamps

The floor/table lamp category covers such fittings as the standard lamp, uplighter, table lamp, desk lamp and Angle-poise.

As these lights are not fixed to floor, wall or ceiling, they offer the greatest degree of flexibility. The traditional standard lamp has come of age – it is now available in a streamlined version, usually made of brass and with a weighted base for stability. Some types even have a telescopic stem, which allows the height to be adjusted – an altogether ideal lamp for use where there is little space and no convenient table upon which to stand a lamp. Table lamps provide a convenient source of decorative lighting, while at the same time introducing a soft (filtered by the shade) pool of light. What better way to illuminate a group of related objects or a flower arrangement on a table top?

## MODERN FITTINGS

Lighting has undergone a revolution in the past twenty years. Unfortunately lighting manufacturers have not been so successful in educating their customers in how to take advantage of these exciting developments. It is perceived that only the professional designer is equipped to benefit from these technological advances and that they are quite beyond the humble home owner – but nothing could be further from the truth. The fittings may have changed, but just as we learned about the performance of low-tech lights, we can also come to understand how the latest models work. Perhaps the most intimidating factor to come to terms with is the sheer quantity and variety of fittings, added to which the multitude of bulbs can easily confuse. To help simplify matters the basic groupings are listed below.

### Downlighters

As its name suggests, a downlighter directs a beam of light downwards, thus focusing attention on the lower part of the room (a useful tool when you wish to distract attention from a too-high ceiling). The width of beam – narrow and intense or wide (flood) – depends upon the lamp and reflector installed, so the one fitting can be made to perform in various ways. Downlighters may be surface-fixed (to ceiling, wall or track), semi-recessed (where there is limited space above the ceiling) or fully recessed (preferable if you wish to 'lose' the fitting).

### Uplighters

Uplighters can come in the form of free-standing models for floor or table as well as pendant and wall-fixed versions. As you might imagine, they produce the opposite effect from that of a downlighter – that is, they direct light upwards. They are especially effective when used to illuminate a beautiful beamed or decorative ceiling. A free-standing model, placed on the floor or on a table (miniature versions are available), can be used successfully to cast a beam of light on an adjacent wall – invaluable for lighting pictures when picture lights and wall washers are not a practical alternative.

*Downlighters above the vanity unit yield extra value when reflected in the many polished surfaces of this marble bathroom.*

## Wall washers

A wall washer is a type of downlighter which, instead of directing light immediately below the fitting, casts a beam of light to the side. Positioned in a ceiling at approximately 1m/3ft 4in away from an adjacent wall, it will flood that wall with light. Where you need to light a large wall hanging or collection of pictures, this fitting would provide the perfect answer.

## Spotlights

Perhaps more popular in the past when it was considered fashionable for such fittings to be visible and very much part of the scheme, the use of spotlights in modern residential interiors has somewhat declined and they have been superseded by more discreet fittings. However, they are an excellent highlighting tool and, being highly directional, allow you to change your lighting arrangement as the room use changes.

## Low-voltage Fittings

Low-voltage fittings are widely used and with good reason. The voltage is reduced by means of a transformer, thus making them much more economical to run. Because of the voltage reduction, the fittings themselves can be miniaturized – very useful where it is not desirable for the fittings to show or there is a limited cavity into which to recess the lights.

Low-voltage fittings can cast an extremely bright, tight and cool beam and are therefore excellent for highlighting displays. On the negative side there is, of course, the additional cost of a transformer and resulting labour charges for installation. Locating the transformer may also present a problem as this has to be positioned within a specified distance. Depending on the voltage several fittings may work off one transformer, and many lights now have the transformer actually incorporated into the fitting itself (though this naturally defeats some of the benefits of miniaturization). The one important thing to remember is that the transformer may at some time in the future require maintenance, so it pays to locate it in an easily accessible position.

Lamps (bulbs) for these fittings are expensive to buy, but because of their longevity are more economical. Never touch the lamp with your bare hands – this causes it to blacken and reduces its life span. The fittings also tend to 'glitter' and, unless this is a desired effect, it is better to choose ones that have the bulb well recessed into the fitting or have a 'lid' to shield the glare. Because of the isolation of the fitting by the use of a transformer, they are a much safer option in bathrooms and kitchens.

If all the above sounds just too complicated, do not despair. A good lighting shop should have on its staff at least one expert who can help you with your lighting queries. If you are able to show them a room plan with furniture drawn in, plus details of any existing electrical installations, this should be of enormous help.

*Focused downlighters 'mould' the shapes of an eclectic table-top grouping while pictures above are highlighted by picture lights.*

## SELECTING SWITCHES, SOCKETS, LAMPS AND SHADES

### Switches

◆ The ideal position for switches to all the lights in a room is at the entrance, so as to avoid the inconvenience of having to find your way around the room in the dark in order to switch on individual lamps. Equally, this arrangement allows you simply to switch everything off upon leaving the room.

◆ The generally accepted height for a wall light switch is at about 1.4m/4ft 6in, but you might like to consider placing the switch plate at a height of about 90cm/3ft. This will result in the switch being nearer normal hand height and will be less intrusive of the wall space. Also, not being at eye level, it will be less noticeable, especially if it can be neatly tucked in above or just below a dado rail.

*Clear acrylic switch plate.*

◆ The average room may contain a number of different fittings. Having these connected to several different circuits (switches) provides the flexibility to illuminate just a few of the lights or, by turning on more switches, to illuminate all the lights.

◆ Try to choose a style of switch plate to go with your scheme wherever possible. If in doubt, install an anonymous-looking clear acrylic one. This will hide the workings while at the same time allowing the wall finish to show through.

◆ Two-way switches are a most useful device. They allow you to switch a light on from one position and off from another. They are particularly suitable for any connecting areas, such as corridors and stairways, and an absolute 'must' for any newly refurbished bedroom (unless you enjoy leaping out of bed last thing at night!).

◆ Attaching a dimmer switch to the circuit will allow you to control the brightness of light – particularly apt for living rooms, dining rooms and bedrooms. The mood can be changed at the touch of a switch!

### Sockets

◆ Always plan for more sockets than you currently need. Over recent years our requirements have increased enormously – who knows what new gadgets we will be using next year?

◆ Wherever practical, install double sockets. They cost pence more than single ones and installation costs may be no more.

◆ By selecting plugs and cables that vaguely match the colours of your decor you will help to eliminate them from view.

◆ To disguise socket plates more effectively, paint them to match your wall decor (use oil-based paint at least for the first coat).

◆ For free-standing lamps located in the centre of a room, a socket installed in the floor will avoid the problem of trailing cables to an adjacent wall. Fitted flush and covered with a hinged plate, this will be invisible when not in use.

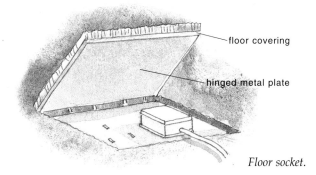

floor covering

hinged metal plate

*Floor socket.*

*Natural daylight, enhanced by full-height mirrors, floods into this south-facing white living room, highlighting its many textures.*

## Lamps

◆ In decorator speak, bulbs are referred to as lamps. They come in dozens of different styles and have two main types of fitting caps: ES (Edison screw) and bayonet.

◆ As a general rule it is preferable for the lamp in a fitting to be shielded from view (candle-type lamps being an exception). It can be extremely irritating and very distracting to be blinded by a badly positioned lamp. Be especially careful if your ceiling heights are low.

◆ GLS lamps (common bulbs) are now available in a wide variety of tints. Use these to give a warm glow to a room or to 'cool down' its colours.

◆ Use of fluorescents should be carefully restricted. These may be highly suitable for work areas (where they provide economical light and cause few shadows to be cast), but are prone to distort colours severely and are likely to give a cold feel to a room.

◆ Handling a bulb shortens its life. Use a cloth or tissue when installing.

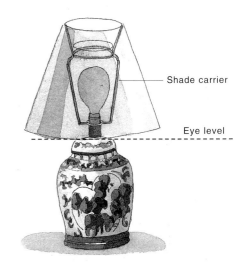

*Correct position for lampshade.*

## Shades

◆ There is only one way to select a suitable-sized shade to go with a table lamp – that is physically to take the lamp base to the shade shop and try various combinations. The popular formula that dictates that the diameter of the bottom of the shade should be equal to the height of the lamp base is not reliable: so much depends upon the shape of both.

◆ The positioning of a shade on a lamp base is determined by the height of the shade carrier. This is a metal structure attached to the base that forms a cradle for the shade to rest on. The correct height for a shade is one that allows all of the base to be visible but none of the metal working parts when viewed from eye level (see above).

◆ Before you buy, be sure to view the shade with a light inside it. Shade colours and materials have a vast effect on the quality of light given off.

◆ The shade shape will affect how the light is dispersed and should be given careful consideration (see left). The three main shade shapes are drum, empire and coolie.

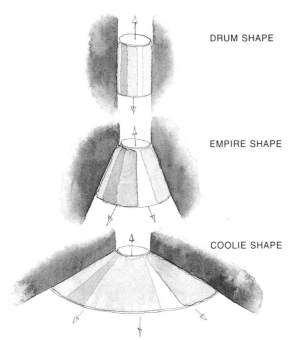

DRUM SHAPE

EMPIRE SHAPE

COOLIE SHAPE

*Light dispersal with various shade shapes.*

# Colour, Pattern and Texture

## COLOUR

All designers, whether professional or amateur, have a magic wand in their tool box. It is called colour and it can:

- make a small room look larger;
- evoke a particular period;
- change the proportions of a room;
- lighten a dark room;
- help to create a certain mood;
- make a room feel 'cool' or 'warm';
- link different objects and areas in a house.

Clearly it would be foolish to ignore such a wonderful device, particularly as a good colour scheme costs no more than a bad one. Paint is relatively cheap and, just as you would not expect to pay more for a chocolate ice cream than for a vanilla one, prices do not vary according to colour or flavour. Historically, though, this was not always the case. Preference for one or another colour in times gone by was often determined by price and, of course, availability of dyestuffs. For instance, the colours identified with Shaker style (see page 246) were very dependent upon economic factors and what could be made or procured locally. Today we have a problem of a different kind. Paint manufacturers, in an effort to assist and inspire homemakers, now produce an almost unlimited array of colours (all at the same price), and our difficulty is how to choose from such an enormous range. This chapter is about how to make colour decisions easier and how to avoid expensive mistakes.

Opting for magnolia in every room is many people's (and many a builder's) way of evading the whole question of colour. Playing it safe may mean the avoidance of disasters, but it also means missing out on so many wonderful opportunities to create a more exciting and successful interior. And, when all is said and done, if your medium is paint and you have made an error over the choice of a colour, this can be corrected by the simple expedient of painting over with a coat of another hue.

Colour can be used very effectively to link different areas in a house and to give it a feeling of harmony. A hallway might, for example, have a carpet that incorporates yellow, beige and tan. This would provide the opportunity to develop schemes based on any one of these colours in the rooms leading off the hall. One room might have a scheme based on the yellow, to which blue might be added; another might be based on the tan, and this could perhaps be combined with cream and dark brown.

Every day of our lives we are influenced by colour. When we see a sweet that is yellow, we expect it to taste of lemon; petrol that comes out of a green nozzle, we conclude, must be kind to nature; and we do not expect a red apple to be anything other than sweet-tasting. Do not imagine that the manufacturers or advertisers arrive at certain colour choices on a whim – on the contrary, all is carefully thought out and our reactions anticipated. In the same way, in your home you can make friends with colour and learn to use it as a tool for creating exactly the room you desire. However, before considering in detail how to use colour, it is necessary to become familiar with its 'grammar'.

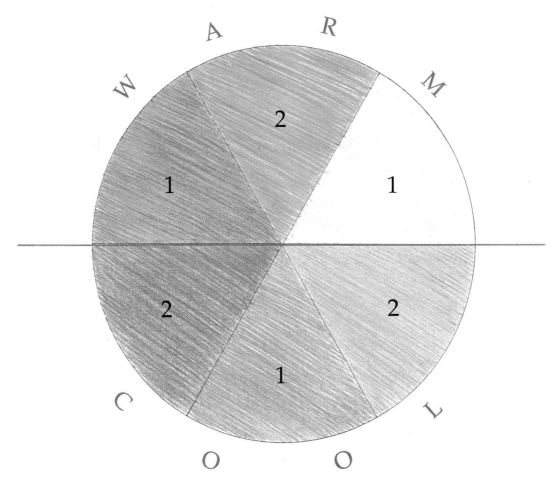

## THE COLOUR WHEEL

There are several colour systems currently used by designers, but all are based upon the work of Sir Isaac Newton who, in 1660, directed a beam of light through a prism to achieve an effect similar to that of a rainbow. Then, by joining the two ends of the spectrum, he developed the idea of the colour wheel.

The wheel is divided into six sections (see above) that can be sub-divided into many more portions. First come the primary colours red, blue and yellow (denoted by '1' on the wheel), so called because they cannot be made up from a combination of any of the other colours. Next come the secondary colours (denoted by '2' on the wheel): these are colours formed by combining their near neighbours – for instance, orange is produced by mixing red and yellow.

The wheel is further divided into two halves, one representing the cool colours and the other the warm colours. Generally speaking, blue, green and violet are considered cool colours, and red, orange and yellow warm colours; however, those near the dividing line can veer either way depending upon the proportions of warm and cool tints – for example, yellow, when it is the colour of egg yolk, would be thought of as warm, while a greenish-yellow has a cool effect.

An important point to remember is that colours from the cool side of the spectrum tend to 'recede' and those from the warm side 'advance'. In other words, if you wish to open out a space and make it appear larger, select a receding colour. Equally, if you want to make a large area seem smaller and more intimate, choose a warm advancing colour.

'True' colour is a myth. Colour is seen by each individual in a slightly (or, in the case of colour-blindness, radically) different way. For this reason designers use actual colour samples and specific colour references and do not risk a scheme by referring to colours by name. Turquoise, for instance, can mean vastly different things to different people.

*Pale shocking-pink stippled wallpaper, edged with a border in a sand colour, adds warmth and drama to this continental sitting room.*

## SELECTING APPROPRIATE COLOURS

To narrow down your choice of colours to a reasonable number, it may be helpful to ask yourself these questions:

- **What is the orientation of the room?** If it is north-facing, you may wish to counteract the coldness of the light by introducing a colour from the warm side of the spectrum. Equally, if the room faces south, this will allow you to base your scheme on one of the cooler colours.

- **Do the proportions of the room need some help?** For instance, painting a ceiling in a darker colour will make it appear lower.

- **Does the size of the room need adjustment?** By painting or papering the walls and ceiling in a warm dark colour, you will make a large space feel more intimate.

- **What is the room's function?** In a bedroom you may find pastel colours more acceptable, while in a child's playroom primary brights might be more appreciated.

- **How much time will you spend in the room?** A strong vibrant colour may be all right for a cloakroom, but unsuitable for a bedroom where more time is passed.

- **What is the period/style of the room?** You may wish to choose from the now fashionable 'heritage' colours, authentic to the period of the room or reflecting its theme.

- **What mood do you wish to create?** Is the living room, for example, to be lively or tranquil? Your colour choice could help to determine this.

- **Will the room be used mostly during the day or at night?** The amount and quality of light can render colours very differently. For a room such as a dining room that is used mainly at night, make sure that your selection looks good in artificial light.

- **What are the colours of existing possessions you wish to accommodate in the room?** These may inspire the starting point for your scheme.

Having answered all of these questions, you should now have an idea of the palette that would most suit your room and your purposes.

Let's take an example of a typical living room in an average house. It is rather small but has a relatively high ceiling. The room is north-facing and has an existing brick-coloured carpet. Your considerations might be:

- to choose a light wall colour to expand the space;

- to select a warm colour to counteract the cool northern light;

- to take the colour over the ceiling in a slightly darker shade to bring down its height.

A pale shade of terracotta might just be the answer.

Now it's time to start thinking about what sort of scheme would be most appropriate.

## TYPES OF COLOUR SCHEME

There are basically four kinds of colour scheme: neutral, monochromatic, harmonious and complementary.

### The Neutral Scheme

The neutral scheme relies almost entirely on the absence of colour and might include such 'non' colours as white, grey, black, brown, beige and cream. It is extremely natural-looking and is the perfect foil for interesting accessories, paintings and so on. The mood created is one of calm sophistication – perfect, for instance, for a formal drawing room.

### The Monochromatic Scheme

As its name implies, the monochromatic scheme is based upon just one colour. Far from being boring, this type of scheme, with its subtle variations of tone and shade and reliance on textures, can be both soothing and full of interest. It would be an admirable choice for a bedroom.

*A study in blue, this conservatory will look fresh and cool even on the hottest of days. A table cloth in two shades of blue complements the blinds in this monochromatic scheme.*

*The inspiration for colour schemes is all around us – nature offering some of the most beautiful combinations.*

## The Harmonious Scheme

The harmonious scheme is composed of colours that fall within one half of the spectrum – for instance, blues and greens, pinks and violets, yellows and oranges. This type of scheme lacks violent contrasts and as such is restful and easy to live with. It is suitable for practically every area in the home.

## The Complementary or Contrast Scheme

The complementary or contrast scheme is formed from colours that lie on opposite sides of the colour wheel, such as green and red, blue and orange. The combination of opposites creates a vibrant lively scheme – great for young people and for rooms that are perhaps not used for long periods at a time. The contrast in colours makes each seem more intense and, for the association to work well, it is preferable for one of the colours to dominate.

## PAINT

Paint is a most wonderful medium – it's simple to apply, comes in any number of shades and finishes, is not vastly expensive and can be manipulated in so many ways. Best of all, mistakes can easily be remedied. Here are ten tips on using paint:

1 **Choosing from a swatch** Go for a colour that appears slightly lighter and less strong than the result you are seeking. When colour is seen in the larger area of a room, it reflects upon itself and intensifies.

2 **Tinting colours** Despite the fact that thousands of colours are available, there are gaps in even the most comprehensive of ranges and it is possible that the paint you have in mind is not on any manufacturer's chart. Tinting your own colours can be great fun. Simply buy either white paint or the colour nearest the one you want and add tints until you achieve the exact shade you desire. Remember always to mix sufficient for your purposes as it will be almost impossible to repeat the recipe.

3 **Magnolia** Beware of this colour! In some lights it appears to have a yellow tinge, in others an incli-nation towards pink. This may be an effect you enjoy – but if not, select another colour.

4 **Matching** Should you require an exact match to a given item of furnishing, some specialist paint shops will custom-mix paint of this colour.

5 **White paint** In an older property brilliant white tends to look too modern and clinical. Choose instead an off-white shade that will give the effect of aged white paint. British standard reference BS 10B15 (Gardenia) would be a good choice.

6 **Woodwork** On woodwork consider using a satin or eggshell finish instead of gloss for a softer effect.

7 **Testing** Always start by painting a test area on a wall in the room where you intend using a particular colour. Check how it looks by day and by night, on a sunny day and on a dull one, before painting the entire room.

8 **Painting tiles** In situations where replacing ceramic wall tiles is beyond your budget, consider painting them. First apply a coat of PVC adhesive that has been diluted 1:1 with water. When dry, this will form a key on to which an oil-based paint can be applied. Once this is in place, finish the tiles with the paint of your choice. If you chose to add painted decorations, such as stencils, it is a good idea to finish the tiles with a coat of clear polyurethane varnish for protection.

9 **Adjusting colour** If you have just painted your walls and they look too bright, too light or too dark, adjust the colour by sponging over the surface with the original colour into which a little white or black tint (depending on which direction you wish the colour to go) has been added. Not only will this help to correct the colour, but it will also give the walls an interesting textured effect.

10 **The right shade** Remember that paint always looks a little darker when dry.

# PATTERN

Design schemes are often referred to as colour schemes, but there are two other ingredients that are every bit as important as colour and without which a scheme lacks depth and interest. It is by the skilful use of pattern and texture that a scheme will be brought to life and given an extra dimension.

Pattern has been used for thousands of years – to decorate dwellings, objects and people – and many of the designs developed in primitive times are still with us today. One of the most beneficial qualities of pattern is that it can be utilized to suggest a given period or style. Flamestitch, for instance, is particularly associated with the Tudor period, a paisley pattern might suggest the continent of India, and 'jazz' designs effectively evoke memories of Art Deco style.

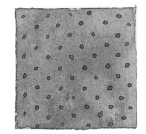

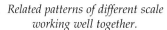

*Related patterns of different scale working well together.*

For the lazy decorator, pattern is a godsend. Designers of wallpapers, fabrics and carpets spend endless time on perfecting colour and pattern combinations. The end results are what you find available on the market. Why not tap into their skills and take your lead from the colours that they have deemed go together well? Try assembling samples of materials that pick out the individual colours featured in your chosen patterned fabric and you will be surprised how quick and easy it is to muster a scheme.

Practice will make you much more adept at forming schemes and you may find the following tips useful:

- By choosing two dominant patterns of the same scale you will find that they 'fight' each other for your attention. Instead, go for patterns of varying scales. Start by choosing one main large pattern, then find medium- and small-scale ones to complement this and fill in with plain colours.

- As a general rule the best results are achieved by arranging for the largest areas (walls, floor, curtains) to take on the largest-scale patterns and the smaller items correspondingly smaller patterns.

- Always view patterns from the distance at which they will be seen in the room. By holding a sample a suitable distance from a mirror you will get the right effect. Remember that small patterns viewed from some way away will merge and appear plain.

- Curtain fabric samples are best viewed with the light behind them rather than facing the light. This will give a better representation of how the material will appear when hung at a window.

- Can't find a fabric, wallpaper or carpet that appeals to you? Consider commissioning one in the pattern and colourway of your choice. Several companies specialize in custom-making materials to the wishes of their clients. You will probably be charged a sum for colour and pattern trials and you may be required to order a minimum amount, but this should not be onerous and the rewards of personally designing your own materials are immense.

- When using several patterns in one room, you will find that they work best when linked.

Choose patterns with colours, themes, motifs or textures in common.

◆ You may wish to place several differently coloured existing possessions in the same room. To make these appear to 'belong' together, find a patterned fabric that includes the colours of the furnishings you already have and you will find that they will be drawn together by the colour links.

◆ When selecting a patterned curtain fabric, it is a good idea to obtain a large sample and drape this in folds as it will appear when made up. You will be surprised how this gathering process can distort patterns – usually in an acceptable way, but not always.

*Pattern-on-pattern works well so long as each is of a different scale, as the soft furnishings on this sofa suggest. Colours and motifs link the individual patterns.*

# TEXTURE

With the growing trend to pare everything down to a minimum, an even greater reliance will be placed upon design schemes containing interesting textures and quality construction. It is possible to spend hours carefully selecting and putting together interestingly coloured and patterned materials; it is also possible to choose highly expensive items. However, neither of these precautions can guarantee a successful scheme if insufficient attention has been given to the textural quality of your choices. A completely 'flat' scheme of materials with similar finishes will lack life and appear dull. Yet by juxtaposing contrasting textures you will create excitement in a scheme. Just think of a coffee table with a polished marble top on a floor covered with rough medieval matting, lustrous chintz cushions on a matt flannel sofa, or a shiny lacquer console table against a wall of suede – all are exciting prospects.

Texture can also have a big influence on how colour is perceived: a matt material such as velvet fabric or emulsion paint will absorb light, rendering it darker, while a shiny one such as chintz or gloss paint, will reflect it and make the colour appear brighter and more intense.

To test the part that texture plays, try making up a scheme using plain fabrics of only one colour – say, cream – and try to find as many differently textured samples as you can. You will be amazed at what an interesting scheme you can compose simply by assembling materials of differing textures.

To get good value from your selected textures, focused lighting is imperative. To demonstrate to yourself how true this is, take a powerful torch and point it at different furnishings within your home. Notice how the beam of light brings out the textural quality and gives objects a three-dimensional 'moulded' effect – that is what you are after.

# Assembling a Scheme

Now that the various elements that go into making up a scheme have been examined, consideration must be given to how these are assembled into a pleasing whole. In fact most of us practise putting together schemes nearly every day of our lives. We get up ... and we get dressed! When dressing, we choose a style that is appropriate for the activities we intend carrying out, we select materials that are suitable and choose colours that flatter us. We decide whether to go for a harmonious outfit or one of contrasts, we determine in what proportions each colour will appear and we may even choose to include a patterned scarf or tie to bring the ensemble together. Finally we pick out appropriate accessories to complement our outfit. Formulating a decorative scheme for your home is very much the same process – so it should hold few fears.

If, however, you feel that you lack inspiration, a good starting point would be to create your own style file. Gather together, from decorating magazines, any pictures of interiors or furnishing details that particularly appeal to you and keep them either in a file or pasted in an album. In this way you will soon see your style preferences emerging. Other starting points for your consideration are your existing possessions. The combination of colours in a favourite painting or a precious oriental rug might inspire a scheme. Lacking these, you might like to seek out an interestingly patterned carpet or fabric to set you on your way. The idea that professional decorators always have a clean sheet to start with is a fallacy. Most, like you or I, have possessions too valuable or loved to discard and which have to be incorporated in any new scheme. Far from finding

*'Blue and green should never be seen' – but rules were made to be broken, as demonstrated in this well-balanced scheme.*

this a limiting factor, they are thankful for the lead it provides.

It should be remembered that no room in your house will be seen in isolation but viewed from an adjacent area and, for your home to have any sense of cohesion, it is important that each room scheme works well with its neighbours. That is not to say that the schemes must all be very similar, but rather that they should have some linking factor. For instance, a dominant colour from one room might be used as an accent colour in the next. It can also be very helpful if connecting areas (hallways, stairs and landings) are decorated in fairly neutral colours. This will allow you to merge easily into any variety of stronger colours in the rooms that lead off the space. In a smaller property laying the same carpet throughout often produces a harmonious result. This tends to lend a greater sense of space and unity to a house and, as a bonus, is often cheaper than buying small quantities of differing colours.

A professional designer takes few short cuts, preferring instead to do thorough research before finalizing a scheme. Skilled at visualizing though designers might be, they still need to see how all the components of a scheme inter-react, and the best way to do this is to make a sample board for each room on which they are working.

Putting together a scheme is in some ways even easier than choosing an outfit to wear. The sight of someone in a shop producing a dress from a bag when buying a hat is familiar. When it comes to decorating, however, we have the benefit of samples. Here are some tips on handling them:

◆ Most manufacturers are willing to provide small cuttings of fabrics, wallpapers and carpets without charge. Either apply at your local decorating store or contact the manufacturer directly.

◆ For a fabric that is pivotal to your scheme and which has a large pattern repeat, a larger sample will better demonstrate how the material will look when made up. Many suppliers will provide a returnable length (say, 1m/1yd) for a small deposit. If one of these bigger samples is not available, it may be preferable to buy 1m for testing purposes rather than having the material made up only to realize that a mistake has been made.

◆ Always view samples in the room where they will appear. Wallpapers can be stuck to the wall with masking tape, fabrics pinned to existing window dressings and paint tried out on a board held up to the wall.

◆ It is vital that samples are seen on the plane on which they will finally appear: for example, carpet flat on the floor, upholstery fabric on a sofa, curtain fabric gathered at a window. Fabric can take on a very different appearance depending on whether it is laid flat, as in a bed cover, or gathered into drapes as at a window.

◆ Gather more different samples than you actually require for any one room. This gives you the opportunity to see how they work together and to reject the ones that prove unsuitable.

◆ Clear plastic file pages are useful for collecting samples. Label each with the title of the room for which they have been selected. When you have all the schemes gathered in, lay each next to the one which it will adjoin in your house. This will allow you to judge if they link together well.

◆ When you are building a scheme around existing furnishings, you will need colour samples of these items so that you can see how your new colours will blend with the old. Where no off-cuts exist, colours from paint charts or strands of wool might be used as a colour reference instead.

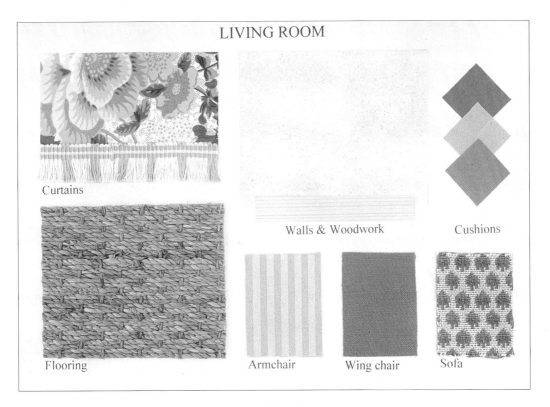

*Sample board.*

## MAKING A SAMPLE BOARD

Just as room plans need to be a true representation of the room in miniature, it is important for sample boards to reflect the right mix and balance of colours and materials in a scheme. When making a sample board, try to position samples according to their location in the room: for instance, carpet at the bottom of the board, wall and curtain samples near the top and furnishing samples in the middle. It is also good to gauge the size of the sample according to the size of area it will cover in the room: for example, your wall covering sample should be much larger than your cushion fabric sample.

Artist's mounting board of A2 size (about 45×60cm/1ft 6in×2ft) forms an ideal base for your display of samples, though any neutral-coloured board of a similar size could be substituted. Simply attach the sample squares to the board – double-sided tape is the easiest method – and label each one with its purpose, 'curtain fabric', 'floor coverings' and so on. If it helps you to visualize the finished room, include any other items that will form part of the scheme, such as illustrations of light fittings and furniture. It is also a good idea to label each board with its room title, especially if you are decorating a whole house.

When your board is complete, you will be quite surprised how well it represents the finished scheme – the mix of colours, the number of textural contrasts and array of patterns all working together. Any anomalies or imbalance should show up now. Perhaps your scheme is too dark or too bland. Perhaps it has too few shiny surfaces or too many patterns. All these elements and more will be demonstrated in your sample board and can be corrected at this early inexpensive stage.

## SCHEME SHEET

As a back-up to your sample board, or when there is insufficient time to prepare a board, there is another system of recording a scheme that professionals use. It is referred to as a scheme sheet and is, in essence, a mini sample board. This scheme colour reference system will fit neatly into a file and can be taken with you on shopping trips. Unlike the sample board,

it requires little artistry and can be made up in no time at all.

The scheme sheet consists of a form, which can be easily drawn up by hand or produced on a personal computer and which slots into a plastic file. This can then be filed in an A4-size ring binder and transported wherever you like. Simply fill in the title of the room at the top of the page and below add in each surface you are going to represent by a sample. In the centre column write any information you consider relevant to describe the finish or material in question. In the last column attach a small sample of the material described. In the case of a patterned material, select a section that shows as many colours as possible – a larger sample can always be kept within a sleeve of clear plastic. And there you have it: a useful sample board in miniature.

*Scheme sheet.*

# Part II

# ROOM-BY-ROOM DECORATING

Are you irritated, when looking at design magazines, that you cannot ask the decorator of a particular room just what was the thinking behind the various design decisions that he/she has made? And, while it may be self-evident that the room decoration is, in total, successful, do you long to take the room apart to analyse the various components that have gone into making up the whole? If so, the following chapters should be of interest as they aim to answer some of the questions that people new to decorating may have.

In this section of the book the eight different room types common to most homes and the special requirements of each are examined. In addition three examples of each of the different rooms are considered in detail – a total of twenty-four rooms in all. The individual elements which make up each one are analysed – because it is by paying attention to every small detail that the total look can be achieved. In each case an actual room has been selected to demonstrate certain design points and the thinking behind that room's design is suggested by the author. A plan of how the room might look is also included so that the reader can see how the rest of the furnishings might be arranged by a designer.

The rooms in a house are very much like members of a family, each varying in size, having different needs and possessing distinct talents and weaknesses, but all sharing a common family likeness. In the same way, when decorating a whole house, it is necessary to look at the requirements of each space and pay homage to the special character of individual rooms while still maintaining a common theme so that each has a sense of belonging to the larger 'family' grouping.

# LIVING ROOMS

Just where do you start with the decoration of a living room? With so many activities to cater for and so many people to keep happy, this room will be successful only if planned meticulously. A good living room is one that on a practical level happily accommodates the various activities you wish to undertake in the space while at the same time being aesthetically pleasing in its role as a reception area.

Your starting point is, as always, to determine exactly what you want from your room as this will dictate how you will arrange the space. Is it to be:

◆ **a leisure room** for quiet reading, listening to music, letter writing, watching television?

◆ **a dining room** for family meals, smart dinner parties, television suppers?

◆ **an entertainment room** for family parties, video viewing, card games?

◆ **a hobbies room** for dressmaking, model making, arranging a stamp collection and so on?

◆ **a work room** for study, wordprocessing, homework, research?

◆ **a mix** of all or any of the above?

These various activities all require specialized lighting, ample storage facilities and suitable furniture. By listing them you will help to focus your mind on what is needed.

When it comes to planning a furniture arrangement, it is important to establish a focal point in your room – a point of interest that can be highlighted and around which furnishings can be gathered. In a living room the most obvious focal point is a fireplace, but if one does not exist another point of interest will need to be selected: perhaps the room has a hand-some window with an attractive view beyond, an important piece of furniture, a collection of paintings or even an antique rug. In a very large or 'double' living room you may have several subsidiary focal points around which you will arrange 'conversation' groupings. These days the television set will also have a vast effect on how the room is arranged.

Selecting a style for your living room should be an easy matter if you live in a period property as the theme may well be suggested by the style of architecture. In a more anonymous modern space you have the choice of imposing a traditional style by the addition of architectural details and furnishings of your selected period or of interpreting a contemporary and perhaps foreign idiom. Your scheme may be inspired by an existing possession – the design of an oriental rug, the style of a distinguished piece of furniture or even the colours in a favourite large painting.

A novel idea, popular in Victorian times (see 'Victorian Style', page 192) and which you might think of reviving, is to change the look of your room with the seasons. Come spring, chair slip-covers, cushions, curtains and upholstery drapes can all be replaced with lighter fabrics to suggest sunnier times. A floral theme can be introduced by painting or stamping designs on to cheap plain canvas using fabric dyes. This material can then be used for a table cloth, chair slip-covers or even curtains. You might also think of adjusting your seating arrangement so that a garden rather than a fireplace becomes the focal point in summer months.

*A beautifully flowered needlework rug provides the inspiration for a pink, green and cream colour scheme in this elegant drawing room.*

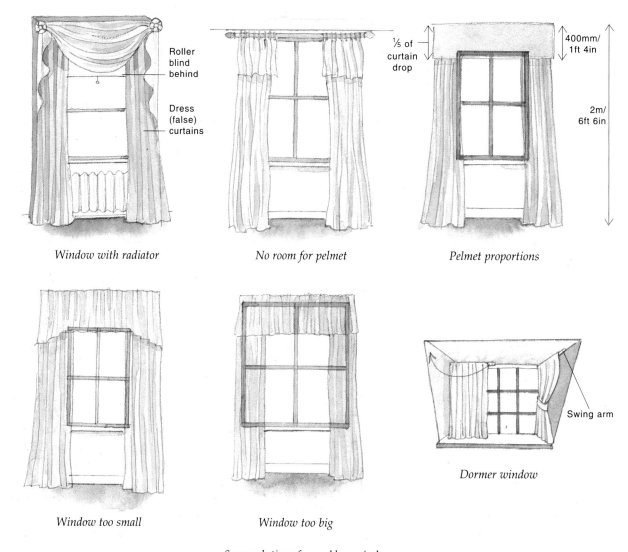

Window with radiator

No room for pelmet

Pelmet proportions

Window too small

Window too big

Dormer window

*Some solutions for problem windows.*

The usually generous windows to be found in a living room offer a great opportunity for decorative treatments, but always check first whether there is a style available that will improve the proportions of your window.

## SURFACES

For many the starting point of a scheme is the flooring as this is where the largest portion of the budget is likely to be spent. Investing in a good-quality carpet or other floor covering will pay dividends as this is the item that will probably outlive many a different scheme over the years. When visiting a carpet showroom, look at the samples in their correct position – that is, horizontally on the floor – and, if possible, borrow a sample to view *in situ* in your home. A carpet with a mix of 80 per cent wool and 20 per cent synthetic material is generally considered ideal from a practical viewpoint, and the use of a good-quality underlay will vastly increase the life of a carpet as well as giving it a more luxurious feel. The suitability of wall surfaces will depend upon the use to which your living room is put. Whatever your choice, the inclusion of a dado bearing a more durable surface, such as paint, will help to protect the wall from damage.

## FURNISHINGS

A single sofa or pair of sofas might be the centrepiece of your seating arrangement. The three-piece suite forms a traditional grouping, but as an alternative consider placing a sofa with two unrelated French bergères or add a wing chair and arm chair to give your room an informal air. This arrangement is particularly suited to the 'country house' look where a matching suite is an anathema. A three-seat sofa offers comfort for two people, but rarely for three. To avoid the inconvenient positioning of seat cushion joins when two people are seated, ask your upholsterer to make up the three-seat size with just two seat and back cushions. Something easily forgotten is that, if you propose to entertain a certain number of people to a meal, the same number of guests will also require seats in your drawing room. Additional seating, to be drawn up when guests arrive, might be provided by upright chairs against the walls and run-up stools slotted under a spacious coffee table. When selecting a curtain fabric, remember to view a large sample draped as it would appear when made up and with the light behind the material (again, as it would appear when at the window).

## STORAGE

A vital ingredient of any successful living room scheme, storage cannot be ignored. If insufficient facilities are provided, all the expense and effort that went into achieving a good-looking living room is wasted if the room is constantly littered with books, newspapers, records, tapes, games and so on. Storage can be in either custom-made built-in units or free-standing items of furniture such as sideboards, bookcases, shelving units and desks. It should be planned at the start of your project and not just introduced as an afterthought. The recesses to either side of a chimney breast provide a useful space for building in cupboards with display shelves above and a window seat that has space for storage within its base offers another solution and has the additional benefit of providing extra seating. Should this be your choice, do remember to select a window treatment to accommodate the seat. A combination of window blinds (festoon, Roman or roller) and 'dress' curtains should fit the bill.

## LIGHTING

Nowadays living rooms have to accommodate so very many activities that providing suitable lighting for each of them can present quite a challenge. Hobbies, eating, watching television, reading, entertaining and relaxing quietly all require very different lighting effects and, in order to satisfy all of them, it is necessary to build in a fairly flexible system that can be adjusted as required. Free-standing fittings such as standard lamps, floor-standing uplighters and table lamps all provide for an easily changed arrangement, and having the fittings on several different (say, three) circuits will allow the opportunity to change effects easily.

The living room is also where you are likely to want to display your most treasured possessions. Be they valuable antiques or family memorabilia, they will all take on much greater 'value' when drenched in light. Pictures can be suitably lit by picture lights or overhead wall washers; collections displayed on a table top can be bathed in light from a downlighter or table lamp. A very successful method of lighting attractive book spines within a bookcase is to install discreet strip lights under or at the side of the shelves, always ensuring that naked bulbs are hidden from view, behind baffles where necessary. Glass shelves within a niche, lit from above or below by a downlighter/uplighter, will give you a wonderful opportunity to display your favourite objects.

Many people are reluctant to part with a central ceiling light, even though this is known to flatten surfaces and kill atmosphere. The reluctance is understandable in view of the attractiveness of some fittings (particularly chandeliers) and the good general light value they provide. So why not keep the fitting, but apply a dimmer to the controls? In this way you retain the decorative value of the fitting and the possibility of using the light for background lighting.

The recommendation to have several light circuits, switched from the doorway, is particularly apposite for the living room. As for the number of fittings to include, this is a difficult question to answer without full information on a specific room, but as a general guide for a mid-sized living room around ten fittings might be considered appropriate.

# Formal Drawing Room

Most people's favourite room when it comes to decorating, a formal drawing room provides the most wonderful opportunity to demonstrate your decorating skills and to express your personality.

In all the other rooms discussed a preoccupation with the practicalities usually has to dominate, sometimes at the expense of aesthetic considerations. Although it has to perform and respond to our needs, the formal drawing room is above all a room for pleasure – to satisfy all the senses. This may involve some subterfuge where there is a conflict between what is needed for comfort and what appeals visually. Here are some examples:

- ◆ A television set cannot be anything but an ugly piece of equipment, yet hidden beneath a round table with a full-length cloth it need not be an eyesore.

- ◆ Radiators are rarely attractive, but can be disguised if encased in a box or painted to match their surroundings.

- ◆ Ugly contours in a room shape can be boxed in to give symmetry and provide storage.

- ◆ A badly proportioned window can have its dimensions hidden behind well-designed curtains (see page 50).

The style of a drawing room is most likely to be dictated by the period or style of the building that houses it; occasionally, however, it can be interesting to go against the architecture and so create drama by a clashing of the centuries. Antiques in a modern warehouse space or contemporary furnishings in a classical Georgian interior are just two examples of the excitement that you can create. Mixing periods within the same room is also a possibility, but needs to be done with skill. The most successful results are produced by combining contrasts: rough aged wood with smooth tubular steel; antique matt velvet with glossy chintz; polished marble with rough medieval matting.

This is a room where many people choose to display their most precious possessions – portraits of ancestors, family silver, collections – and it is important to bear this in mind when deciding upon a scheme. It is all too easy to go overboard and cover every surface with pattern, only to find that when accessories are placed they disappear against a dominant background. To avoid this an experienced designer will always gather together the accessories right at the start (or, if they are not yet accumulated, will have them in mind) and will think of them as part of the overall scheme. If you like your furniture, accessories and guests to star, select plain surface treatments and create a 'blank canvas' backdrop for your features.

Should flowers be your passion, leave space for a judiciously placed vase, and when planning flower arrangements, always take into consideration their surroundings – give thought to their colour and form within the context of your scheme. Try mixing fresh blooms with artificial greenery to make your bouquets go further and have in reserve further silk imitations for when fresh flowers are not to hand. If no flowers are available, try sprinkling flower essences in your room – you will find your guests searching for the bouquet.

When arranging furniture in a drawing room, view the room from every direction before settling on a format. Make sure that from each position you have a pleasant vista. The view of the room you get upon first entering is particularly important and sometimes this can be much improved by rehanging the entrance door on the opposite axis (see page 17), so that it opens flat against an adjacent wall and you are able to view the whole room immediately.

*Pretty pastels and modern furnishings contrast with traditional architecture in this light and airy drawing room.*

# HOW THE ROOM MIGHT LOOK

## THE PLAN

This large room with its pleasing proportions provides an elegant space for a modern formal drawing room. The area is divided, courtesy of the furnishings, into two separate conversation areas, which has the effect of giving balance to the room and making a large space seem more intimate. This is primarily a receiving and entertaining room and so does not have to cater for other activities associated with family living. Storage (to house audio equipment and so on) is minimal in order to maintain a look that is uncluttered.

Scale 1:60

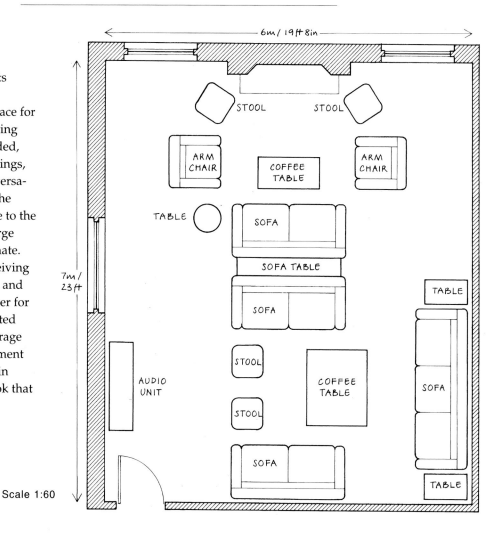

## DESIGN DECISIONS

1 **Scheme** This exercise in pastels was inspired by the large abstract paintings.

2 **Polished wood floor** Practical and elegant, this reflects any natural light coming into the room, thereby increasing the feeling of airiness.

3 **White area rugs** These contribute to the lightness of the room and help to define the conversation areas.

4 **Sofa table** Minimal in width, this table between the backs of two sofas provides a useful surface for placing flowers and lighting.

5 **Mirror-faced coffee table** This adds to the light and airy feeling in the room and, although large, the mirrored surface helps it to disappear into its surroundings.

6 **Two double-cushion stools** While taking up very little room, these stools provide extra seating for visitors.

7 **Window treatment** Deliberately understated, the curtains allow the contours of the arches and the wrought-iron work beyond to speak for themselves.

8 **Lighting** Picture lights have been eschewed in favour of discreet, modern, recessed wall washers to highlight the pictures, while more traditional fittings have been included in the scheme to provide a welcoming ambience.

9 **Accent** Touches of black found in the smaller picture, the two vases, the garment hanging on the larger painting and the fireplace, provide a contrast to the pastels and give the scheme some definition.

10 **Accessories** Few, well chosen and all linking in some way with their surroundings, these are kept to a minimum so as not to destroy the purity of the room.

11 **Flowers** These well thought-out arrangements co-ordinate with the scheme and add a sculptural quality to the room.

# Open-plan Family Living Room

For many people deciding whether or not to join two or more small rooms to create one large living space presents a major dilemma. Historically, and particularly in Victorian times (see 'Victorian Style', page 192), many houses were built with a room at the front for entertaining and receiving guests and another separate one to the rear for family use. This arrangement no doubt suited life in the nineteenth century, but now our need is for more flexible living areas and for larger multi-purpose spaces.

You may wish to set aside areas for study, play, cooking, dining or perhaps a library, while at the same time still retaining the facility to open up these areas to form a larger space when required. Opening one room into another makes sense, but do remember that there is more to think about than just the size of the new space you are creating. What about noise, smells and untidiness – are you prepared for people using one area to be exposed to these elements from another?

For maximum flexibility and comfort build in plenty of storage so that toys, files and dishes can be quickly removed, install an efficient ventilation system to remove odours, and plan on plenty of soft surfaces to absorb sound. You may also wish to exclude children and pets from certain areas and these might require a barrier of some kind.

Once you have made the decision to join two or more rooms, it is necessary to think about just how much communal living will suit you. It is possible to go the whole hog and open up the spaces permanently (depending upon structural limitations), or you may wish to retain some form of separation to be put in place occasionally when required. A permanent solution might involve the use of an arch, a squared-off opening or even the complete removal of any traces of a dividing wall between two areas. Whatever your choice, do remember that this newly formed room is part of a larger architectural structure. Be careful not to create an imbalance in the distribution of space within your home as a whole and take care to continue any architectural theme already in place. This may mean installing columns at either side of an opening in a classical interior or perhaps fixing decorative corbels to an arch in a Victorian home.

Should you wish to retain the ability to shut one room off temporarily from another, there are various methods that can be employed. Doors (double, sliding or concertina) can be hung at the opening, a folding screen placed at the dividing line, a piece of furniture strategically located or curtains/blinds hung between the two rooms. If the quality of light in one room depends upon a

*The colours of blue and terracotta combine happily in this open-plan family living area that invites you in and encourages you to relax.*

window in the other, you might also like to consider glazed doors that will allow the light to be shared between the two spaces.

It is important that the vista from one room through to another be a pleasant one, so avoid placing furniture with its back facing an adjoining room. If you must position a sofa thus, place a sofa table at its rear to enhance the view. Ensure also that your passageway between the two rooms is unhindered. Flexibility will need to be built into any furniture arrangement and lighting scheme so that when you wish to use the rooms as a single unit, this can be done with a minimum amount of effort. A proportion

of free-standing lighting and furniture on castors will do much to help.

It is vital that the decorations in these individual spaces that have now become one act together harmoniously and that there is a strong sense of unity between the areas. This doesn't mean that the schemes have to match exactly, but they should relate to one another. For instance, a fitted carpet might be installed in a sitting area while a patterned area rug incorporating some of the carpet colours might sit on a wooden floor enclosing a dining area in another. Window treatments of the same fabric and similar style will also aid a feeling of cohesion.

# HOW THE ROOM MIGHT LOOK

## THE PLAN

Three distinct areas are opened up to form a comfortable living space where the whole family can commune. The division between the kitchen and dining room is defined by a row of units that runs across the 'border' and which contain tableware – handy for table laying opposite. The sitting area is separated off by a tall cupboard that opens into the dining area. Another large storage unit (is it possible to have too many?) nestles neatly next to the chimney breast and houses books, audio equipment and a television.

## DESIGN DECISIONS

1  **Scheme** Neutral colours and natural surfaces dominate in this easy-to-live-with, all-purpose scheme. Blue highlights provide a good contrast to the terracotta flooring and introduce a feeling of country freshness.

2  **Flooring** Sealed terracotta tiles provide a tough, easily maintained flooring that reinforces the country feel of this open-plan living area. An oriental-design rug links the

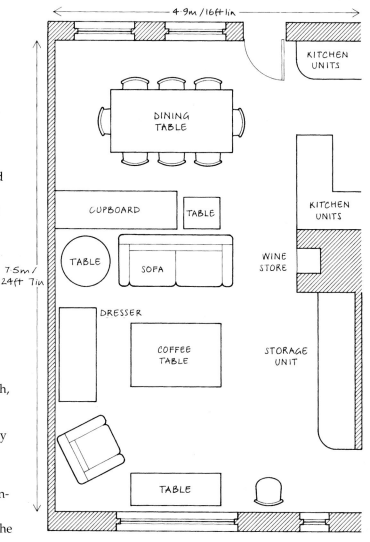

Scale 1:60

blue of the sofa with the tan of the flooring and brickwork. This also serves to soften and define the seating area.

**3 Kitchen units** The blond wood of these units is followed through into the other areas, being reflected in the finish of the dining table, tall cupboard, coffee table and storage unit.

**4 Lighting** Eyeball spotlights in the ceiling critically direct light where needed. Although the bulbs show, these are unlikely to cause glare because of the height of the ceiling. A traditional pendant light over the dining table provides plentiful light in that area and underscores the period feel of the room.

**5 Sofa** Foam-filled sofa seat cushions ensure that the sofa will take plenty of abuse and still remain in good shape. The patterned fabric cover discourages marks from showing. If this were treated with a sealant, removing dirt would be a matter of merely wiping over with a damp cloth.

**6 Soft furnishings** The off-white fabric chosen for the window and door treatments blends well with the walls and so does not conflict with the many architectural details (beams, leaded windows and so on).

**7 Blue highlights** The blue of the tiles and decorative plates in the kitchen reflects the sofa upholstery colour, thus helping to link the areas.

**8 Accessories** Kept to a minimum, these give a clean uncluttered look while at the same time suggesting a relaxed country air.

**9 Wine storage** This is provided by a group of clay pipes cunningly placed within a chimney. A strategically positioned downlighter turns this storage problem into a design feature.

*In contrast to its city-centre location, this Gothic-inspired Chelsea conservatory introduces more than a hint of country elegance.*

# Conservatory Living

**C**an you imagine the joy of spending late autumn afternoons warmly lounging in the midst of your garden, of growing and harvesting your very own tropical fruits and of twilight summer suppers that are guaranteed rainproof? No, this is not a description of life on a faraway tropical island, but a glimpse of the bliss to be had when you own a conservatory.

Yet another inspired Victorian concept that we are revisiting and appreciating anew, despite the disparity of lifestyles between then and now. A conservatory gives life a new dimension. It allows us to enjoy a garden year-round and stretches the living areas of our homes. All age groups can benefit: it provides an ideal space for a toddler to play in (the semi-outdoor finishes should stand up well), for an elderly person to relax in out of season, and for people of any age to enjoy atmospheric dinner parties.

Should you be on the brink of deciding to construct a conservatory, be sure to pin down your ideas well in advance:

- ◆ How much do you want to spend? A finished conservatory may cost more than you imagine and such extras as heating, lighting, wall and floor finishes, furnishings and plants can add considerably to an initial estimate.

- ◆ How will the finished conservatory look from outside? Do you wish its style to reflect the architecture of your home?

- ◆ Which direction do you wish your conservatory to face? A southerly orientated conservatory will be full of sunshine, but unless a good ventilation system is installed and shade provided (by blinds or by painting the glass), it is likely to overheat in summer. A north-facing glass house will receive little sunshine and so will require an efficient heating system for cooler days.

◆ To what purpose will you put your conservatory? Is it to be a place for indoor gardening, relaxing, dining, cooking or playing?

◆ Do you wish your conservatory to become an integral part of an interior living area and/or to open up to and become one with your garden or terrace? The larger your opening on to either or both of these areas, the more linked they will appear. Double, sliding or folding-back doors will help to achieve the connection you desire.

Because the conservatory represents a link between the house and its exterior, the most appropriate furnishings will be those that reflect this connection. Well-designed garden furniture, softened with table cloths, cushions and upholstered seats, will help to blur the line between inside and out, as will rattan, wicker or cane furniture. A floor of flagstones, scrubbed wood planking or terracotta tiles will underscore the connection. Accessories can provide a similar link – garden statuary, urns, plants and terracotta pots are all particularly suitable. The best window treatments are ones that do not detract from the view or interior planting. Tailored blinds or curtains of muslin or calico in a simple style are ideal.

When it comes to selecting a colour scheme for your conservatory, the choice is yours – but do remember that the exterior views will become your 'wallpaper' and indoor plants your 'accessories', so choose colours that blend well.

Lighting a conservatory is a relatively easy process so long as electrical points have been well positioned and there are sufficient sockets for free-standing fittings. Wall- or ceiling-mounted lanterns will look good, as will discreet spotlights focused on features. A well-lit garden will form a magnificent backdrop at night and a dining table might be lit by a simple country-style chandelier or candles in glass hurricane lamps on the table. Free-standing uplighters placed behind plants will add some magic to the room.

## HOW THE ROOM MIGHT LOOK

### THE PLAN

Despite space limitations and its modern construction, this upper floor of a two-storey conservatory in central London manages to create a feeling of airiness and tradition. A three-seat sofa and wing chair provide seating in this all-purpose living-space-cum-studio. A coffee table and round side table are provided for the convenience of the occupants and a large antique chest offers generous storage space.

### DESIGN DECISIONS

1 **Scheme** Cool cream and green form the basis of this deliberately simple, fresh, rural scheme. The designer's use of country-style fabrics and natural materials are entirely apt in this 'back-to-nature' space.

2 **Conservatory style** The gracefully arched, glazed sections are mirrored in the contours of the railings outside the conservatory to give the room an air of elegance. A panelling detail to the lower part of the walls and doors adds interest.

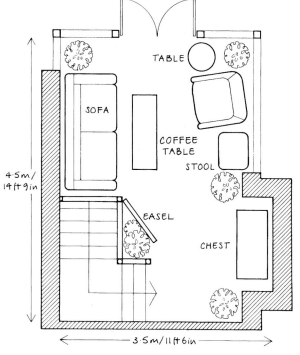

Scale 1:60

**3 Walls** Washed with palest cream to provide a perfect background for botanical prints, a choice of colour that encourages a feeling of spaciousness.

**4 Flooring** Sisal matting contributes a strong textural quality to the scheme and provides a robust floor covering for this indoor/outdoor surface.

**5 Upholstery** A deep and comfortable three-seat sofa encourages leisurely relaxation, and a profusion of cushions with check and zoological-patterned covers shows up well on the dark green striped cover fabric. On the opposite side a plaid-covered wing chair is draped with a length of green checked fabric to soften the chair outline.

**6 Blinds** Operated by a system of cords on cleats, cream-coloured fabric blinds continue the unified look and keep the sun's rays from damaging furnishings and overheating the room.

**7 Lighting** Table lamps and a naive metal chandelier were chosen to reflect the traditional styling of this conservatory and to give it a homely air.

**8 Door furniture** Fine details are the hallmark of the professional designer. Here, handsome brass bolts, handle and hinges lift the whole scheme and give it a quality finish.

**9 Planting** The variegated greens of the foliage blend well with the overall scheme and help to link inside with outside.

# KITCHENS

The kitchen has taken on a much more strategic role in modern times. Once purely an 'engineering' room, it is now more often regarded as the social centre of the home. In line with its new function a typical modern kitchen is more likely to be decorated in an altogether warmer, homelier style. Gone are all traces of laboratory lighting and outhouse floorings and in their stead have come a wealth of living-room attributes.

This does not mean to say that the primary purpose of a kitchen – cooking – can now be ignored. Food preparation must of course be at the forefront of any design decision made for this very important room. One of the most difficult rooms to organize (mistakes will irritate on a daily basis), it requires loads of common sense and forethought to eliminate wasted energy and to make the room a pleasure in which to work and play.

If you are starting from scratch, choosing the right-sized room for your kitchen can be critical. Too small a room and you will have difficulty in accommodating all that you require. Too big and the preparation of each meal will involve you in a marathon. Sometimes the use of two inter-connecting rooms can provide the best answer, the main one being reserved for cooking and the secondary

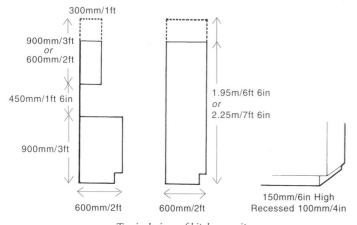

*Typical sizes of kitchen units.*

*Hi-tech metal shelving sporting beautifully arranged kitchen paraphernalia and hardwood units provide all the decoration needed in this serious cook's kitchen.*

one for food storage, laundry, dining or other activity.

It is always a good idea to start by listing all the activities you wish to cater for in your kitchen. Apart from the obvious ones related to cooking, you may wish to launder and iron clothes, arrange flowers, serve informal meals, store party equipment, accommodate a central-heating boiler, provide space for a child to play and so on. If your kitchen has a door to the exterior, you may also need to allocate space for the storage of outdoor clothing, and if there are pets in the house, finding them a corner in which to curl up may be a priority. When you have completed your list, it's time to draw up another detailing all the equipment and storage requirements necessitated by the various activities you have listed.

Having established exactly what is required in the way of equipment, workspace and storage, the easiest way to determine the best position for everything is to draw up a scaled plan of the room (see page 15), remembering to mark in the positions of windows, doors and service points as these will have a strong influence on the location of major items. Then, using tracing paper over your plan, you can try out different arrangements, always starting with the most important items – the sink, cooker and refrigerator. When you have finished, it is advisable to track the movements around your kitchen that might be involved in preparing, serving and clearing away a typical meal. Can any of these journeys be avoided by switching the positions of any items of equipment?

Easily forgotten is the matter of waste disposal. A small skip might be appropriate in some kitchens, but a more practical solution may be the combination of large swing-bin (preferably housed within a unit) and a waste disposal unit attached to the sink. A waste compactor will also help minimize the volume of waste for disposal. Ventilation is another aspect easily overlooked: do you really want to be reminded of what you ate for dinner last night?

There are various solutions – a vent in a window or exterior wall or an extractor system over a hob that recycles the air through filters. Best of all, however, is an extractor that wafts kitchen vapours directly to the exterior.

Once all the important planning decisions have been made, it's time to decide upon the style you wish to adopt. Perusal of kitchen magazines and brochures plus visits to showrooms should fill you with inspiration.

## SURFACES

Paint is probably the most suitable wall finish in a kitchen, but this doesn't have to be boring old flat cream. Choose from any number of decorative finishes – stipple, rag or other broken surface. Conjure up a country-kitchen feel by the use of stencils or create your own faux finish to complement your kitchen units. Wallpaper, so long as it is washable and is well adhered, can also be used.

Surprisingly in a kitchen the floor, being a relatively uninterrupted surface, often offers the best opportunity for a design statement. First fashionable in the 1960s and 1970s, cork is probably one of the most appropriate floorings. It is quiet, soft underfoot, doesn't readily show dirt and is easily cleaned. A vinyl woodstrip flooring (vinyl with a thin veneer of natural wood) performs as well as any synthetic floor but has the advantage of having a natural look. Cushioned vinyl floorings are popular and old-fashioned linoleum is enjoying a revival. All these floorings can be cut to your own design in any number of shades or have a contrasting border incorporated. Other hard finishes such as quarry tiles, flagstones and ceramic tiles are all suitably durable, but may be noisy and a little tiring on a busy cook's feet.

The most common finish for worktops is laminate. A much-improved product, this is now

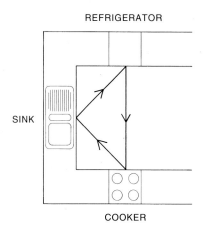

REFRIGERATOR

SINK

COOKER

*The working triangle.*
*For convenience your passage*
*between these three main elements*
*should ideally form a small triangle.*

*Kitchen lighting.*

able to stand up well against hot pans and sharp knives. It looks particularly smart with a deep, post-formed, rounded edge. As an alternative, various types of stone (granite, slate, marble and so on) can give a touch of luxury. To save on cost and weight, these surfaces can be relatively thin, with a double depth at the edge to fool the eye into believing that a greater thickness has been used. Wood is a wonderful material and makes an attractive top for a country kitchen. Tiled tops have found favour, but are difficult to keep clean and care should be taken to avoid germs being harboured within the grouting.

## FURNISHINGS

Furnishings are best kept to a minimum so as not to hinder movement around the kitchen. Tall stools (with a seat height of about 70cm/27in) are suitable for under a standard worktop and provide for spontaneous meals or a rest for the tired cook. It is advisable, for both aesthetic and acoustic reasons, to introduce some soft finishes into this otherwise rather hard-edged room. Padded seat covers for the seating and your choice of a textile window treatment will help. Curtains are not always the answer – the window recess may be shallow and curtains might dangle inconveniently over the worktop surfaces – and blinds generally prove to be a more acceptable solution. Whatever your choice, all fabrics should be washable.

## STORAGE

Frequency of use should be a strong determining factor when planning storage. High and low levels are best left for rarely used items, while eye-level spaces should be reserved for items that are used every day. In many instances a ceiling can provide useful extra storage space. A rack can be fixed from which can be suspended any number of objects (preferably items that are both practical and at the same time decorative).

## LIGHTING

As with all good planning, practical considerations come first. In this case the preparation of meals must be top of the list. The mistake most frequently made is not in the selection of fittings but the siting of light sources. It is vital that light beams are cast exactly where you want them and that they are not interrupted by shadow. To ensure this the light source must come from directly above the work surface rather than behind the person working at that position. Avoid spotlights on a centrally positioned track as almost inevitably this will mean you are working in your own shadow. Instead consider ceiling-fixed downlighters over your work surfaces or strip lights fixed to the underside of wall units and shielded from view by baffles.

To create a more social atmosphere in dining/relaxing areas of the kitchen it is advisable to have at least one other circuit of lighting which can be switched on when food preparation is completed and the lighting over work areas is extinguished. A rise-and-fall pendant fitting over the dining table provides a most suitable light, as does a downlighter. And for those special occasions, nothing beats the intimacy and cosiness of candles. Additional soft lighting around the room could come from a combination of table lamps and wall lights.

# Cook's Kitchen

The kitchen takes on so many roles in modern times that it is sometimes easy to lose sight of its primary purpose. The starting point when planning a kitchen for the dedicated cook has to be the equipment. Whereas many kitchens may have only a basic oven or microwave, the true cook will undoubtedly be seeking altogether more specialized appliances.

Cooking, it should be remembered, is a physically tiring process and everything possible should be done to minimize unnecessary work, travel around the kitchen and wear and tear on the cook. The layout of the working cook's kitchen is unlikely to have units simply ringing the room. A central island or 'peninsular' unit is a most important factor in the reduction of kitchen traffic. A mobile unit on castors is also a useful addition to kitchen furnishings.

In the serious cook's kitchen, storage may well be without doors and open to the elements – quick and easy access obviously being a priority. To ensure that the vast array of exposed equipment and worktop space is kept impeccably clean and does not become covered with a fine film of grease resulting from the cooking vapours, a heavy-duty ventilation system is essential. When planning your storage requirements, do not forget to allow a slot for cooking manuals.

The surfaces within the well-used kitchen will be chosen for their robustness and ease of maintenance. Stainless steel is a favourite work surface and, as well as being tough, easy to clean and hygienic, it can look extremely smart in a modern setting. A bright idea for the busy cook is to set a cutting board into the worktop as a permanent fixture – so much easier than having to seek out a loose one from within a cupboard.

For walls and ceilings, a paint finish that will stand up well in humid conditions (seek individual manufacturers' advice) is likely to be your first choice. Dark colours are rarely seen in a kitchen but, with the right artificial lighting, can provide a stunning background to complement your food. The area between wall and base units is generally faced with ceramic tiles – a good finish that can also provide an opportunity for decoration.

Any floorings discussed in the general introduction (page 66) would be suitable for this busy kitchen, but do take care that the surface beneath the floor covering is well prepared in the first place. Any faults in the under-floor will soon show through and with time the flooring will wear unevenly.

When we think of a chef's kitchen, the most likely image is of a very modern, streamlined room devoid of any decoration or charm. But there really is no reason why a country kitchen (see page 76), centred around an old-fashioned range, should not serve the same purpose so long as certain essentials are in place: namely, good working appliances, plenty of clear work surfaces and masses of accessible storage.

For ideas on how to equip your kitchen, visits to the showrooms of catering kitchen manufacturers can provide inspiration. Here you will see a vast array of equipment and appliances rarely displayed in a domestic supplier's showroom and you can seek out advice from the professionals.

*Everything in this clean-cut kitchen, with its many serviceable surfaces, shouts 'We mean business.'*

# HOW THE ROOM MIGHT LOOK

## THE PLAN

The island unit in the centre of this working kitchen provides a useful extra work surface as well as somewhere to serve informal meals. Its positioning also means that cooker, refrigerator and sink are never more than a few steps away from the working/serving area. Notice how the sink has been located in front of the window so as to provide maximum natural light and a view, and the cooker is positioned so that vented smells can easily be trunked to the exterior.

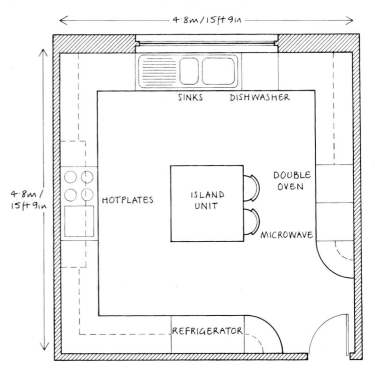

Scale 1:60

## DESIGN DECISIONS

1 **Scheme** More about materials than colours, this simple scheme centres attention on blond wood, stainless steel, marble and brick.

2 **Flooring** Wood planks provide a warm, easily cleaned, hard surface perfectly in keeping with the use of natural materials in this kitchen.

3 **Island unit** A convenience for both the cook and the diner, this unit, with its handsomely proportioned top, allows plenty of overhang to ensure room for seating comfort. An inset section made from the same marble as the worktop elsewhere in the kitchen is convenient for chopping, pastry-making and laying down a hot pan. A channel around the perimeter catches any loose liquid. The brick of the unit base adds a contrasting texture to the smooth stainless steel and polished wood.

4 **Stools** Two in number and sleek of design, these allow the busy cook to rest or to enjoy an informal meal in company. When not in use, they slot neatly beneath the worktop.

5 **Sink** One-and-a-half sinks are surrounded by a stainless-steel top and have a useful swing-arm mixer tap. A waste disposal unit beneath the half-sink ensures that kitchen garbage is kept to a minimum.

6 **Cooker hood** Faced with stainless steel and of serious proportions, this hood ensures that cooking odours linger less.

7 **Window treatment** Venetian blinds provide a no-nonsense window treatment that is neat, practical and continues the hard-edge look.

**8 Lighting** Pendant space-age fittings located over the island unit and sink are well targeted and their sculptural quality reinforces this kitchen's modern theme. Pin-hole downlighters, discreetly recessed into the ceiling, lift the overall level of lighting

**9 Metal racks** To either side of the cooker hood, these make use of 'dead' space and provide long-term storage for pans and other cooking utensils.

**10 Wine rack** This stylish criss-cross unit not only stores bottles but also provides a design feature in this aesthetically and ergonomically planned kitchen.

**11 Wall clock** An essential ingredient for the time-conscious cook.

# City Kitchen

For some the preparation of meals is a task to be reduced to a minimum. This might be from choice, priority time being given to work commitments, study or social activities outside the home, or it may be caused by the simple lack of space. Whatever the reason, to cater for your needs it will be necessary to refine your kitchen operations and equipment in a minimal kitchen.

While the best space in an apartment is likely to be devoted to reception rooms and bedrooms, the kitchen is frequently relegated to the remaining area. This might be under a staircase, in a corridor, off a hallway or in some small internal room. Having decided on where the kitchen is to be sited, the next matter for your attention is whether to have the kitchen exposed or cleverly concealed from view. Cupboard doors, a screen or blinds can all be used to good effect in this regard.

Overcoming lack of space and natural light are likely to be the biggest problems faced in a small kitchen. However, much can be done with careful selections:

◆ Pale, cool, reflective surfaces will visually enlarge the space, as will the use of similar colours for all surfaces – details can be added in contrast to give interest.

◆ Space can also be saved by swapping a conventional door at the entrance to the kitchen for one that takes up less space. This might involve a sliding door, double doors (which open in half the space) or concertina doors.

◆ Clean lines and constant levels help to give a kitchen a streamlined appearance, as will the installation of an unfussy window treatment (Venetian, roller and Roman blinds are particularly suitable).

◆ Artificial lighting can be used to advantage. Plan on providing a good balance of light in your kitchen – any areas remaining in shadow will visually disappear, thus making the room appear smaller. Ceiling-fixed recessed down-lighters and strip lights fixed to the base of wall units will provide excellent lighting conditions. Should your kitchen have a disproportionately high ceiling, this can be disguised to some extent by concentrating light in the lower portion of the room.

◆ The effect of placing mirror tiles on the wall between the base units and upper units is most impressive. They add glitz, increase any natural light and visually open up the space.

◆ It may be tempting to go for reduced-sized appliances (as supplied for boats, caravans and so on), but select full-size equipment if you possibly can. This will allow you a greater variety of items to choose from and, should you later move on to a larger space, your equipment will be reusable.

◆ The microwave cooker has revolutionized our lives and is particularly suitable for the small city kitchen. Not only does it take up a much smaller space than a conventional oven, but it also simplifies the cooking process.

◆ To enlarge your worktop space, incorporate pull-out extending surfaces that slot under a normal worktop.

To increase storage space, build in extra-high wall units. The upper portion of these can be used for longer-term storage and fold-up steps for reaching can be kept nearby. Extra storage can also be eked out of the wall space between the upper and lower units if a racking system or cup hooks are installed. In a tall kitchen the ceiling space could also be brought into use as a storage area with cooking utensils hung from hooks suspended from the ceiling.

*Walls of high-gloss Devonshire cream and an arrangement of classical busts give nothing away in this hallway kitchen of a London apartment.*

# HOW THE ROOM MIGHT LOOK

## THE PLAN

Sculptures in this entrance hall kitchen take their inspiration from the exhibits in the Soane Museum in London and help to disguise the room's rather surprising dual role. Cupboards to either side of the desk open up to reveal a far more domestic purpose than first appearance might indicate.

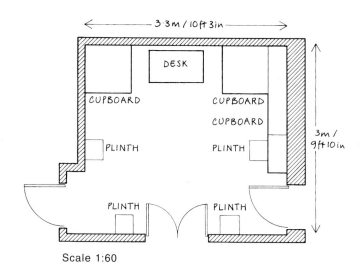

Scale 1:60

## DESIGN DECISIONS

1 **Scheme** Glossy walls of pale yellow enlarge the space and create a soft background upon which classical busts are displayed.

2 **Flooring** Coir matting provides textural interest and a robust finish suitable for this 'traffic' area.

3 **Desk** A shelf pulls out from the underside of the Victorian standing desk to provide a useful work surface.

4 **Cupboards** Flanking the desk, these are built in and finished in the same way as the walls so that they appear to be part of the structure. Note how the cornice and skirting/base board has been continued across the cupboard fronts and sides so as to complete the illusion.

5 **Lighting** Strongly focused down-lighters highlight the wall-hung plaster busts, while wall-fixed swing-arm lamps illuminate the desk. The cupboards open to reveal additional downlighters to light the contents.

# AN ALTERNATIVE KITCHEN

## THE PLAN

Squeezed into 'dead' space on a landing with stairs leading off, this narrow kitchen is both decorative and functional. The units are full depth and cleverly accommodate all that the minimal cook might require. Fitted against one wall, this slender kitchen takes full advantage of the airy space above the stairs.

## DESIGN DECISIONS

**Scheme** Whatever the season, this spring-like scheme, with its sponged pale yellow walls and jade units highlighted with white, will always feel fresh and bright.

**Flooring** Practical pale green linoleum tiles are bordered by a darker green to give the area definition.

**Units** Chosen for their decorative quality, these Gothic-inspired units are painted in a delicate shade of green.

*This smart landing kitchen, with its elegant units and pretty colours, does not need to be concealed.*

**Shelves** Filled with decorative objects, these help to give the kitchen a less-than utilitarian look.

**Lighting** Four eyeball spots focus on the kitchen worktop and on pictures on the wall opposite. Additional working light is provided by strip lights under the wall units.

**Pictures** Positioned high up on either side of the prettily arched window, the two paintings ensure a pleasant view from the kitchen.

**Plants** Artificial foliage suspended from the ceiling to conceal an air vent continues the country theme.

# Country Kitchen

What a wonderful picture the term country kitchen conjures up: visions of flowers drying over an Aga cooker, dogs curled up in a corner, home-made orchard-fruit preserves in pots on a rustic dresser, freshly gathered garden-grown vegetables in a basket and the smell of newly baked bread permeating the whole house. The room reeks of tradition, wholesome food, country values and a sense of permanence, summing up an altogether more tranquil approach to life – an attitude that seems ever more desirable in times of pressure, insecurity and rapid change.

Of course, such a kitchen style is best suited to a house or cottage set in a rural location, but this does not preclude it from being adopted in a more urban situation. The urban kitchen might open out into a conservatory rather than a picturesque cottage garden and a cat might replace the hunting dogs, but there is no reason why the essential elements of country style should not be embraced in the city.

The essence of country-kitchen style is that everything should look as though it has had a chequered past. This is best demonstrated by including old items that have in fact been used over generations – perhaps bought at country auctions, purchased from antique shops or haggled over at car-boot sales. Newly constructed articles, manufactured to modern standards and 'distressed' to give an instant feeling of age, can also be incorporated. These may well have the advantage of offering a better performance while still evoking times gone by. A gas-, oil- or electrically-powered range will suggest a bygone age without requiring stoking, and modern units behind doors of aged wood will be easier to keep clean and will not warp.

Units are best when they appear to have evolved rather than having been installed all at the same time and from a matching suite. Although it is preferable for the carcasses to be modern, the facings can be manufactured from aged timber and, for the correct look, should be free-standing rather than in a continuous run. A central wooden table and a large ceramic Belfast sink with wooden drainer and old-style taps will help to reinforce the style.

Surfaces within the country kitchen are most likely to be natural or at least natural-looking. Wood dominates and can be used for units, worktops, flooring and even walling. Flagstone floors are traditional and terracotta tiles will give a similar country feel to a kitchen. Painted wall surfaces are in order and nature's rich colours – leaf green, earthy terracotta, sunny buttercup yellow and gentian blue – provide a perfect background to complement all that timber.

This is one kitchen style for which curtains might be the preferred choice of window treatment. Unpretentious materials such as cotton gingham, ticking, butter muslin and calico make a strong rural statement when used for simply gathered country-style curtains.

The most suitable lighting arrangement here would be to combine high technology with simple country-style fittings. The modern fittings should be discreet and provide a good working light (recessed downlighters and/or strip lights behind baffles are a suggestion), and traditional wall lights, table lamps and old-fashioned overhead pendant fittings will help to set the mood.

Although we tend to think of the country kitchen as being essentially English, there is no reason why you should not create your own Portuguese, American, Mexican, Italian, Moroccan or other ethnic kitchen (hints on ethnic style can be found in 'Global Style' on page 216). What fun could be had in collecting implements, crockery and other cooking kit in foreign lands and finding ceramic wall tiles, cupboards and floorings from far-away places.

*Cream and buttermilk combine with blue to offer a warm welcome in this fresh country kitchen.*

# HOW THE ROOM MIGHT LOOK

## THE PLAN

A country-style dining table forms the centrepiece to this spacious, traditional kitchen. The Aga cooker on the right nestles neatly in the chimney and units to either side house pans, baking tins and so on. On the opposite wall a dresser, laden with china, provides additional storage space. The 'sink with a view' makes full use of natural light in its position under the window and a dishwasher is accommodated nearby. Double entrance doors are flanked to one side by a refrigerator and on the other by a tall cupboard. The door on the right leads to a butler's pantry and that on the left to a dining room.

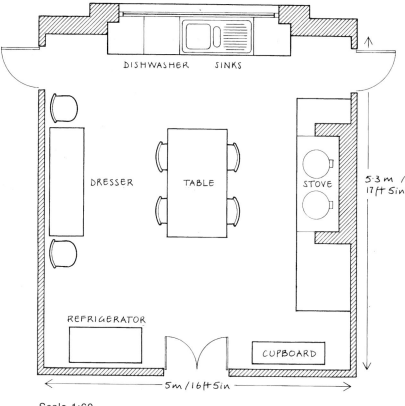

Scale 1:60

## DESIGN DECISIONS

1 **Scheme** Fresh creams bring sunshine into this north-facing kitchen and blue china plates 'paper' the walls to provide interest and contrast. A blue border neatly contains the wall space to give the room a tailored appearance. A dado of wooden boarding reinforces the country feeling and continues the worktop line.

2 **Flooring** A natural-coloured hard floor surface is practical, especially in cooking and washing up areas, while a cotton rug brings softness to the dining area. The colours of its stripes help to bring the scheme together.

3 **Units** Panelled doors and simple brass knobs give these units a country feel and the cream-painted fronts help them to disappear into the wall surface.

4 **Work surfaces** Slabs of hard-wearing granite provide a touch of luxury. Notice how it is also used for the splash-back around the sink and how it forms a useful shelf behind the range.

5 **Furniture** A country-style table and chairs provide a suitable setting for informal meals. Wooden seats are softened by tie-on cushions with blue-checked covers.

**6 Window treatment** The lack of a soft finish to these windows is no loss when handsome architraves are on display. A border of blue completes the treatment.

**7 Lighting** Modern technology and traditional fittings combine for an apt lighting arrangement. The charming old-style wall lantern is electrified and the Victorian-fashion pendant fitting over the dining table has a rise-and-fall mechanism to allow height adjustments.

**8 Shelf** Formed from a length of cornice, the shelf above the Aga provides a surface for display and has under it a pole for drying kitchen cloths.

**9 Accessories** Great control has been exercised in the selection of accessories. Their common blue colour helps to give this kitchen a sense of unity and order.

# DINING ROOMS

Unlike our Victorian ancestors who believed in each room in the home having a very specific purpose, today we tend to think of dining as a movable feast to be undertaken wherever most convenient or wherever the television is located. It is not so long ago that the dining room was considered very much the heart of the home and few houses were constructed without one. It was where families assembled on a daily basis and where all important festivals and rites of passage were celebrated. But times have changed and in most modern homes the kitchen has in many respects supplanted the dining room as the family gathering room. The dearth of house servants to transport and serve meals, the hectic and conflicting timetables of family members and the general lack of space have all rendered the dedicated dining room, for many, a disposable luxury.

However, the kitchen can provide a most excellent space for dining. Generally the warmest room in the house (an important factor in cooler climes), it allows food to be served directly from the preparation area and also enables the person preparing the food to enjoy the company of others fully as the meal is processed.

Other areas you might consider for a dining role are a portion of a living room, a hallway, a study or even a conservatory. It makes little sense to deprive a child of his/her own bedroom, a spouse of his/her study or guests an overnight stay in order to preserve a room that otherwise might be used only for occasional entertaining. But there is no reason why a room cannot serve two functions. With cleverly chosen lighting, the selection of dual-purpose furnishings and inventive use of storage, a room might provide a space for several purposes most successfully.

If you are in the happy position of being able to reserve a room specifically for dining, how do you go about selecting a space within your home? It goes without saying that for convenience this needs to be sited in close proximity to where the food is prepared. Our ancestors may have found tepid tea and lukewarm lunches acceptable when houses were larger and servants plentiful, but today's busy lifestyles yield little time for scuttling along corridors and space is not easily given up for that piece of furniture appropriately known as a dumb waiter. Hatchways through to the kitchen, once much favoured, are currently rather less fashionable and are being replaced by open-plan kitchen/dining rooms. The size of room is obviously a factor for consideration, as is the view from the window if the room is to be used primarily during daylight hours.

When deciding upon a style for a dining room, think carefully how it will marry up with your/your family's eating habits and your desires for entertaining. You need to ask yourself:

- What household members need to be accommodated (numbers and ages)?

- When will the room mostly be used – day or night time, summer or winter?

- How many people do you like to entertain at any one time?

- Do you prefer to entertain formally or informally?

- What mood do you wish to create?

*Pleated raspberry fabric, with a gilt fillet edging, lines the walls of this colourful dining room lit by a Dutch-style chandelier with tall candles.*

## SURFACES

The treatment of surfaces will very much depend upon your style of dining. For a family they will naturally have to be fairly resilient to stand up to daily wear and tear. The floor merits special attention. This needs to withstand the scraping of chairs (take care with stretchable natural floorings and any that are not stable or well adhered to the floor itself). The acoustics of the room should not be ignored. Half a dozen small children dragging wooden chairs on a hard floor surface can be quite deafening, especially if there are few other soft surfaces in the room.

## FURNISHINGS

The centrepiece of the room is naturally the dining table and much will depend upon your choice of the most suitable shape and size for your purposes. Many people favour a round table, which has the advantage of eliminating disputes as to who should sit at its head. It also allows conversation across the table to be enjoyed between all diners rather than only between those positioned adjacently as is the

case with a rectangular table. An additional benefit is that there is greater possibility for squeezing in an extra guest, especially if your table is a pedestal type (that is, one with a central pillar rather than legs around the perimeter). The table size is also critical: too small and it will not happily accommodate all your dishes and diners will not be able to eat in comfort; too big and conversation will be difficult and traffic around the table may be hindered.

## STORAGE

The main items requiring storage are likely to be table mats, napkins, silverware and glassware, and it is a great advantage to have these stored where they are easily to hand. A sideboard will provide conventional storage, but perhaps cupboards and shelves might be constructed within niches to either side of a chimney breast. The bulk of your items could be placed within the cupboard space, while the more decorative items (pretty china, glass and silverware, for example) could occupy the display shelves. An unused fireplace can

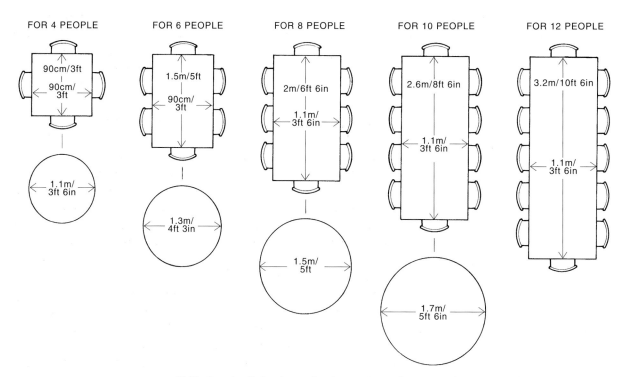

*Table sizes for dining in comfort (approximate dimensions).*

*Bouquets of stencilled flowers border the sloping ceiling and carry the eye upwards in this pretty country setting primed for breakfast.*

provide useful storage for wine. Simply fill the space with clay pipes (see page 57) and store bottles on their sides within the pipes.

## LIGHTING

Dining rooms probably offer the greatest opportunity for planning creative and dramatic lighting effects. As they are frequently used at night and for entertaining, a little theatricality is not misplaced. The star feature in any dining room will inevitably be the table and, of course, the diners – and flattery of both is your aim.

Traditionally the table would be lit by an overhead light fitting – frequently a chandelier type – which, although adding to the decorative value of the room, may not provide ideal lighting conditions or even a controllable source. To overcome the deadening effect of light cast from such a fitting, a dimmer could be attached to it and downlighters installed to provide more easily manipulated light sources.

The highlight of your table, apart from the dishes you serve, will no doubt be a centrepiece and, whether a humble bowl of fruit or an elaborate flower arrangement, this will benefit enormously from being swathed in light. A recessed low-voltage downlighter casting a narrow beam will highlight this beautifully. The addition of candles, be they in smart silver candlesticks or within a hurricane glass, will soften the effect and cast a pleasing glow on guests' complexions.

Of critical importance is that nothing should interfere with cross-table communications. Attention therefore needs to be paid not only to the height of any table decoration but also to the position of light fittings over the table. A rise-and-fall system attached to an overhead pendant light will allow you to adjust the height precisely, and candle sizes can be selected to ensure that they do not cause a distraction. A crown-silvered bulb will help to prevent glare in guests' eyes.

To complete your plan, softly focused lighting around the perimeter of the room will ensure that the table does not appear in a vacuum; it can also be useful in illuminating a serving area.

Get the lighting right, and at the flick of a switch your 'café' will turn into a sophisticated restaurant!

# Dedicated Dining

A licence to entertain! Formal dining is all about theatre, drama – a performance. We are continually being told that the dinner party is dead and that, in modern life, a dining room is a luxury we can all live without. True, we can get by without one, we can invite friends for supper and entertain them in the kitchen surrounded by all the clobber of cooking, but anyone who possesses a room dedicated to the pleasures of eating and entertaining knows how much it adds to the richness of home life. For a few hours we can suspend reality and pretend that the world is a wonderful place where every sense is pampered and everyone is beautiful.

For a start it presents the most amazing opportunity for showing off – for bringing out grandmother's china service, for polishing the family silver, for decorating the dining table with exotic floral delights and for wearing the most glamorous of outfits. We all need to escape, especially after a hectic, distinctly unglamorous day.

The decoration of your dining room can be quite idiosyncratic – it is part of your theatre and the set you create will depend upon the tale you wish to relate. Think of all the restaurants you really admire and enjoy lingering in. Would the style of any of them translate well into your space? Is your taste for a sophisticated, cool, modern look? Or perhaps French rustic style? Write down half a dozen words that best describe your favourite look and use these as your starting point.

Choosing a colour scheme for a dedicated dining room can be great fun. Banished are the restraints that pertain to some of the other rooms in your home. There is no need to select a safe calm scheme here – the likelihood is that you will occupy the room for only relatively short periods and so can afford to go for a stronger statement than, for instance, in a bedroom or even in a living room. If your room will be used primarily at night, the problems associated with balancing natural light need no longer limit your choice. Colour psychologists will tell you that red stimulates the appetite (did the Victorians know something we claim to have recently discovered?) and it is certainly a colour to encourage animated conversation. Whatever your choice decision, it is vital to try out the colours/materials in the light in which they will be seen.

Lighting is probably the most important factor when it comes to setting the mood in a dining room. As your guests enter the room, a great theatrical trick is to limit the lighting to just one very strong narrow beam (preferably from a recessed downlighter) directed over the centre of the table where you have placed a most magnificent centrepiece. Even the humblest bowl of herbs, presented in this way, will take on altogether new dimensions of interest. As all the guests assemble, you can then switch on other lighting sources to continue with the meal.

When dressing the table, never think of its accessories in isolation. Whatever you put on the table in the way of centrepieces, cloths, mats, napkins, china, glassware and so on will instantly become part of your overall scheme, and each piece should be chosen with this in mind. It is therefore necessary to practise some restraint when selecting a scheme to ensure that, when all is in place, the two most important elements – your guests and your food – are complemented by and not in competition with your decorations.

*Dressed to entertain: this traditionally styled dining room promises pleasure.*

# HOW THE ROOM MIGHT LOOK

**THE PLAN**

This fortunate space happily accommodates a dinner for ten with room to spare. The door on the left leads to the kitchen, while double doors open on to a hallway. A tall ceiling results in elegant proportions suitable for a grand treatment. Items of antique furniture fill the spaces to either side of the fireplace and a Regency sideboard occupies the wall opposite. Gilt console tables flank the double doors in this pleasingly symmetrical room.

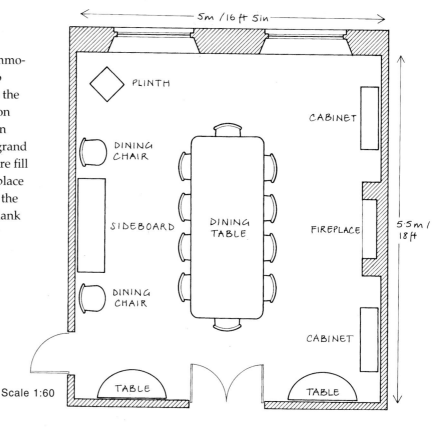

Scale 1:60

**DESIGN DECISIONS**

1 **Scheme** Green has been chosen as the basis for this scheme in a south-facing room. The cooling effect of this colour is diluted by a traditionally styled, cream wallpaper bearing a trellis pattern covering the wall above dado level. Below the dado rail, green paint has been applied and the horizontals that this treatment creates help to lower a very high ceiling.

2 **Flooring** Beige Wilton carpet fitted to close cover has a luxurious feel and provides a soft background against which the stunning table setting is seen.

3 **Window treatment** Generously proportioned windows provide a perfect setting for a grand swags-and-tails treatment. A tartan silk has been used to line the tails and trim the leading edge of the curtains and a deep bullion fringe finishes the swags. The loss of natural light from this curtain style is acceptable in a room facing south and having such handsomely proportioned windows. The brightness is further filtered by the use of sheers.

4 **Lighting** The dramatic effect of focused lighting from downlighters above the table is softened at night when candles within hurricane lamps are lit.

5 **Dining chairs** A stunning green-and-beige fabric has been used for the upholstery and it is shown off well on these high-backed chairs. The antique close-nailed finish to the backs and seats reinforces the room's traditional style.

**6 Tableware** Continuing the period theme, cut glass and fine china have been laid out with napkins to complement the scheme.

**7 Flowers** An important ingredient to dress any dining room and to perfume the air, the flowers on the table and mantel reflect the room colour scheme, while topiary trees of dried flowers complete the window dressing.

# Family Dining

Family dining is all about happy, relaxed times spent enjoying wholesome food with family members. It is not about going into a cold, little-used, unwelcoming room where ritualistic behaviour is required. Family meals may provide the only time in the day when all gather together and proper conversation is possible, so it is vital to make this assembly as convenient, enjoyable and relaxing as possible. Decorations chosen with this in mind will go a long way to encourage just such an atmosphere.

For the space to work it needs to be practical, so that a glass of spilt juice does not cause a catastrophe or dropped food a drama. In this regard your choice of floor covering may be critical. A hard floor, from a maintenance viewpoint, is ideal. Ceramic or terra-cotta tiles may be easy to clean, but perhaps a little hard on the feet and noisy. A cushioned flooring of sheet vinyl, cork tiles or wood may be a more comfortable solution and one that is slightly warmer in appearance. If you have a partiality for soft finishes, an area rug that can be easily cleaned may be the answer. A fitted carpet is not out of bounds – especially if treated (when new) with a sealant to prevent the absorption of spills. Natural floorings are not recommended for families with anything less than the best behaved children – they tend to absorb liquids (unless treated) and hold crumbs and their unstable character can cause them to ruck up where chairs are dragged over their surface.

Other surfaces within the dining area may need to be child-proof too. A table with a laminate surface that can be cleaned very easily is one answer, and a wooden one, treated with a clear varnish, will perform almost as well. Should your table surface be of not such a suitable material, the use of an oil cloth will help to protect it. Always provide mats (cork or padded fabric are a good choice) for hot plates.

*Neutral furnishings in this practical family dining area allow the many beautiful wood finishes to shine through.*

Where smaller children are involved, it pays to use a resilient wall finish should this be within 'firing distance'. Gloss or other washable paint is suitable, as is vinyl wallpaper or wooden boarding.

When considering the decorations for a family dining area, you will, of course, also need to take into account any other purposes for which the room is intended. Wherever a family dining area is located, (near a food preparation area, for preference) the aim should be to create a space that is bright, cheerful and informal.

The lighting in a family dining room needs to be relatively bright and perhaps less dramatic than in a formal dining room. The dining table may well also be used for other purposes – homework, hobbies and so on, and these activities require good lighting con-

ditions. A pendant fitting (or two, in the case of a long table) would be suitable, provided that either the bulb is not visible or that it is of the crown-silvered variety. It may be wise to avoid table-top lighting as it may interfere with work and hobbies, although this could be brought out for evening entertainment purposes.

To define your dining area it may be necessary to divide this portion of the room from the rest. You can do this in a variety of ways. A piece of furniture (such as a sideboard, a floor-to-ceiling shelf unit or a kitchen unit) could be placed appropriately between the two functions; an area rug, somewhat larger in size than the table, could be laid under the eating position; or screens could be used to obscure the cooking area of a kitchen.

# HOW THE ROOM MIGHT LOOK

## THE PLAN

This medium-sized room is visually enlarged by the glazed doors opening it up to the adjacent space. Perfectly suited to the needs of a growing family, the table is well proportioned to the size of room and ample storage space is provided in the dresser and sideboard opposite. The symmetry has been maintained by the central positioning of the table, giving this room a casual but controlled feel.

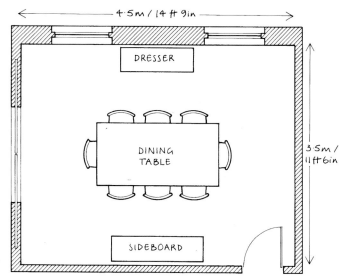

Scale 1:60

## DESIGN DECISIONS

1 **Scheme** The neutral scheme based on natural materials in the dining room is repeated in the adjoining sitting room, which helps to make the two areas work well together.

2 **Flooring** Not only is parquet wood a highly practical finish but it also echoes the light colour

of the wood of the table, chairs, dresser and sideboard, helping to harmonize the scheme.

3 **Table** Well weighted and sturdy, this timber table happily accommodates eight in comfort and visually looses its bulk against a background of a similar colour.

**4 Chairs**  A harlequin set of similarly styled chairs is more interesting than a matching set and is much more fun to assemble. Tie-on cushions aid comfort and can be easily removed for cleaning when required.

**5 Dresser**  Traditional in style, this gives the room a country look and provides useful storage for tableware.

**6 Sideboard**  Placed opposite the dresser, this provides additional storage and maintains a sense of symmetry.

**7 Windows**  A stained-glass panel rests within the frame of each of the two windows to provide a decorative statement.

**8 Window treatment**  Curtains are slotted on a brass pole running the whole length of one wall. Unlined, they allow sunlight to filter through, giving the room a light and airy feel.

**9 Double doors**  These glazed, sliding doors provide a division when required and slot neatly within the adjoining walls when drawn back. The glazing allows light to pass between the two rooms when the doors are closed.

**10 Lighting**  Rise-and-fall pendant lights, providing convenient illumination for dining or doing homework, can be adjusted upwards when more overall lighting is required.

**11 Plants**  These reinforce the country message.

# Occasional Dining

As dining rooms are increasingly requisitioned for what are seen as priority uses – a study, a playroom, a guest room or a nursery – we are having to become ever more ingenious in seeking out a space for dining activities. Even if a dedicated space already exists, there may still be a call for some small corner for dinner *à deux* or even for solo suppers.

What, then, are the possibilities? In a living room a coffee table might be utilized for a casual television supper with friends, or perhaps a small round table normally covered with a full-length cloth could be given a new role as the centrepiece of a smart dinner for four. That often-neglected area, the hallway, offers many possibilities. Two semi-circular tables normally positioned separately against a wall and displaying collections of pretty things might be joined together to form a round table for a smart supper for six. A kitchen peninsular unit plus several stools might provide an easy space for an informal lunch with friends, and a garden suite in a conservatory could become the site of magical midsummer candlelit suppers.

Where space is limited, there are several measures that can be taken to make the area seem larger:

- A small dark basement room with a door leading to a garden can be transformed with the help of sheet mirror attached to the walls and faced with garden trellis. A suite of well-upholstered garden furniture, lots of shade-loving foliage and dozens of candles complete the picture.

- Banquette seating takes up far less space than individual chairs – an excellent way of creating a dining area within a bay window or small kitchen corner. In addition, if the seats are constructed with hinged tops, the space beneath can be used for long-term storage.

- A glass-top table will virtually disappear against background decorations and will not dominate the space it occupies.

- A good idea from the Shaker movement is to incorporate pegboards into a room scheme (see page 246). These are excellent for storing fold-up tables, chairs and other items when not in use.

- For occasional larger parties, a small round table can be temporarily extended with the help of a hinged circular top made of MDF (medium-density fibreboard) or similar weighty material in a size in excess of the existing top.

- Other space-saving tables are: drop-sided tables; tables that will accommodate additional drop-in leaves; gate-legged tables; trestle tables.

Accommodating dining chairs when they are not in use can be a problem in a small apartment. A great idea is to scatter them throughout your rooms, covering each drop-in seat with a fabric to match the scheme of the room where the chair is located. When they are gathered together for dining purposes, the chairs can be transformed with temporary covers all made of the same fabric to give the appearance of a matching set.

The quickest and easiest way to inject a transient eating area with a sense of occasion is by clever use of focused lighting. A floor-standing swing-arm lamp directed over the table will do the trick, as will a group of candles massed at the centre of the table and scattered around the room. A floor-standing uplighter placed in a corner behind a large plant will create some evening magic. Remember that by focusing light on the table, the room's main purpose will be to some extent disguised.

*Neo-classicism is the theme for this grand hallway in a Mediterranean villa that happily
changes its role to that of dining area for up to twenty people grouped around the two tables.*

# HOW THE ROOM MIGHT LOOK

## THE PLAN

The hallway is entered from a portico on the left and acts as a lobby to the grand salon to the right. A small sitting room is located at the top of the plan and opposite is an entrance to the kitchen – a perfect arrangement both for every day and when entertaining. In the classical style, symmetry permeates the plan, giving the room a great sense of order. When it is used in its capacity of dining room for a large party, the two granite-top tables are set with fine china and lit by candles. The side tables are used for serving and additional chairs are gathered from other locations in the villa.

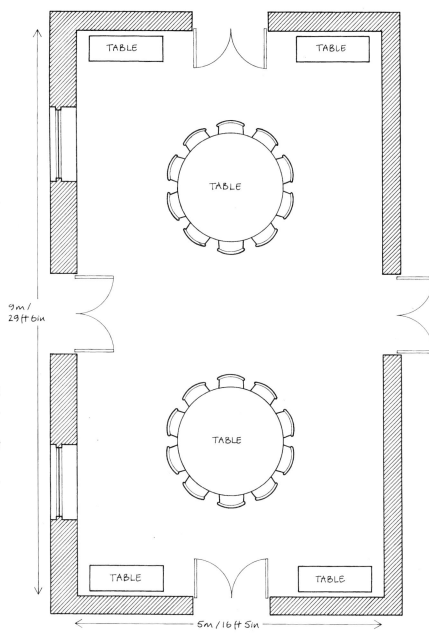

9m / 29ft 6in

5m / 16ft 5in

Scale 1:60

## DESIGN DECISIONS

1  **Scheme**  Deliberately neutral to contrast with the boldly coloured schemes of the rooms which lead off from it, this large space is made more intimate by the colour rendering of both walls and ceiling in the same pale corn hue.

2  **Flooring**  Teak, bush-hammered stone and brown glazed tiles combine geometrically to form this dramatic entrance-hall flooring which is both practical and attention-seeking. The pattern is enclosed in a border of the plain stone to ease the transition to other floor surfaces in the rooms leading off.

3  **Architectural details**  An over-scaled broken cornice, keystones and bold architraves add impact to the room and reinforce the classical theme.

4  **Doors**  Four sets of almost full-height double doors give the room a sense of importance and grandly frame the views beyond.

**5 Tables** Two granite-top round tables with plaster tripod bases provide a surface for books and baskets of dried flowers in their everyday role and can each seat ten people for large dinner parties.

**6 Chairs** English-style Portuguese chairs with a limed finish are scattered throughout the house and assembled whenever a large dinner party is planned.

**7 Side tables** Two classically inspired tables with stone tops sit at either end of the room to provide a surface for decorative objects during the day and serving areas for dinners at night.

**8 Mirrors** Flanking the double doors into the salon, these two highly decorative, gilt looking-glasses from the eighteenth century bring a sparkle and sense of occasion to the room, especially when candles are lit at night. They are carefully positioned to reflect the attractive exterior view and help to amplify the natural light in this otherwise slightly dim area.

**9 Pictures** Twenty splatter-work silhouettes from the mid-eighteenth century litter the walls in a symmetrical fashion, all positioned with a common baseline.

# CONNECTING SPACES

The arteries of your home, connecting spaces should be awarded all the respect normally given to individual rooms. They not only greet you but also serve to lure you into the rooms beyond. The hall, stairs, landings and corridors of a house have a pivotal role to play and it is through the framework they form that you will view all the other rooms. Often characterized by their mean proportions, irregular shape and lack of light, these areas require very careful attention if they are to become the convenient welcoming spaces they should be.

The designer's first consideration should be the actual structure enclosing the space. By highlighting any features that are perfectly proportioned or well balanced, you can bring a sense of symmetry to what otherwise is often a rather disorganized area. Perhaps the floor has a regular outline: this could be emphasized by giving the chosen floor treatment a border in a contrasting colour. Alternatively, if the ceiling height is pleasing, an attractive cornice or border could be introduced to enhance the line where ceiling meets wall. A bold treatment at a good-looking window has a similar effect. You can disguise features that are less pleasing by reducing their details or painting them out (that is, in the same colour as their background). If the area is totally lacking any redeeming features, you might consider creating a 'blank canvas' of the same colour on all surfaces and then applying points of interest superficially on the walls (with pictures) or on the floor (with area rugs) or by introducing interesting loose furnishings.

It is important to establish a focal point in each area – something pleasing for the eye to rest upon. It might be a handsomely surrounded fireplace, an impact-making picture, a well-proportioned window or a stunning carpet. Whatever it is, be sure that it is well positioned and given real star treatment with the help of some thoughtfully designed lighting.

When it comes to selecting colour schemes for these transitional spaces, people have a tendency to veer towards bland mid-range colours and, because of sometimes restricted space, strong patterns are avoided. But the opposite approach often produces the most successful results. A boldly patterned carpet, for instance, can add an enormous amount of drama and excitement to what otherwise might be a very characterless area, and because people are generally only passing through the room there is little danger of tiring of such a strong statement. Because these spaces impinge upon one another – the hall leading to the stairs and the stairs then leading on to a landing and so on – it is important to establish strong links between the schemes in each. Laying the same carpet throughout these connecting areas is an excellent way to give your house a sense of unity. The only limitations to bear in mind are the effect of heavy traffic on your chosen colours and the possibility of clashes with individual room schemes.

Where light is restricted you have two choices: either to fight for light (by using reflective surfaces, light colours and mirrors) or, more unconventionally, to accept the darkness and play up to it. By painting such an area a wonderful rich dark colour and incorporating some clever lighting effects, you can sometimes produce a magical effect.

Because there may be less to distract the eye in these connecting spaces, attention to details becomes paramount. Door handles and panelling, architraves and cornices, light switches and socket plates – these all deserve your special attention.

*In this 'continental' entrance hall natural materials are to the fore. Note how the chandelier cleverly reflects the lines of the table base.*

*Using stippled wallpaper in yellow banded with chocolate, the designer David Hicks lends character to his cornice-less English country house hallway.*

## SURFACES

The highways of your home have to cope with much wear and tear and will soon appear tired if hard-wearing surfaces are not installed. For floors a robust treatment is required. If your choice is carpet, this should be at least of heavy domestic quality, and a twist or loop pile carpet will show less evidence of shading than a cut pile. Natural floor coverings, such as sisal, coir and seagrass, may well provide the robustness you need, but care should be taken when applying these on stairs as some of them can be rather slippery (seek the advice of manufacturers when in doubt). Hard floors like wood, stone, marble, terracotta and vinyl can look stunning in hallways and corridors and can be covered with area rugs for warmth and sound insulation, but do take care that the combination is not a lethal one from a safety viewpoint.

Walls can be tricky in connecting areas when it comes to deciding where one finish should end and a new one start, particularly when stairways are involved and you wish to link two different schemes harmoniously. In general, priority should be given to the more important ground-floor scheme, but if there is a logical architectural break between the two areas this is the obvious point at which to make the change. If your choice of wall treatment is a little delicate – wallpaper, for instance – you might consider installing a dado rail and treating the area below it with a more resilient paint finish.

## FURNISHINGS

Because connecting areas generally offer few opportunities for the placement of furniture, each piece will stand out and therefore requires very careful selection. Consider particularly how items will appear when viewed from different angles. For example, a chest may be seen from below when positioned on a landing at the top of a stairway. Corridors, landings and hallways can appear rather bleak without the interest furnishings create, but remember that no item of furniture should be allowed to hinder the passage of human traffic.

## STORAGE

Even in the very smallest of connecting spaces you can often find a cranny where storage can be accommodated. In many cases, by filling in a recess in this way, the architectural symmetry of a room can be much improved at the same time. Drawing up a room plan (see page 15) will reveal just where these spots are. If you want these newly created housings to appear as part of the structure, the surface of the door front should be treated in exactly the same way as the rest of the wall space (wallpapered or painted) and the door furniture should be minimal. Book storage in a home is often a problem, but corridors offer an excellent site. Being narrow in depth and decorative in appearance, books can be happily accommodated in passageways, lobbies and hallways – but do remember to light them appropriately, so that books can be removed and examined in comfort. A valuable space for storage that is often ignored is the area above a doorway. Although not easily accessed, this space can be useful for the long-term storage of items infrequently required.

## LIGHTING

Safety considerations should be top of your list. Arranging for at least one light that can be left on overnight in each connecting area is important. This could either contain a low-wattage bulb or, better still, be controlled by a dimmer switch for minimal overnight lighting. A timer switch attached to, say, a hall light may also deter would-be burglars in your absence. You may well think that because there are no specific activities being undertaken in connecting spaces, there is no need of 'task' lighting, but the act of circulating through your house does require good lighting if it is to be done in safety. In particular light should be directed towards floors so as to highlight

any change of level (this especially applies to stairways). A system of two-way switching that allows you to switch on a light from one position and off upon leaving the area from a different exit is essential. Exterior lighting at a front door is often neglected, yet it is needed not only to offer a warm welcome to visitors but to also illuminate the knocker/door bell/letterbox, and to allow you to view your visitor before opening the door.

*Tricks of the trade that visually widen and shorten a long, narrow corridor.*

# Entrance Hall

The old adage 'You never get a second chance to make a first impression' is a reminder of the importance of the entrance to our home – the introduction to ourselves and to how we live. It is from here that we welcome the world, and leave the first (and last) impression with family, friends and sundry visitors. Outside it may be dark, cold and hostile, but inside we offer warmth, light and comfort and, whether the hall be grand or humble, this is the message we would like to convey upon opening our front door. Probably because so many are dark, small and badly designed, hallways are often considered a waste of time. But with a little help from some interesting decorations and clever lighting, this unloved space can become our welcome sign to the world.

The range of floorings suitable for an entrance hall are numerous and offer wonderful opportunities for decorative treatments. In a traditional home, hard floorings such as stone flags, marble, terracotta tiles or wood are all fitting choices. Should you be lucky enough to live in a Victorian house (see page 192), you may well find some marvellous encaustic tiles beneath a more modern covering and their colours may provide you with the key to your scheme. Carpeting is also acceptable, but do ensure that a door mat (preferably set within a well so that its surface is flush with the rest of the floor covering) is installed at the entrance to prevent dirt being trampled all over the house.

Lighting plays an important role in setting the mood in an entrance hall. An exterior light (perhaps a lantern for a traditional home and a downlighter for a more modern approach) will signal your presence and guide the visitor to your door. In the hall itself a good level of light is needed and this should be directed towards whatever you have chosen to highlight – a beautifully stencilled floor, a piece of sculpture on a plinth or a massive vase of fresh flowers: the choice is yours. Table lamps offer a very homely, soft light, while a floor-standing uplighter behind an impressive plant will produce shadows that dance across the room.

The furnishings you include in this room will very much depend upon the space available – what you want to avoid, at all costs, is anything that will hinder the circulation of traffic through this 'terminal'. Important items to include are: somewhere to set down mail/newspapers/house keys and so on; a receptacle for umbrellas; a place to hang coats; and, space permitting, at least one chair. If coats are to be stored in a cupboard, remember to ensure that this is ventilated (louvred doors are perfect) to help air damp clothing. A wall mirror is also very useful for last-minute adjustments and this will have the added benefit of introducing a feeling of space and light into what otherwise might be a rather dim

*The simplest of decorative schemes, on a limited budget, encourages light to flood into this once-gloomy Victorian hallway.*

area. Chair backs will be highly visible against the walls, so choose furniture for its decorative quality.

Although it is traditional for furnishings to ring the perimeter of a hall, if space allows, it is a great idea to place a round table at the centre of the room. When topped with a collection of beautifully bound books or prettily framed photographs, and perhaps a large bowl of dried or fresh flowers lit from above with a downlighter, this can form a stunning focal point and serve as the centre to your 'roundabout'.

The spacious hall can be made to feel more homely and less sparse if furnishings are to scale – that is, as grand as the room – and if lighting is concentrated upon the lower portion of a tall room. A grouping of upholstered seating placed around a fireplace forms a welcoming sight and deep, warm, advancing colours (see page 34) on the walls and ceiling will enhance the feeling of cosiness and intimacy.

If space is a problem – you might possess one of those frequently seen, narrow, rather dark halls – much can be done visually to counteract its limitations. Exchanging a solid door for a glazed one will much improve the availability of natural light, as will the introduction of a fan-light above the door. Mirror, framed or in sheets, will enhance whatever light falls naturally into the area and at the same time will help to open out the space. To maximize the feeling of spaciousness visually, go for plain reflective surfaces in cool pallid colours (see page 34) and bring interest to your scheme by the introduction of contrasting textures. A combination of rough matting, gloss paint, pale matt stone and polished blond wood, for instance, could look stunning. (For other ideas on visually enhancing space see page 18).

The style evidenced in a hall will set the tone for the whole house, so its selection is most important. As always the architectural period/style of your home will be your first prompt, and for your house to have any sort of cohesion the theme you choose should relate to that running throughout the rest of the building. Global (travel posters, suitcases, wall masks) and classic English country house (flagstones, wellies, architectural prints) are just two themes that adapt particularly well in a hallway. As this room forms the meeting point between exterior and interior, why not bring the outside in? Terracotta pots positioned upright and on their side, a giant urn full of grasses, a watering can crammed with contorted twigs, even a garden bench – these are just a few ideas to inspire you.

## HOW THE ROOM MIGHT LOOK

### THE PLAN

Furnishings are kept to a minimum so as to avoid traffic snarl-ups in this compact Victorian hallway. Instead great reliance is placed upon the architectural features that have been retained to provide decorative interest. The radiator cover plays a dual role – to conceal the radiator and to provide a useful surface for lighting and decorative objects.

### DESIGN DECISIONS

1 **Scheme** Well away from the original Victorian palette, a bright neutral scheme brings this hallway bang up to date. The wallpaper, with its stripes of two pale yellows, emphasizes the elegant proportions of the space without adding confusion to the already interrupted wall area.

2 **Architectural details** The decorative arch, glazed entrance door, handsome cornice and embellished balustrade all contribute to the period feel.

3 **Flooring** Seagrass is selected for its toughness in this high-traffic thoroughfare. Its textural quality and natural colour add much to the scheme, while the stair carpet of a similar colour causes no distraction. A mat of coir positioned at the entrance relieves shoes of dirt and an oriental rug in the main area adds a colourful touch.

4 **Lighting** A combination of downlighters and two blond wood candlestick lamps bring brightness to the hallway. Notice how the three-dimensional quality of the plaster bust is emphasized by the

light falling from the candle lamps. During the day, a mirror amplifies any natural light entering the area from the glazed front door.

**5 Internal door**  Treated in a modern way, this is stripped of paint and waxed to show off the beautifully figured pine grain.

**6 Radiator cover**  This trellis-fronted box serves to hide a radiator discreetly, at the same time providing a surface for decorative objects and the setting down of keys, letters and so on. The glass top with its reflective surface and the open base both contribute to the overall feeling of space and light.

# Stairways

The staircase in your home may not be equal to that featured in *Gone with the Wind*, but may nonetheless be of sufficient architectural interest to form the focal point of your entrance. Graciously curving hand rails, handsome newel posts, elegantly proportioned steps and elaborately cast or turned balustrades – these are all details that merit attention. If more modest in size and lacking decorative detail, your stairway will, at the very least, offer space to create your very own picture gallery or perhaps a print room, and will become a pleasurable transitional space between floors.

*Glass shelves within window reveal.*

The major decision you have to make is whether or not to 'star' the stairway and, if so, which elements merit special treatment. Whichever parts are coloured in contrast to the rest of the scheme, these are the details that will stand out. Remember also that wood has a colour and it is a good idea to try to match other timber furnishings in the surrounding areas to this colour.

It is impossible to think of a stairway without considering the rooms with which it connects – in particular the hall from which it probably emanates. Because the two areas will inevitably be viewed together, it is important that the colour schemes of both are closely linked, if not entirely the same.

The space beneath a stairway offers a wonderful opportunity for storage, either closed in and housing unsightly items (such as cleaning implements and bicycles) or open and perhaps forming a mini library or bar. In a space-pressed home, a miniature office might even be accommodated.

For practicality surfaces need to be tough. If carpet is your chosen floor covering, ensure that it is well attached to the stairs either by a gripper rod beneath or stair rods above. Stair rods are an old-fashioned but decorative idea and many styles, particularly those in brass, are still being manufactured. A stair nosing will protect stair edges in situations where there is particularly heavy wear. Delicate wall surfaces can be protected by the introduction of a painted dado at the lower level.

Lighting is an important element of stairway design. This does not need to be especially bright, but the risers and treads should be bathed in sufficient light to ensure that they can be distinguished. Ceiling-fixed downlighters provide ideal lighting so long as suitable fixing points are available. Alternatively, wall-fixed lights (either downlighters or uplighters) will provide good illumination, but these should not protrude dangerously into the stair space and care should be taken to ensure that glare from bulbs is not viewed while either descending or ascending the stairs.

The small landing formed where stairs change direction can provide a useful platform for an interesting decorative treatment. If space permits, a grouping of console table and one or two chairs will transform this otherwise rather boring area.

Stair windows come in all shapes and sizes – sometimes in the form of a feature to be embellished upon, but all too often an architect's disaster to be disguised. If you are lucky enough to possess one of elegant proportions, much can be made of this. The contours of an interestingly shaped window are best preserved by fixing the treatment within the reveal, and this is one situation where a festoon blind or

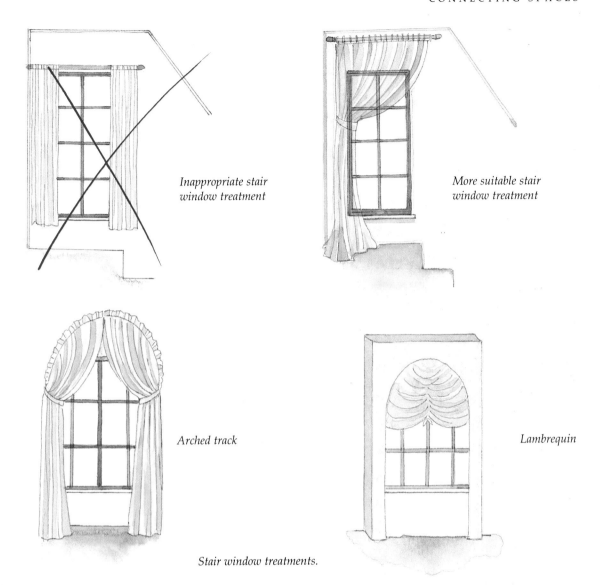

*Inappropriate stair
window treatment*

*More suitable stair
window treatment*

*Arched track*

*Lambrequin*

*Stair window treatments.*

festoon curtain can be deemed appropriate. Curtains do not look good if they stop half-way down a wall or if they dangle aimlessly over a top step. In such cases a single drape, swagged to one side with a chunky rope tie-back can look most effective. Shutters offer another solution and can take on decorative importance if echoing the outline of an attractively shaped window. Should privacy not be of concern, an unadorned window can be framed with a painted stencil border on the surrounding wall. Another suggestion involves fixing glass shelves across the front of the window to display a collection of beautifully coloured glassware or healthy plants. The best way of dealing with an unattractive window is to minimize

its importance by treating it in the simplest manner possible and by selecting a fabric to blend in with the surrounding wall colour. The eye can be further distracted from an ugly window by hanging dramatic pictures on adjacent walls or by fitting an attention-grabbing floor covering.

Spiral staircases continue in popularity. They offer a solution where space is at a premium and can look most decorative. But beware: they take up more space than you might imagine and are generally not as easy to negotiate as conventional stairways. It pays to plan ahead – if you intend to introduce children or the elderly into your home, this style of staircase may prove a hindrance.

# HOW THE STAIRWAY MIGHT LOOK

## DESIGN DECISIONS

**Scheme** Shades of grey have been chosen to ensure that all attention is on the white silhouette of this superb modern interpretation of a late seventeenth-century balustrade.

*Shades of grey throw into sharp relief the magnificent contours of this late seventeenth-century-inspired stairway.*

**Flooring** Polished marble in the entrance hall mirrors the classical garden feature and bounces daylight in all directions. On the stairs a grey cord carpet with a darker border defines the route.

**Archway** To add symmetry to the stairway, an arch to the right-hand side half-way up the stairs has been echoed on the other side by the use of sheet mirror.

# AN ALTERNATIVE STAIRWAY

## DESIGN DECISIONS

**Scheme** Basically neutral, this scheme takes its lead from the wall display of hats. White-emulsioned walls provide a plain matt background and dark beams add definition.

**Flooring** Tough coir matting reflects the neutral theme and echoes the texture and colour of the straw hats.

**Landing** Continuing the natural theme, nests of grain rest on wall brackets and long twigs add to the wall decoration. A metal chair completes the grouping.

*Hats of every shape, size and nationality provide amusement and textural
interest on this cottage stairway.*

# Corridors and Landings

S o often a dumping ground for furnishings not wanted elsewhere, corridors and landings deserve better treatment – in fact, they deserve their very own schemes and to have furnishings purchased specially. They form areas we are likely to pass through on a daily basis and so are worthy of our care and attention.

Because landings frequently have their wall space haphazardly interrupted by openings off, it may be necessary to tidy up the space aesthetically in an attempt to bring to it some sense of order. This may involve making a badly positioned doorway 'disappear', which can be done by creating a jib door. Here all evidence of the door (panelling, architrave, finish and so on) is removed and instead it is finished in the same way as the surrounding walls, including a continuation of the skirting/base board (see page 18). Where doors are pleasingly symmetric in their placement, you may wish to highlight them. By adding well-scaled mouldings to the face of flush doors, painting panels in different shades, painting the doors in a contrast to the walls or by running a border around the door frames you will direct the eye to these pleasingly placed features.

In a narrow corridor, furnishings may prove difficult to accommodate. As with all traffic areas, it is vital that circulation is not hindered. You might consider incorporating some small upright chairs with elegant backs and pretty cushions, a shallow console table laden with decorative accessories or a fitted bookcase. However, if space precludes even these, you might think of forming a 'shelf' table that fits neatly against a side wall and takes up no floor space

*Grandeur is added to this classically themed small space by the use of over-scaled accessories.*

at all. It could be constructed from a strip of marble – say, 15cm/6in deep from front to back – supported by two reinforced plaster corbels and attached to the wall at 'table height'. A beautifully framed mirror fixed above completes the arrangement (see page 99).

One of the secrets of successful corridor decoration involves the visual breaking-up of the space so that a passageway does not appear to meander aimlessly on and on. There are several ways to achieve this:

- The creation of pools of light rather than all-over light will provide both contrast and interest. Narrow-beamed downlighters directed at a decorative floor treatment (such as patterned carpet, checkerboard tiles or a stencilled wood floor) will achieve just such an effect.

- By the judicious selection of wall colours you can visually change the proportions of a corridor. To push out the side walls select colours that recede, and for a corridor to appear shorter add an advancing colour to the end wall (see page 34 for advice on the functions of various colours).

- Mirrors fixed to side walls will magically open up the space and make it appear much wider and lighter. These can be in the form of sheets made into a wall of mirror or in panels placed between doors. Cut to shape, mirrors can be used to back recesses/niches, and framed sections can be hung at intervals.

- The placement of an item of interest at the end of the corridor will have the effect providing a focal point as well as stopping the eye. You may choose to display a piece of sculpture, a stone urn or perhaps a decorative vase on a plinth. A stunning framed painting, stencilled walls or a *trompe l'oeil* painted effect will serve a similar purpose, as will an item of exquisite furniture.

- Floor coverings that emphasize the horizontal will also help to break up the space. A continuous carpet that has a trellis pattern or is divided into panels will be effective, as will individual area rugs placed at intervals on to either a hard floor or fitted carpet.

- Interest can also be created on side walls by hanging pictures. Not only will they make your passage through the space more pleasurable, but the reflective surface of their glass fronts will help to bounce around whatever natural light is available. A decorator's tip to stabilize pictures hanging in a traffic area is to fix each picture at two points (that is, with two hooks) instead of one.

Structurally breaking up the space may involve only slightly more work. The creation of arches along your corridor will not only break the 'journey' but will also provide an attractive frame through which to view the scene beyond.

The key to a winning scheme may well lie with some existing possession. A tribal runner carpet, a particularly dominant painting, an exotic screen or a gorgeous piece of painted furniture – any of these items could be used as a trigger for a successful scheme. By picking out and repeating a colour element from your furnishings, you will instantly draw attention to them and give them a sense of belonging.

On the matter of safety it is important for sufficient light to be provided to signal any changes of floor level, and that lights can be switched on and off at either end of a corridor (that is, two-way switched). It also is essential that loose floor coverings be well attached to the underfloor (special webbings are available for loose carpets placed on either hard or soft floorings), and for hard floor surfaces to be non-slip, especially where there are children or elderly people in residence.

# HOW THE ROOM MIGHT LOOK

**DESIGN DECISIONS**

1 **Scheme** Walls of glossy cream 'snakeskin' help to enhance the minimal amount of natural light falling into this potentially dull space and provide a blank canvas against which bold accessories and prints are displayed.

2 **Flooring** Reed matting continues into the adjoining rooms to create visual unity and provide a robust floor covering in this high-traffic area. The fact that its colour is near to that of the walls encourages a feeling of space.

3 **Chairs** A pair of pigskin-covered chairs join their 'mates' when required in an adjoining dining room.

4 **Accessories** Bold and linked by a classical or natural theme, these well-scaled objects have been chosen to provide plenty of passing interest.

## *AN ALTERNATIVE LANDING*

**DESIGN DECISIONS**

**Scheme** The choice of vertically striped wallpaper adds elegance to this connecting area and the selection of neutral colours allows for maximum leeway in the schemes for the rooms leading off.

**Flooring** The trellis-patterned carpet reflects the style of the radiator grille and directs the eye away from the length of the corridor.

**Lighting** Huge brass lanterns continue the bold theme and visually break up the area by creating pools of light.

**Prints** Beautifully framed, these prints are grouped together for impact.

*Bold but neutral, this scheme has impact without limiting the schemes in adjacent rooms.*

# BEDROOMS

It is quite extraordinary to think that we devote so little attention to the planning of a room where we are likely to spend half our day if not half our life! Of all the rooms in a house the bedroom is perhaps the most important – a private space in which we can recoup and recharge our batteries, ready to face the onslaught of another day.

We think nothing of spending endless hours on the careful planning of a kitchen. It may not occur to us that the bedroom requires every bit as much attention. But the positioning of a dressing table and the establishment of the correct depth for a wardrobe are equally as critical for our comfort and convenience as deciding on the height of worktops and a location for the refrigerator.

Listing the activities that will be taking place in the bedroom is the starting point. Apart from the obvious one of sleeping, we may, for instance, wish to be able to read, exercise, take breakfast, write letters, or play or work on a computer. Chronicling these at the start of your design project will help concentrate the mind – because it is not until these have been established that you can plan for the space, lighting, furnishing and storage facilities each requires.

## FURNISHINGS

The bed is the main item of furniture in the room and should always be considered first. It is best sited where there is sufficient room to manoeuvre around it (a minimum of 45cm/1ft 6in is recommended), where there is good natural light and from where there is a pleasant view. Other considerations are the electrical points (can the existing ones be utilized in the new arrangement?) and, not to be forgotten, in

*'Less is more' – demonstrated by designer David Hicks in this Portuguese villa guest bedroom dressed in shades of white.*

which position will the bed look best when viewed upon entering the room?

Careful thought should also go into the choice of bed head. Wood and metal are currently favoured materials, but are comfortable only if plenty of pillows are also supplied. A padded type, provided it is covered with a resilient or patterned fabric, may be a more suitable selection. A decorator's tip is to attach the bed head to the wall instead of to the bed itself: this will result in a more stable bed head and will mean easier bed-making.

The most important considerations when it comes to the choice of bed cover are how it will look when in place, and how it will fare when folded. Quilting a fine fabric will do much to give it body and will help preserve its new appearance for longer, and having a suitable receptacle at the end of the bed on to which to fold back the spread will also encourage good care. A long stool will serve the purpose, but a blanket box will have the added advantage of providing storage for cushions and extra blankets.

## STORAGE

In a bedroom there is so much to accommodate and never enough space. A walk-in closet is undoubtedly the most practical solution, but not always an option for those owning a smaller or older property. Additional storage capacity may have to be found wherever possible. Perhaps a cupboard could be located in the hallway outside the room or an adjacent small bedroom converted into a dressing room?

Clothes are likely to be the most pressing problem, with the need to store items both horizontally on shelves and vertically on hangers. Hangers require a space approximately 60cm/2ft deep, and it is important to position the rail at a height which will allow for garments to clear the base of the cupboard. A

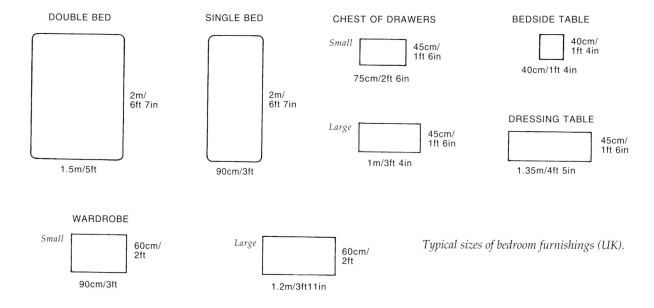

**DOUBLE BED**

2m/6ft 7in

1.5m/5ft

**SINGLE BED**

2m/6ft 7in

90cm/3ft

**CHEST OF DRAWERS**

*Small*

45cm/1ft 6in

75cm/2ft 6in

*Large*

45cm/1ft 6in

1m/3ft 4in

**BEDSIDE TABLE**

40cm/1ft 4in

40cm/1ft 4in

**DRESSING TABLE**

45cm/1ft 6in

1.35m/4ft 5in

**WARDROBE**

*Small*

60cm/2ft

90cm/3ft

*Large*

60cm/2ft

1.2m/3ft11in

*Typical sizes of bedroom furnishings (UK).*

system of wire baskets within a framework could offer the most flexible shelf solution (and, being free-standing, could travel with you when you move on).

A built-in wardrobe unit spanning floor to ceiling will generally provide greater capacity than a free-standing cupboard. This built-in type of housing can also be more easily disguised if you apply the same treatment to the door fronts as to the walls of the room (even going so far as to run the cornice and skirting details along the top and bottom).

### LIGHTING

In many ways the rules applying to lighting the living room can be applied to the bedroom too, but perhaps in a more subtle fashion. It is important to create a calm restful atmosphere and to avoid glare. Light diffused by the addition of silk shades will give just the right soft glow.

As well as achieving a relaxing mood, it is also vital to ensure that the 'task' lighting is doing its job. Of primary concern must be the bedside lighting. Position here is everything: the light source should be at least 60cm/2ft above mattress height if the 'hotel bedroom syndrome' is to be avoided (where the carpet by the bed is beautifully illuminated, but there is simply no chance of any of those rays reaching our book in bed!). Buying a sufficiently tall bedside table

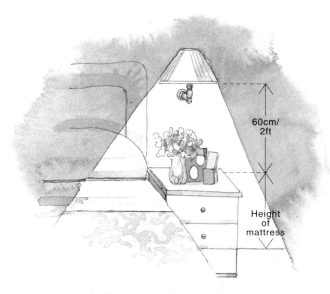

60cm/2ft

Height of mattress

*Example of correct position for bedside light.*

(of, say, approximately 50cm/1ft 8in for the average mattress height) is a good starting point and, so long as the light source is at a sufficient height, it does not matter whether this is a free-standing table lamp, a wall fitting or a headboard-mounted lamp. Many consider the angle-arm wall fitting to be the perfect answer. This frees the bedside table space and can be adjusted for reading in bed or swung back against the wall for bed-making. For double occupancy,

*Stars painted on the ceiling of this gorgeous blue-and-cream bedroom are reflected in the lantern hanging from its centre.*

separate lights to each side of the bed will allow one person to sleep undisturbed while the other reads in bed. These lights, for the sake of convenience, should be two-way-switched between bedside and entrance door so that they can be illuminated on entering the room and extinguished from the bedside .

If a downlighter or pendant fitting is used to provide general lighting, ensure that this is not positioned too near the bed head or the glare will be visible by anyone in the resting position.

Locating a dressing table in front of a window certainly helps with day-time grooming, but at night it will be necessary to ensure that there is an adequate light source between the person sitting at the dressing table and the mirror. Twin candle lamps provide an excellent solution. The same applies for a full-length mirror, although in this case wall lights to either side or a downlighter fixed directly above may be the answer.

Strip lights fitted within wardrobes and with an automatic switch in the door jamb will make the selection of clothing much easier. Alternatively, and provided that the cupboard door exteriors are attractive, a ceiling-fixed wall washer will serve the same purpose.

# Main Bedroom

As our lives become ever more frenetic, the haven a bedroom offers becomes more and more inviting – and not just for sleeping. Quiet reading, television viewing (for the programmes *we* want to watch!), enjoying a peaceful light supper, letter writing – these are all activities that may be best suited to that special private space. Whether accompanied by a partner or not, we should consider our own bedroom the one area where we are obliged to please no one but ourselves (the words indulgence and pampering spring to mind). It therefore makes good sense for the 'best' bedroom space available in terms of area, shape, view, orientation and access to dressing and bathroom facilities to be reserved for this purpose.

At last the benefits of self-containment have been realized. We expect to pay a premium for a hotel suite, so why not plan permanent accommodation on similar lines, with areas set aside for hobbies, relaxing, dressing, bathing and of course sleeping?

When it comes to deciding upon a scheme, it really is a question of whatever takes your fancy: remember, this is *your* room! For preference, though, many people opt for soft colours and quiet patterns as these are considered less tiring on the eyes and more conducive to rest and relaxation (see page 34). An obvious area of contention is when two people of different persuasions try to concoct a scheme to suit both. This problem can usually be overcome by the skilful selection of colours and patterns mid-way between the two tastes. Botanical prints do not necessarily mean acres of pretty pink roses, and in any case pink does not have to be pale and feminine. Some of the most successful bedroom schemes rely on neither interesting colours nor bold patterns. Picked for their blandness, neutrals provide a wonderful backdrop for relaxation and can be sparked up

*Cream forms a calming background for this fresh country-house-comes-to-town scheme.*

by the introduction of pretty bed linen, stylish furniture and sharp accessories. Here you have the chance to buy that really fine, delicately coloured carpet of your dreams (thought to be far too impractical for other traffic-heavy areas). The one requirement is that, whatever covering is selected, it should be kind on the feet. Fashionably modern, natural floorings rarely meet this criterion, but the situation can be saved by laying mats of more friendly materials at bedside 'landing spots'.

There are many styles of dressing table, among which the fabric-covered type is a timeless favourite. The most important factor, however, is its positioning so that as much natural light as possible falls upon the face of the person sitting at the dressing table – beneath a window is ideal.

If you enjoy the feeling of being cocooned, bed drapes are for you. Whether emanating from a corona, half-tester or full tester, they give a wonderfully secure, enclosed feeling and look extremely attractive into the bargain. Always devote careful thought to the lining of any such bed treatment as that is what will be most often seen by the person lying in bed. A smaller repeat of the face fabric pattern can produce a very pleasing result, as can the use of ticking fabric in a co-ordinating colour.

Everyone has their personal preference when it comes to the choice of bedside table or cupboard. There are, though, some common principles worth considering. First, for convenience, it is best if the unit is approximately the same height as the top of the bed mattress. This will vary, but will most usually be around 50cm/1ft 8in. Ideally there should be enough space within the unit to accommodate all that you might wish to store at the bedside: this will help prevent a cluttered top with nowhere to set down that occasional cup of tea or perhaps a posy of fresh rosebuds. A sheet of clear glass cut to the outline of the top of a cloth-covered table will help to prevent staining and dust gathering on the fabric surface.

# HOW THE ROOM MIGHT LOOK

## THE PLAN

The bed is positioned facing an attractive conversation grouping of sofa and easy chair and provides a good view of the garden through the bay window. The availability of natural light was the determining factor when locating the dressing table. Two antique chairs to either side of this complete the group. The sofa is flanked on one side by a cloth-covered circular table (a suitable site for a lamp) and on the other by a

bookcase to house reading matter. The coffee table provides a useful surface for magazines, flowers and meal trays. On the left-hand wall a built-in cupboard spanning nearly its full length provides approximately 4m/13ft of storage divided into shelving and hanging space with long-term storage above. A 'corridor' between the cupboard and the rest of the furnishings has been deliberately left to allow easy passage to the adjoining small dressing room and bathroom.

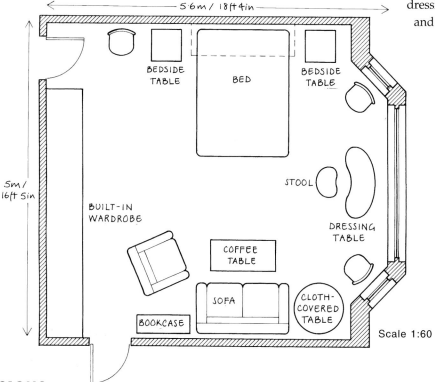

## DESIGN DECISIONS

1 **Scheme** Everything an ideal bedroom scheme should seek to be – clean, calm, light, balanced and relaxing. The floral print helps to bring the garden element into the room.

2 **Main fabric** Controlled use of the floral pattern on the walls and for the bed treatment is balanced by masses of plain fabric to prevent the scheme from appearing too busy. Unusually, the patterned fabric is used to line the inside of the drapes, while plain fabric is used for the exterior.

3 **Fabric-covered walls** These help to cushion noise, giving the room a hushed luxurious feel. Fixings are concealed by a smart dark trim.

4 **Carpet** The choice of cream, a rash decision in any other room where traffic is heavier, is perfectly apt here. The pale colour also helps to give the room a very light, airy feel.

5 **Bed treatment** The generously proportioned, decorative half-tester echoes the serpentine outline of the curtains, adding to a feeling of harmony.

**6 Bed cover** Fitted and box-style, its straight lines are in contrast to the frillier elements in the room.

**7 Bed base** Finely pleated, it perfectly finishes this pretty bed treatment.

**8 Bedside tables** Traditional in style, these painted tables are of a good height and just big enough to stow bedside necessities.

**9 Dressing table** Perfectly positioned for maximum natural light. The kidney shape of the table is replicated in the accompanying stool.

**10 Curtain and bed valance headings** Deep smocking gives interest to these perfectly proportioned but otherwise plain curtains. A pretty navy-and-cream fan edging neatly finishes the base.

**11 Chairs** The positioning of these against a pale background helps to emphasize the magnificent curves of the chair backs.

**12 Lighting** The bedside lamps carry a light source at a suitable height for reading in bed and the use of silk coolie shades helps to spread and diffuse the light (see page 32).

# Occasional Guest Bedroom

A world-famous hotelier is reputed to commission the decoration of his hotel bedrooms only after the interior designer has produced a mock-up of the proposed scheme and after he, the hotel group president, has slept in the sample room for two nights. These are extreme measures for a host to take to ensure the comfort of his guests, but should we do anything less for the enjoyment of our personal visitors?

Few households these days can afford to dedicate bedroom space for the exclusive use of a sporadic guest. Space in many houses will simply not permit it and, more often than not, this room will have to double up with some other function. A study or dressing room could probably most easily be converted to serve this additional purpose with the minimum of disruption, or perhaps a little-used dining room might be considered. Whichever space is selected, take care not to compromise the room's main purpose to any degree for the sake of the occasional visitor. With clever planning it should be possible to devise a room to take on both roles without difficulty.

Should you ever wish to issue an impromptu invitation for an overnight stay, it is important that the room can be readied quickly – no guests like to think that they are putting a host/hostess to any trouble. The conversion therefore needs to be achieved without major furniture movements or storage adjustments.

Beds, when not in use, can be disguised in a variety of ways:

- Convertible chair- and sofa-beds are sold in their thousands and are extremely popular, but be aware that some seating comfort may be compromised by the bed mechanism.

- The fold-away type which emerges, ready-made, from a wall cupboard is easy to erect and is unobtrusive when not in use.

- A fold-up camp bed is cheap and useful for visiting children, but may not offer sufficient comfort for an adult. There is also the problem of housing the bed when it is not in use.

- A day bed is for many the most satisfactory solution. When dressed with bolsters during the day, it provides useful seating and can be handsomely draped for decorative impact. Bedding may be contained within drawers beneath the divan or in a separate blanket box or chest.

- If your need is to provide for two guests, one of the best solutions is a bed with collapsible legs which slips beneath a second bed when not required.

Lighting in this dual-purpose room needs to be carefully thought through if it is to serve both uses adequately. Incorporating free-standing lights such as table lamps and standard lamps (see page 27) will allow you to make swift minor adjustments to your arrangement. Always ensure that there is some form of lighting which can be switched from the bedside.

A wash basin in a guest room is a boon, giving independence to the guest and relieving pressure on a family bathroom. A nearby radiator could have a temporary rack attached for holding towels and a folding screen might be employed to hide the basin when it is not in use.

If the dual role of the room is to be disguised, good storage will be needed. A desk in a study might house stationery, and when the room is required as a bedroom, this could be covered with a full-length cloth and a mirror placed on top for use as a dressing table. Where there is no room for a wardrobe, a coat stand or hooks on the back of a door should suffice for the short stayer. Somewhere will be needed to set down a suitcase. A folding luggage rack, painted to co-ordinate with your scheme and crossed with pretty braid, is an ideal solution.

*A vision in red, this study-cum-guest room offers a warm welcome, even on the coldest of nights.*

Having a guest in your home is all about giving pleasure – those little touches that count for so much:

- ◆ Guest towels sprayed with cologne and presented in a basket on the end of the bed.

- ◆ Fresh flowers on a dressing table.

- ◆ A decanter of mineral water and small tin of biscuits freshly provided by the bedside.

- ◆ Recent magazines or children's story books left on a small table.

- ◆ Tea/coffee-making facilities (the kettle must be small enough to be filled from a basin tap) on a tray placed near a socket.

- ◆ A television, radio and alarm clock for entertainment and information.

- ◆ A hair dryer in a dressing-table drawer.

- ◆ A mirror – full-length, if possible, to aid grooming.

- ◆ A basket of bathroom goodies – perfumes, shampoo and so on, plus a minute bottle of detergent for washing 'smalls' (airline and hotel give-aways are perfect for this purpose).

# HOW THE ROOM MIGHT LOOK

## THE PLAN

This useful space was eked out of a central London maisonette to provide both a work area and accommodation for an occasional overnight guest. The sofa doubles as a bed, and opposite a wall of deep shelves and cupboards houses files and books. The room is also used as a small sitting room, and entertainment is provided by a television and audio system concealed within the wall units.

## DESIGN DECISIONS

1  **Scheme** Warmth is introduced to counteract the cool light entering a north-facing room by the use of bold brilliant red in this monochromatic scheme.

2  **Sofa** Covered in a red-and-white pattern to relieve the masses of solid red, this quickly converts to a bed when required. As a sofa, it is perfectly positioned for television viewing.

3  **Chairs** Positioned at either end of the sofa, a pair of folding wood and cane chairs double up as bedside tables.

4  **Window treatment** A festoon curtain with a handsome swag softens the light entering through the large window. An Indian-inspired pattern is used and is reflected in the ornaments below. A border in a darker red provides definition.

5  **Lighting** Lots of lighting is needed in this room, where the wall surfaces are finished in a dark matt colour. A pair of wall lights, created by the designer, reflect the architectural subject of the prints and are perfectly positioned for reading in bed.

6  **Prints** Old architectural prints are mounted on red card to link them to the scheme.

3m / 9ft10in

SOFA / BED

TABLE

SHELVING UNITS

Scale 1:60

2·5m / 8ft2in

# AN ALTERNATIVE GUEST ROOM

## DESIGN DECISIONS

**Scheme** Neutral and elegant, the scheme encourages the eye to rest upon the attractive view of the garden beyond.

**Flooring** Off-white ceramic tiles 30cm/12in square have been laid diagonally for added interest and are a perfect surface to lead out into the garden.

**Cupboard** Handsomely styled, this cupboard gives few hints of its contents.

*This simply decorated hallway gives no hint of its dual role – until the cupboard doors are opened.*

**Lighting** Uplighters positioned in the corners throw into relief the contours of two pretty chairs. General lighting is provided by the pendant light. When the space is used as a bedroom, integral downlighters illuminate the bed-head area for night-time reading.

# Elderly Person's Bed-sit

Having an elderly relative living in your home can often benefit the whole family. The cost of professional care is becoming beyond the reach of many and, for the older person, living with an extended family can provide continued interest, security and the best possible care. The accommodation of a member of a different generation within the home, it has to be admitted, is potentially fraught, but with a little care and good planning this should not prove to be too disruptive.

The room you choose for the older person will, ideally, be at ground level so as to minimize difficult journeys and should if possible allow space for more than just sleeping. If it also has a large window with an interesting view, this should make your decision easy. The provision of areas for relaxing, bathing, cooking and dining will allow the senior citizen to remain active and somewhat independent from the rest of the household – a situation that is likely to suit both parties. Dividing these areas of activity (by employing screens, curtains or items of furniture) is important for the occupant so that he/she can appreciate the changes in his/her day and can entertain without private areas being on view.

Designing a room for an elderly person is best done by placing yourself in that person's shoes and by thinking through how to compensate for the possible limitations imposed upon their lifestyle. You don't want to be too pessimistic, but it also pays to plan for days when the person's capacities may be reduced. Some of the more obvious provisions are:

- A comfortable, easy-to-get-out-of chair for the room occupant and seating for guests.

- Bright lighting to help cope with failing sight. Wall and ceiling-fixed lights plus well-weighted table and floor-standing lamps are suitable. A bedside switch is helpful, as is a low-wattage light that can be left on overnight. Remember to highlight any changes in floor level. Perhaps also consider positioning sockets and switches nearer to hand height.

- Warmth – older people generally require warmer temperatures than the young. Central-heating radiators and open fires need to be easily controlled and well guarded.

- Storage at an easily accessed level and with openings that are not too difficult to operate.

- The elimination of all sharp corners for safety reasons, and the removal of any electrical cables that could be tripped over. A smoke alarm is another wise precaution.

- In the bathroom, grab rails and a lockable medicine cupboard. You might also like to consider fitting an 'engaged' door sign rather than a lock. Mixer taps and a controlled-temperature shower system will help avoid extremes of water temperature.

- Curtains on a corded track, operated from the side, to ease opening and closing.

- Non-slip flooring and well-attached loose coverings. A fitted carpet of the type that can be easily cleaned is ideal.

The decoration of the room in a familiar style (most likely to be traditional) and the incorporation of existing possessions will help to make the elderly person feel quickly at home. Inviting them to make decoration choices will involve them further. Pretty patterns and cheerful colours will do much to lift their mood and the addition of plants and even a pet will bring life to the room. In addition certain electrical gadgets, such as remote control for lights and curtains, could well smooth the life of an elderly person.

*Country casual is the theme for this comfortable all-purpose room for an elderly person.*

# HOW THE ROOM MIGHT LOOK

## THE PLAN

The view upon entering this well-planned self-contained accommodation for an elderly person is of the comfortable sitting area straight ahead. To the left units enclose the kitchen area. The bedroom area is cleverly divided from the sitting room by means of a high-backed banquette seating unit and next to the bathroom is a useful dressing area containing a wardrobe and full-length mirror.

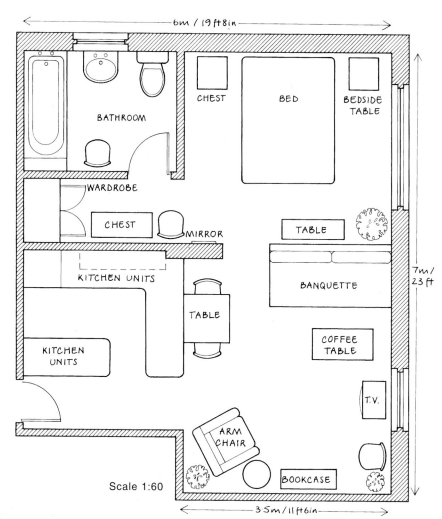

Scale 1:60

## DESIGN DECISIONS

1 **Scheme** Cream walls provide a blank canvas against which country-inspired decorations are displayed. Warm colours predominate and are encapsulated in the border that runs around the sitting room at picture-rail height and which is echoed in the bedroom at dado height.

2 **Flooring** Non-slip ceramic floor tiles in a warm terracotta tone run throughout the space. In the sitting room an oriental rug defines a conversation grouping and is echoed by a smaller one next to the bed.

3 **Banquette seating** Ideal for visiting guests, this seating arrangement is so positioned to partition off the bedroom area. Easily converted into a bed, it is useful for overnight guests or perhaps, in years to come, could provide accommodation for a carer. The base stores bed linens and pillows.

4 **Table** Perfectly sized for the lone diner or small group, this sturdy pine table fits in conveniently next to the kitchen.

5 **Chairs** Continuing the country theme, these have rush seats and a soft cushion for that bit of extra comfort.

6 **Kitchen shelves** The height of these shelves and their lack of door fronts mean that items can easily be reached by an elderly person.

7 **Windows** Stretching almost from ceiling to floor, these large windows provide a generous view of the garden (especially from the bed) and ensure that the room is rarely gloomy. On sunny days the windows can be slid back and entrance to the garden gained.

8 **Window treatment** A blind, headed by a length of paper border on the wall above, gives the windows a simple out-of-the-way treatment.

9 **Lighting** Traditional in feel, the various fittings give a warm glow to the room while ensuring that tasks are targeted. In the bedroom area a bedside lamp is easily reached at night and a Victorian pendant light improves the overall light level. The sitting room is lit by a similar combination and in the kitchen area a candle lamp casts light on the nearby dining table.

10 **Wall clock** Without a busy programme, an elderly person can easily lose track of time: this pretty ceramic clock will act as a helpful reminder.

11 **Flowers** Both dried and fresh, these reinforce the country theme and bring life to the room.

# BATHROOMS

The greatest test of a good bathroom is to ask yourself whether you like to linger there. If the answer is no, it's time to convert that cold, sad, clinical space into something much more pleasurable.

Why the bathroom should be given such low priority by most people and why architects and developers pay so little attention to this vital room is a mystery. Often allocated the meanest of budgets and constructed from what little space remains after all the 'important' rooms have been decided upon, the typical bathroom is frequently small, misshapen and possessing the very worst of views (if, indeed, it has a window at all). From this it can be deduced that we need to be very skilful if we are to create a warm practical room that invites us in.

If you are in a position to start from scratch, you have a wonderful opportunity to customize the space to your exact requirements. Allocate to a bathroom the largest area you can afford and position it for your convenience, even if this means sacrificing a rarely used guest room. Then decide exactly what functions you want the room to perform. These days, as well as being a room for bathing, it may well be used for exercising, beauty treatments, child's play, dressing, reading and relaxing as well as functioning, in some cases, as a laundry.

The placement of the essential equipment of a bathroom is critical – decorations can be changed at whim, but the bath, WC and wash basin will outlive many a scheme. To help you decide upon the best positions, draw up a scaled plan on graph paper (see page 15) and be sure to have this checked out by a specialist plumber before proceeding further. It may well be that by lining up all your equipment on one wall, less disruption will be caused and a smaller proportion of your budget spent. Consider rehanging the entrance door on the opposite axis if this will aid your plan. Alternatively a sliding door or double doors may give you those vital extra few centimetres which will allow you to accommodate all that you need. The space around each item of equipment requires careful planning too, if you wish to carry out the various functions in comfort. Don't forget to consider also how things will work when more than one person is occupying the space (see page 130).

Convention dictates that the bath should run along a wall, but why not be adventurous and place it coming out into the room from a wall or even position it in the centre of the room? Not a new idea this – some of the first baths were so placed to be near an open fire. On which subject, if you have the opportunity to retain an existing fireplace or to construct a new one, think how cosy this could make your bathroom.

The bathroom is a perfect place for incorporating fitted furniture. Not only will it help to hide away much of the 'engineering', but it will also give your room a smarter, more tailored appearance. Incidentally, never overlook the view that you will get while sitting in the bath – from that low level much that is not particularly attractive (the underside of the basins and so on) is revealed.

Some bathrooms need little more than a face lift. In such cases the addition of co-ordinating towels, the introduction of a carpet or the adjustment of lighting systems can sometimes transform at little cost. Ugly dominant ceramic tiles can be disguised by painting over (see page 39) and a discoloured bath re-enamelled. Sometimes a bathroom can take on a new lease of life if you simply clear away the clutter. Enclose the basin in a vanity unit or attach a wall

*Pleated silk shades surround brass wall lamps and are echoed in the mirror-framed Roman shade at the window. Brown walls show off the beautifully figured marble vanity top.*

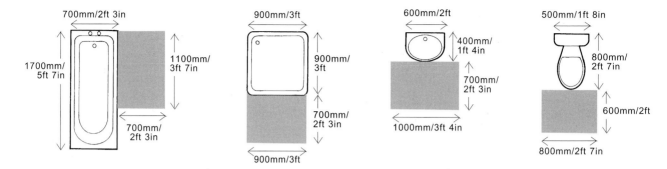

*Typical sizes of bathroom fitments and recommended spaces for activity.*

cabinet and much of the bathroom paraphernalia can be stored out of view, greatly improving the overall effect.

The choice of style for your bathroom is very much a personal decision. As with all other rooms, if you follow the architectural style/period of your house, you probably won't go far wrong. Many fittings from bygone eras are still being reproduced: an Art Deco-inspired bathroom (see page 204), for instance, in a 1920s or 1930s house could look stunning. One thing to avoid is a colourful over-stylized bathroom suite that will not only date but will also limit future schemes.

When it comes to thinking about the decorative details, a tired palm, fluffy loo seat cover, 'fishy' plastic shower curtains and a dish of broken shells will not suffice! Not only are these features hackneyed, but they bear little relation to each other and add up to nothing short of a mess. Instead choose a theme for your room and follow it through.

### SURFACES

Wall coverings must, above all, perform well in humid conditions. Papers can be used but must be securely fixed and have a spongable surface if they are to survive. Non-vinyl papers can be rendered more resilient if coated with a layer of clear varnish. Around basins, showers and baths a sheet of clear acrylic can be fixed to form a transparent splashback. If marble is used, care should be taken to ensure that protruding corners have polished edges. More popular choices are ceramic tiles (aesthetically more pleasing when full-height) or paint. Ceramic tiles can be used on the floor, but make sure that they

are specified for floor use and are of a non-slip variety. Alternative hard floor treatments are cork, marble, wood or cushioned vinyl. In each case the fewer the joins (where water can accumulate), the better. If covering a hard floor with a rug, ensure that it will not slip or trip anybody up. Carpet is also a popular choice: this is obviously softer on the feet but is less easily cleaned.

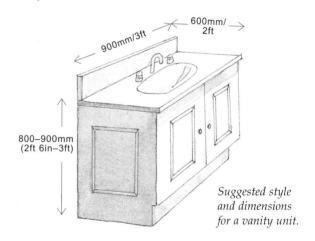

*Suggested style and dimensions for a vanity unit.*

### FURNITURE

The basic items of the bathroom suite (bath and/or shower, WC, wash basin and optional bidet) will no doubt take up most of your budget and so should be carefully selected. A classic white or cream suite is often the preferred choice. Taps should be easy to manipulate, even with wet hands, and a mixer arrangement will aid temperature control. Roll-top Victorian-style baths with claw feet are a current favourite but should be reserved for the larger bathroom where they can be viewed to advantage. The panelled-in type is more common and gives a neat fitted look (especially if you continue the skirting/wainscoting detail around the base of the unit). A vanity unit to surround the wash basin will give a similar effect, but in this case a recessed plinth is required (as for kitchen units) to enable the person using the basin to stand close to it. Be as generous as you can with the size of vanity unit to give plenty of elbow room when washing and to increase storage capacity. Apart from these essentials, other items to add to bathroom pleasure are: a heated towel rail; a chair or stool; and a chaise longue for ultimate luxury.

## STORAGE

Most bathrooms suffer from a lack of storage, so it is no wonder that they appear cluttered and disorganized. In general, bathroom necessities are not attractive and display surfaces should be left free for more decorative items such as perfume bottles and so on. Bath cleaners and the like can be found a home in the base of a vanity unit if this is included in your scheme – behind doors or a curtain, these items remain handy but out of sight. Additional storage can be located in other fitments or a free-standing chest. A stool with towelling cover and lift-up seat combines a useful piece of furniture with extra storage space. Extra loo rolls don't have to be hidden away: heaped in a basket or other suitable container, they can take on decorative importance. How many times have you turned round in a hotel bathroom only to find no place to hang a dressing gown? Hooks on a door or wall space cost little and add considerably to convenience.

## LIGHTING

As well as providing good 'working' light conditions, consider introducing hints of glamour – even perhaps Hollywood-style with 'film star' lighting around a mirror. Safety, however, must be your primary concern: whatever your choice of fitting, ensure that it has been passed for bathroom use. Safety also plays a role when it comes to switching and regulations may require that, if a switch is

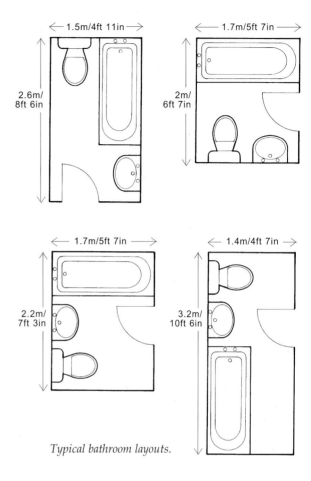

*Typical bathroom layouts.*

located within the bathroom, a pull-cord type is used. Low-voltage lights (with their transformers that help to isolate the fitting) are particularly suitable for bathroom use, and sockets, with the exception of specially designed shaver sockets, are not permitted at all within the bathroom.

Think carefully about the surfaces in your bathroom. They may well be white and have a polished reflective finish that will cause glare if overlit.

As suitable surfaces on which to attach lighting may well be limited, sealed bathroom-rated downlighters may prove to be the most useful fittings to light bathroom activities. As in the bedroom, ensure that light is positioned between the person using the mirror and the mirror itself. The standard fitting for this situation is a strip light, but a ceiling-fixed downlighter or wall lights to either side of the mirror may provide a more aesthetic solution.

# En-suite Bathroom

J ust as there is a trend towards connecting the kitchen with living/dining areas for social reasons, so it is with the bedroom and bathroom. As families become more and more fragmented because of increasing time spent away from home pursuing work, study and pastime commitments, time actually spent in the home has become a precious commodity and the desire for the company of family members strong. The en-suite bathroom in modern times is a necessity rather than a luxury. Not only does it allow for bathroom functions to be carried out in privacy, but provides a more companionable ambience if you wish.

If you are considering forming an en-suite bathroom where none has previously existed, you might think of cutting into the bedroom space if the conversion of an adjacent room is not feasible. If you choose to follow this route, take care not to compromise both rooms by spoiling the architecture of the bedroom and providing too small a space adequately to accommodate all the bathroom equipment you need. If space is very limited, building in a whole wall of cupboard units within the bedroom, one to house a basin and WC, another for a shower and perhaps a further one for hanging clothes may prove the most aesthetically pleasing configuration.

Because the en-suite bathroom is likely to be for the sole use of the occupant(s) of the adjacent bedroom, it can be tailored to their needs without consideration for others. The adult en-suite bathroom can be styled without regard to the assaults a family bathroom is likely to undergo. Wallpaper might be considered and the bedroom carpet continued into the bathroom (with mats to protect potentially wet areas). Pictures might be hung and more items of furniture incorporated. Drapes around the bath might also be considered. If this is your approach, ensure that there is adequate ventilation (to the exterior where practical) to prevent condensation. Internal bathrooms (without a window) are required to be vented and this is frequently operated automatically with the light switch.

If the bathroom and bedroom are to work successfully together, their schemes need to relate, while at the same time maintaining their own individual character. An effective way of achieving this is by reversing the bedroom scheme in the bathroom – that is, taking the bedroom accent colour and using this as the main colour for the bathroom, and adopting the main bedroom colour as an accent colour in the bathroom.

As more and more husbands and wives now both work, bathroom 'collisions' become increasingly likely. To prevent these it is a good idea,

*Style, understatement and elegance – this classically inspired, user-friendly bathroom made for two has it all.*

where space and budget permit, for facilities to be doubled up. A double sink arrangement, a bath and a shower and two WCs will all help to make preparations for the day or for sleep a speedier and more convenient process. For the ultimate in luxury, the inclusion of a dressing room in your suite, if at all possible, will not only free cupboard space in the bedroom but will also allow for one partner to dress without waking the other.

When planning a kitchen we are accustomed to thinking in terms of fitted furniture, so why not in the bathroom which also has to house unsightly equipment and cumbersome plumbing? A framed and panelled bath with drapes, a basin enclosed in a vanity unit, and built-in shelves around a hot water tank or to fill an awkward recess all help to relieve storage problems and give the bathroom a more streamlined profile.

# HOW THE ROOM MIGHT LOOK

### THE PLAN

Perfectly arranged furnishings in this spacious bathroom provide amply for a busy couple with clashing schedules. Double doors at the entrance are faced with 'his' and 'hers' full-height mirrors and a decorative sofa forms a pleasing focal point upon entering the room. Twin basins beneath the window are well positioned to take maximum advantage of any natural light. Curtains at the entrances to the two WCs offer privacy and the centrally placed bath is easily accessed from either side. A shower in one of the WC cubicles offers an alternative bathing facility.

### DESIGN DECISIONS

1 **Scheme** This cool, neutral, grey scheme is both calming and suggestive of classical times. Black accents have been introduced in the bath surround, WC seats, curtain poles, vanity top and picture frames to give the scheme definition.

2 **Theme** In this case, classical – as emphasized by the urn on the bath, the Piranese print, the dish on the vanity top and the vase of fresh lilies.

3 **Flooring** The choice of this off-white carpet is justified in this adult bathroom where wear and tear are likely to be minimal.

4 **Bath** Centrally placed, this adds to the classical symmetry of this smart bathroom.

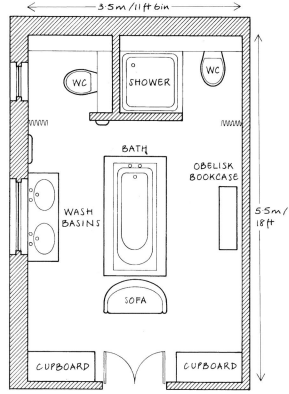

Scale 1:60

5 **Cupboards** Fitted storage cupboards to either side of the double entrance doors and beneath the basins ensure that clutter is housed out of view. An obelisk bookcase opposite the window accommodates bathtime reading matter.

**6 WC cisterns** These unsightly pieces of equipment in the two cubicles are neatly boxed in and hidden from view.

**7 Lighting** Principally provided by recessed down-lighters, this gives an otherwise fairly bland room added drama without making a feature of the fittings themselves. The value of the light from the downlighter over the bath (which is positioned slightly off-centre to avoid a structural beam in the ceiling) is intensified by reflection from the white enamel of the bath.

**8 Skirting** Notice how this continues around the fitted elements to give them the appearance of being integral.

**9 Curtains** At the entrance to the WCs and shower, these simply styled, goblet-headed curtains are suspended from decorative, crook-ended metal poles.

**10 Towel rail** Positioned vertically near the basins and easily accessed from the bath, this towel rail with heated bars ensures that towels are always warm and dry.

**11 Telephone** Essential for busy people, this colour-blending telephone is sited for maximum convenience.

*Clean lines distinguish this modern stylish bathroom scheme in black,
grey and white relieved by vivid yellow.*

# Family Bathroom

They may be queuing to get in, but are you sure this is as an indication of the attractiveness of your family bathroom? Might it not simply mean that your home could really do with additional facilities?

It may be a long time since we had to make do with a tub before the fire and a hut in the garden, but it seems that we are slow to recognize the vital role a bathroom plays in the smooth running of family life and it is only now that houses are being constructed with bathrooms matching bedrooms something like *pro rata*. A recent survey by house builders has revealed the somewhat unsurprising information that what most appeals to the current house-buying public are big kitchens and 'lots of bathrooms'.

When it comes to planning a new bathroom or refurbishing an old one, the criteria that apply to bathrooms in general (see page 128) apply especially to the family bathroom. In addition there is a need for even more stringent safety precautions in view of the wide range of ages likely to be using this bathroom. A lockable cupboard for the storage of medicines is useful and an out-of-the-way space will be needed for storing caustic cleaning materials if the household contains young children. Locks on windows and the elimination of sharp corners in the bathroom will also help maintain safety. Non-slip surfaces should be incorporated wherever sensible and grab rails are a useful addition if there is an elderly person in the house. Taps need to be chosen carefully: they should be easily manipulated, even with wet hands. A mixer-tap system will help prevent bathroom users from being exposed to extremes of temperature and, incidentally, will make for easier hair washing.

The furnishing of the family bathroom will depend very much upon the size of room at your disposal. As it is likely that the bathroom may be occupied by more than one person at a time, keeping the room as clear as possible (especially around the bath) will be a priority. Twin wash basins housed in a built-in unit are ideal and, if space allows, a separate shower could prove an invaluable alternative bathing facility. A chair or stool (possibly with a lift-up seat and storage below) will give you somewhere to sit or lay down clothes as well as providing a surface for a small child to stand on when reaching a basin. Privacy is often a sensitive subject with growing children and if you can provide some minimal form of screening around the WC (a low projecting wall, a screen or curtains will suffice), this will do much to help. If possible, a separate WC should also be available for when the bathroom is occupied. It is not possible to over-estimate how long a teenager will spend in the bathroom!

The best decorations for a family bathroom are simple, bright and cheerful (some children may need encouragement to enter!). If the bathroom is for use by both adults and children, try to avoid deliberately childish themes, especially in any permanent fixtures (you, and your children when they are older, might regret those teddy-bear tiles). One idea, though, would be to introduce a younger theme in a replaceable shower curtain. Buy a fabric of your choice and line this with a plain plastic lining. However, by choosing a seashore, nautical or botanical theme, you might well suit all tastes. Surfaces, if they are to remain looking good, will need to be resilient. Ceramic tiles or a paint finish (with stencilling, if you like) are best for walls and sheet vinyl is probably the most serviceable covering for the floor. An easily removed, non-absorptive carpet might also be considered.

Useful extras for the bathroom would be plenty of mirrors, as large a heated towel rail as you can accommodate – there is little so uncomforting as a damp towel – and a wall-mounted hair dryer located near a mirror (but away from sources of water).

# HOW THE ROOM MIGHT LOOK

## THE PLAN

Space is not a problem in this good-looking bathroom, planned for adults and older children. A pleasant view is assured from the bath by positioning it under the window. The WC and shower are separated from the body of the room by a low wall and the provision of a separate shower and double sinks allows for the bathroom to be occupied by more than one person at a time.

## DESIGN DECISIONS

1 **Scheme** Clean and crisp, this sharp scheme combines black, grey and white with bright yellow. The whole is softened by the introduction of green foliage.

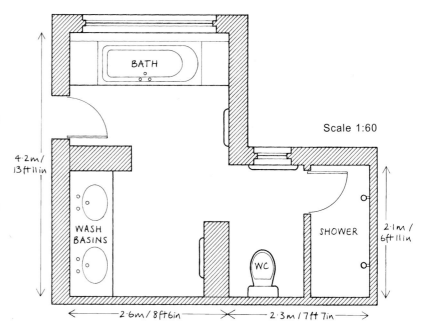

2 **Walls** Pale grey and black tiles provide a good wall protection while being aesthetically pleasing and bringing a sparkle to the room.

3 **Flooring** Made to withstand drenching, polished marble tiles are easy to maintain.

4 **Lighting** Utilitarian safety lamps in this context take on a stylish look. Light-coloured reflective walls mean that rather less light is needed than in a room with dark matt surfaces.

5 **Wash basins** Side-by-side double basins are practical when bathroom facilities are in demand.

# AN ALTERNATIVE BATHROOM

## THE PLAN

Roof space has been reclaimed to form this bathroom for the exclusive use of junior family members. The floor level steps up to leave a void for essential plumbing while at the same time creating some additional interest.

*Primary colours form the basis of the scheme for this bathroom dedicated to the younger members of a family.*

## DESIGN DECISIONS

**Scheme** Primary colours ensure that this bathroom always offers a bright welcome to entice possibly reluctant bathers.

**Walls** White ceramic tiles are applied to the lower portion of the walls to take 'the worst of the wet'. The choice of a wallpaper with a similar white background successfully distracts the eye from an uneven ceiling line.

**Bath** The round shape and blue colour of the bath give all the appearance of a paddling pool, inviting youngsters to jump in. The setting of the bath provides two sides for maximum access and allows an adult to reach bathing children easily.

**Wash basins** Double basins are always useful where multiple occupancy is envisaged.

**Mats** These are placed near to the WC, bath and basins to help prevent carpet damage.

# Cloakroom

Often regarded as a dull little room, a cloakroom should instead be a room to treasure. Sadly neglected by many home owners, cloakrooms all to frequently become a dumping ground for broken bicycles, discarded footwear and malfunctioning deck chairs. If treated with a little (but not too much) respect, your cloakroom will serve as a useful convenience for your guests while allowing you privacy in your own bathroom (where your wrinkle cream, old school face cloth and worn-out toothbrushes remain for ever a secret!).

Requiring minimal space (an area as small as 1×1.5m/3ft 4in×5ft will accommodate the essentials), a cloakroom can be sited practically anywhere so long as suitable provisions can be made for the plumbing and, if it adjoins a living room or kitchen, there is a lobby between the two. A space on the floor below an existing bathroom will in many cases minimalize disruption.

What does the good cloakroom contain? Essential, of course, are the WC pan and cistern. From a decorative point of view, a built-in cistern is neater and also provides a shelf on which accessories can be displayed. Should your cistern not be built in, you can still install a removable shelf supported on brackets over it. If space is limited, you will need to fit either an extra-small hand basin or one that will fit across a corner position. In a larger cloakroom it is a good idea to select a more generous basin with a swing mixer-tap arrangement – so useful for filling a bucket, watering can or kettle. The basin can also be set into a vanity unit to give it a less utilitarian appearance and to secure extra storage below. If space allows, the inclusion of a shower unit may help to relieve pressure on a main bathroom.

In addition to these basics you will need a well-lit mirror (preferably full-length), toilet paper holder, towel rail and wall hooks for coats. Heating a room that is used for such short periods may seem wasteful, but is essential for the comfort of those visiting the room and can easily be combined with a heated towel rail. Grooming aids such as a nail brush, perfumes, hair brush and comb set, paper tissues and a clothes brush are thoughtful additions, as are magazines for the amusement of visitors.

Because your cloakroom is likely to occupy only a small area, you have a wonderful opportunity to consider more exotic finishes that might be thought of as extravagant or overpowering in a larger space. And, as the time spent in this room is likely to be brief, you can afford to make a much stronger decorating statement than might be considered prudent in, say, a family bathroom. It's the optimum room for cracking a visual joke to a

*Cartoon magazine covers form a colourful and amusing theme for this small cloakroom.*

captive audience – where else can you display your achievements (your 'Oscar', degree, war medals, parachute jump certificate or peace prize) without seeming immodest? Give some thought to the following ideas:

◆ If there are many pipes exposed, how about making a feature out of them by painting them rainbow colours?

◆ What about covering your walls with sheets of newspaper containing amusing headlines?

◆ If your cloakroom has a dull view from the window (or indeed no window at all), why not use the opportunity to create you own scenes with a touch of *trompe l'oeil*?

◆ Consider leaving the walls fairly plain and using your cloakroom as a trophy room, museum or art gallery.

Whatever your style selection, be careful not to combine too many ideas in this small space or the room will lose impact.

## HOW THE ROOM MIGHT LOOK

### THE PLAN

Minimum space has been used to maximum effect in this *New Yorker* cloakroom. Attention has been drawn away from the irregular contours of the room by means of the colourful 'wallpaper'.

### DESIGN DECISIONS

**1 Scheme** With attention centred on these brilliant magazine covers, there is little need for other distractions. Their content is there to amuse and their colours to brighten the mood. If you wish to copy this theme, paste the covers either directly on to the walls using wallpaper paste or on to lining paper which can then be applied in the usual way.

**2 Wall trim** Red tape is used to edge the 'wallpaper' and give it a finished look.

**3 Lighting** Appropriately dramatic, a powerful downlighter in the ceiling over the basin gives this room a sense of theatricality.

**4 Wash basin** This corner basin has been chosen to take up the minimum amount of space. Plumbing essentials below, which, unless concealed, would provide a less-than-attractive view from the WC, are cleverly hidden behind a panel.

**5 Fittings** Simple, stylish, chrome fittings do not distract from the main theme. Mixer taps at the basin help to control water temperature.

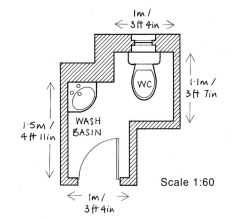

# AN ALTERNATIVE CLOAKROOM

## THE PLAN

To distract the eye from an oddly shaped space, this cloakroom has been given a highly decorative treatment. The translation into 'potting shed' is perfectly executed and, using the existing room contours, the whole effect is carried off with great aplomb.

## DESIGN DECISIONS

**Scheme** *Trompe l'oeil* has been used to magical effect in creating this horticultural haven. The addition of some real plants adds to the credibility of the theme.

**Lighting** Downlighters above the WC and basin provide light where it is needed. Because the fittings are recessed they cause little distraction from the outdoor theme.

**Mirror above basin** This is well positioned to reflect an attractive view.

**Towel rail** A hook-on rail is added to an existing radiator to provide a good space for hanging towels and ensuring that they are always dry.

Trompe l'oeil *is employed to turn this otherwise ordinary cloakroom space into a charming 'gardener's retreat'.*

*A large sheet mirror over the basin at one end (see left) reflects the whole room and doubles the effect.*

# CHILDREN'S ROOMS

'I need my own space' is a familiar cry of the late twentieth century. But very rarely do we relate this lament to our children's lives. We are so often tempted to relegate them to the smallest rooms (where there is, in theory, less room to make a mess) and somehow we don't imagine that their little lives could possibly be so full of confusion and clutter as to require a well-thought-out, organized, private space all to themselves. We forget about the pressures brought on by bickering brothers and sisters, the claustrophobic life of the school room and the confrontations of a competitive playground, not to mention the constant attention of parents who 'don't understand'. If children are to survive and to develop into sane adulthood, they need all the help we can give them and if, by allocating them their own special quiet space, we can help this along, then so much the better.

The thought process needed for the planning of children's rooms is very similar to that required for the other rooms in a house. First naturally come the practicalities: the activities to cater for, the storage to accommodate and comfort and security to attend to. Then there are the aesthetic considerations – also very important. Who, for instance, cannot recall the wallpaper of their room of formative years? So pause a moment to think before reaching for that book of clown wallpaper prints. Careful planning before you start decorating will ensure that your child will be safe, comfortable and happy.

What activities is your child likely to perform in his/her room? To name but a few – sleeping, eating, playing, craftwork, study and, last but not least, entertaining. It is a good idea to create separate areas for each activity so that the child who may spend many hours in this one room has some contrast between the different activities and so that 'messy' areas do not intrude into other parts of the room – though this, of course, will depend upon the space available. If two are to share one room, efforts should be made to allocate specific areas for each child which 'belong' to him/her and for which he/she is responsible. This will help to encourage growing children to feel more responsible for their room in the future.

The planning of children's rooms does differ from other rooms in two important regards. First, whatever materials you select for your scheme are likely to be severely tested. Water may be splashed, food dropped and wall surfaces scuffed, so your choice of finishes and fabrics will have to be very carefully considered and their ability to stand up to wear and tear must be a priority. Second, children have a habit of growing up very fast and at each stage they seem to develop an allergic reaction to the scheme that just a couple of years ago was deemed so appropriate. Durability and adaptability are therefore the keys to satisfying the young person's growing requirements and evolving taste.

The safety provisions required will to some extent depend upon the age of the child. But whatever his/her age, the danger points to pay particular attention to are: any electrical installations (sockets, switches, wires and so on); light fittings (these may be knocked over or skin burnt on an exposed bulb); heating appliances (with their danger of scalding or setting fires) and windows. Security glass in a window will help and good locking devices are a must, but grilles need to be considered in the context of a fire outbreak (that is, they must be easily removed in an emergency). Attention should also be

*There's no need for story books to prime a child's imagination in this charming 'underwater' bedroom.*

given to the choice of furniture. This should be stable, of a suitable size, without sharp corners or rough surfaces, and be made of a non-shattering material. Care should also be taken to avoid the use of paints containing lead.

Cleanliness and hygiene have a high priority – especially where the small baby is concerned. Scrubbable surfaces and the avoidance of crannies where dirt may lurk will help, as will the use of washable materials.

## SURFACES

Children will be children – and to expect them to have the same reverence for your home as you have is a tall order! Rather than installing vulnerable surfaces, tough resilient finishes will give you more peace of mind and your child greater freedom. Hard, splinter-free flooring in a young baby's room may prove the best solution. Area rugs (non-slip) to give a feeling of comfort can be added, and later a fitted carpet installed once the child has left the 'messy

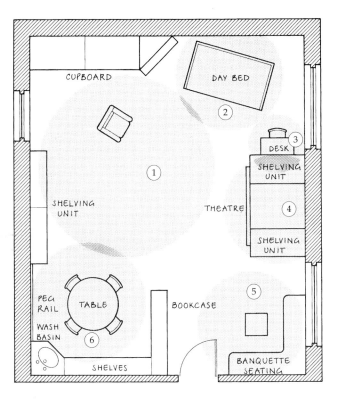

*Activity zoning in a playroom. 1: floor play, 2: resting, 3: writing, 4: play acting, 5: quiet reading, 6: craftwork and eating*

years' behind him/her. When it comes to walls, cute wallpapers, attractive as they may be, do not necessarily provide the ideal finish. Paint surfaces, on the other hand, are easily cleaned, can be renewed without too much trouble and form a great background for both baby effects and the older child's posters. The focus of many a non-sleeping hour, ceilings are frequently neglected: they offer the most wonderful opportunity to fill your child's mind with the material of sweet dreams – of the Man-in-the-moon, Superman or Peter Pan.

## FURNISHINGS

Whether or not to scale furniture to the size of the child is a personal decision. Although child-sized furniture may offer greater comfort and safety to the young child, it will inevitably be outgrown in a very

*Pine pieces against a plain background do all the decorating that is necessary in this back-to-nature children's sitting room.*

short time. Perhaps a mix of miniature and full-sized furnishings (which will stay with the child through later years) may be the best solution. Seating for the visiting adult should not be forgotten.

## STORAGE

With all the activities likely to be undertaken in this room come the inevitable paraphernalia and resulting storage problems. Forward planning in this area will mean that the child has few excuses for untidiness and unsuitable items are not left out for him/her to misuse (ten minutes with a tin of baby powder and a child can make quite an impression on a room!). It is recommended that some hidden storage (behind doors, screens, in bags and so on) is provided for a quick tidy-away, while other areas are left open for the display of favourite toys and books.

*A peg rail is a useful addition to storage facilities.*

## LIGHTING

Safety cannot be overemphasized where lighting is concerned. Although many table lamps are attractively designed for use in children's rooms, these should always be carefully positioned, out of reach of the young child, and trailing cables should be avoided. Good overhead or wall lighting is what is needed, but care should be taken to ensure that the resting child is not blinded by the glare from an unshielded bulb. A glowing night light kept on till morning offers much reassurance to a young child when nightmares loom. Although few electric sockets may be required for the very young baby, remember to install sufficient for future needs as he/she grows up. These can be blanked off until required.

# Baby Nursery

Anticipating the arrival of a new baby can be such an exciting time and the temptation to concentrate on the pretty details of the nursery decoration hard to resist. However, if your baby is to be healthy, comfortable and safe, it is essential that adequate thought be given to some practical elements before anything else.

Safety must always be the first consideration – see the introductory section to this chapter for guidance. In addition it should be remembered that the small immobile bundle of joy will, in a matter of months, double in size and will attain a high degree of mobility, not to mention curiosity. Although few electrical sockets will be required in the nursery at this stage, they should be planned for with an eye to the future and those not currently required can be blanked off until needed.

Temperature is an important factor for the comfort of your baby. Controllable central-heating radiators are probably the most successful way of safely heating a child's room, but these should be out of reach if possible, either hidden behind an item of furniture or protected by a guard. It is often forgotten that a young baby is just as vulnerable to overheating as to the cold. For this reason it is important to provide adequate ventilation (at a safe height) and to ensure that a baby's cot is positioned well away from any direct source of heat.

A wash basin with running water in a nursery is often considered a luxury, but when it is seen in the context of the lifetime of the room, the benefits become more evident. The nursery may soon become the child's playroom, then a teenager's bedroom. Finally it may even become a guest room. In each of these guises the inclusion of a wash basin could be considered a bonus. If the basin is housed within a vanity unit, shelves beneath can be used at this first

*A prime example of a nursery achieved at minimal expense and with future adaptability firmly in mind.*

stage for the storage of the baby's necessities and later perhaps for storing toys.

Few items of furniture are needed in the nursery of a very young baby. A cot, chest of drawers (the top of which, when covered with padding, could be used for changing the baby) and an easy chair with low arms for the nursing mother are all that are required. Shelves for displaying pictures, toys and books help to decorate the room. A trolley to house the baby's nappies, cream, powder, a bucket and so on is a useful addition and can be put to other use when no longer required in the nursery. Later on, as the baby develops, a small wardrobe, high chair and play pen might be purchased.

The decoration of the nursery need not involve great expense. Plain painted walls that allow for surface decorations to be added and changed as the child matures are a good idea. Pictures, stencils, mobiles, paper borders and pasted cutouts are all decorations that will inspire the imagination of your child. Colours should be bright and cheerful, and in these enlightened times there is no need to be restrained by the 'blue for a boy, pink for a girl' dictum.

When it comes to floors, hygiene, ease of maintenance and the child's comfort and safety can all be served by laying such materials as cushioned vinyl, cork or hard wood (so long as it is splinterless). The addition of easily washed play mats will soften the hard floor effect.

It is preferable for curtains not to drop to the floor as these may well be used by the child to support himself/herself. The addition of a blackout blind or curtain lining may help your child to sleep in the early evening and will help prevent him/her awakening with the dawn.

# HOW THE ROOM MIGHT LOOK

## THE PLAN

The layout is extremely simple and yet caters for all the needs of a new-born child. Storage is provided by a free-standing chest, and shelving units attached to the right-hand wall. The shelves have been cleverly designed, leaving a space where a cot might be sited at a later date. Seating in front of the window allows mother to cradle her child in comfort and to enjoy the view. A second chair is for guests or for laying out clothes for the following day. The room remains uncluttered – essential for the baby who will soon be crawling.

## DESIGN DECISIONS

1 **Scheme** Sunshine yellow is contrasted with navy blue to give this room a bright cheerful feel suitable for either male or female offspring.

2 **Walls** Softly stippled, washable paintwork is easily cleaned and provides a perfect background for childhood decorations.

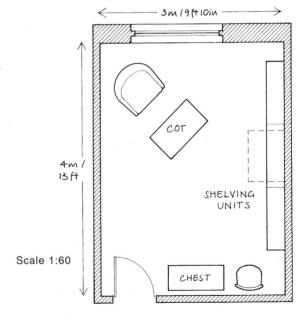

3 **Paper frieze** This charming animal border handsomely decorates the walls and can be easily changed for one with a more mature theme when the child is older.

4 **Flooring** Wood veneer planks sealed with a coating of vinyl are both practical and attractive. It can be treated as any other vinyl flooring and upkeep is minimal.

5 **Easy chair** Bought second-hand and painted smart navy, this Lloyd loom chair with its comfortable cushion and low arms is perfect for the nursing mother.

6 **Shelving system** Basic in conception and execution, these beautifully dressed shelves are securely attached to the wall and will easily adapt for the child's future needs. The choice of navy-striped fabric to enclose them is inspired – smart and yet not tying the room to babyhood.

7 **Storage baskets** Ideal for all baby's kit, they can be removed for easy access and transported to laundry or car.

8 **Changing table** An essential item, this one is cantilevered off the wall at a convenient height and its colour co-ordinates well with the chosen scheme.

9 **Window** A lever operates the opening of the top windows to provide ventilation without placing the baby in a draught. A blind will cut out the light when required.

10 **Radiator** Currently exposed, this can easily be enclosed once the child is mobile.

11 **Mobile** A decorative feature, strategically placed for baby's amusement.

12 **Electrical socket** Well hidden in an unobtrusive corner, this is blanked off anticipating a toddler's curiosity.

# Pre-school Playroom

Anyone who has cared for children of between the ages of one and five years knows all too well just what are the important things to remember when planning a playroom. For a mother to remain relaxed about her child spending time in this room, supervised or unsupervised, she needs to know that the child cannot damage himself/herself or the room and that he/she will be entertained for a reasonable length of time. It is also important that, after playtime, the process of cleaning up can be carried out with the minimum of effort, mother and child both having better things to occupy them. At this age of maximum mobility and minimum attention span these are tough demands.

A gate as well as a door at the entrance will help ensure that the child is contained within the room and within earshot when mother's back is turned. To lessen noise from the playroom, install plenty of soft finishes within the room.

The creation of zones for different activities will help punctuate the child's day as he/she moves from one activity to another, and will help with the organization of storage associated with each occupation. For example, in one corner a table and chairs might be positioned on plastic sheeting to protect the flooring and craft materials stored nearby. Other areas might be dedicated to eating, quiet story-telling, play-acting, resting and so on.

To enable you to keep the room in reasonable order, plenty of storage facilities will be needed. In general these are best housed in fitted units – apart from them being more stable and less likely to trap tiny fingers, such units will give the room a neater finish. A blackboard might be attached to the front of one, a pinboard to another, and perhaps a third might carry a plastic mirror. Any free-standing units, so long as they are well weighted, could be used to divide areas within the room. Additional storage could be provided in chests, in boxes on castors, in baskets or even in a hammock (especially if this were

to fit in with the theme of your room – for instance, 'Treasure Island'). If the child is also to use the room for sleeping, a bed and some kind of wardrobe will, of course, be needed. Although initially a child might not need hanging space, it is wise to allow for this as he/she will soon be into clothing that will require more than just shelves. A really useful tip for a playroom is to fix a pegboard with hooks, as found in Shaker homes (see page 246), at dado-rail height (90cm/3ft). This could be used for hanging clothing, small chairs or drawstring bags, or for displaying decorative items.

As children mature they need the company of others to develop their social skills fully, and so it is important to make provision for visiting friends. A small table with several chairs where they can gather is a good idea – useful for both play and meal times. And as children seem to simply love to stay over, you might consider bunk beds or some other novel sleeping solution.

The decoration of a playroom can be great fun – you'll be amazed at what can be achieved with a staple gun, a few metres of fabric, some pots of paint, several sheets of MDF and a fertile imagination. Create your own circus tent, underwater world or Indian camp! An alternative approach would be not to have a specific theme in mind but to use strong bright colours as a background for constantly changing visual shows. These temporary decorations could be attached to walls by means of removable adhesive, mobiles could be hung from the ceiling and prints suspended from a picture rail. To help develop your child's taste ask him/her to make selections from a range of ideas you deem suitable.

*In this bright and cheerful playroom, walls have been kept plain so as to permit surface decorations to change and to allow for the room to grow with the child.*

# HOW THE ROOM MIGHT LOOK

## THE PLAN

The furniture in this well-organized playroom has been zoned to allow for areas of different activity. A theatre divides a drawing/writing area from a quiet story-telling corner with banquette seating (plus storage beneath the seats) and a low bookcase encloses a craft/dining area. A shelving unit for display, a day bed and full-height storage cupboard complete the furnishings.

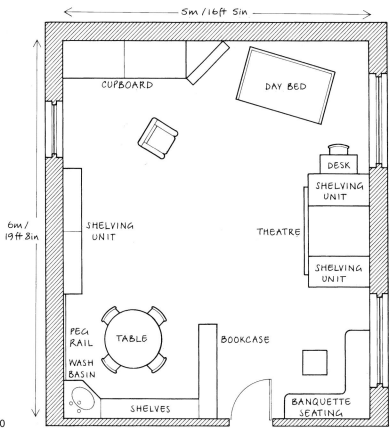

6m /
19ft 8in

5m / 16ft 5in

CUPBOARD

DAY BED

DESK

SHELVING
UNIT

SHELVING
UNIT

THEATRE

SHELVING
UNIT

PEG
RAIL

TABLE

BOOKCASE

WASH
BASIN

SHELVES

BANQUETTE
SEATING

Scale 1:60

## DESIGN DECISIONS

**1 Scheme** The simplest of painted walls form an uncluttered backdrop for primary-coloured furnishings and toys. In this south-facing room the cool blue is compensated for by the warm natural light entering from the two large windows.

**2 Animal theme** Represented by the picture on the wall and echoed in the cushions, soft toys, window blinds and floor mat.

**3 Flooring** A polished wooden plank floor is easy to maintain and warm in feel. A mat is provided for when a 'soft landing' is required.

**4 Furniture** The blond wood of the floor is reflected in the finish to several items of furniture.

**5 Day bed** This doubles up as a cot for the young child to sleep in. When the child is older, it can be converted to a bed.

**6 Cupboard** A full-height fitted cupboard provides masses of storage. Later a hanging rail can be fitted to take the growing child's clothes.

**7 Desk** This extends from one of the tall, wall-fixed units and is bathed in natural light from the nearby window.

**8 Table and four chairs** This grouping forms an assembly point for meals and play. Proportioned for little people, the table has a polished wood surface varnished with clear protective lacquer.

**9 Theatre** Two tall wall-fixed units combine with a theatre front to form a secret space where plays can be performed.

**10 Building blocks** Giant foam 'bricks' are light and safe to use. They help to develop the child's creative abilities and to exercise young muscles. When not constructing, the child can use the blocks as seats.

**11 Lighting** In a co-ordinating style, this pendant light can be adjusted so that it is always out of the growing child's reach. Similar lights focus on the craft table and the reading area.

**12 Blackboard** Children will always be tempted to scribble on walls, so why not provide a special surface for the purpose? The pedimented shape of the board echoes that of the theatre and the building blocks.

# Teenager's Den

You may be lucky enough to have a perfectly behaved teenager living in your home or you may belong to one of the millions of families with typical, slightly out-of-control offspring. The teenager will probably want to make too much noise, be unlikely to see the merits of being tidy and have ideas on decoration that involve sticking things other than wallpaper on walls. He/she may well develop into a proud home owner in the future, but meanwhile, accepting that 'teenagers will be teenagers' will go a long way towards harmonious living in the home you share with a child-adult going through a prolonged youth crisis.

Deciding upon just how much isolation each of you wants or thinks is desirable is a matter for negotiation and the outcome will probably determine which room in the house is selected for the teenager's room. A converted loft or basement could provide an ideal self-contained space where neither party's life impinges too greatly on the other – a place where friends can be entertained, noise made and privacy maintained.

The teenager's involvement in deciding upon the decoration of the room is very important if he/she is to have any respect for his/her surroundings and if he/she is to be encouraged to maintain them well. Teenage years are a great time for experimentation and, although mistakes will surely be made, it is hoped that lessons will also be learned. An interior designer specializing in young people's rooms has been quoted as saying: 'Ask them what they want, then bargain!' This seems a fairly sensible approach to adopt.

As in the younger child's playroom, it is a good idea to create zones for different activities within the teenager's den. In the sleeping area, duvets are an easy solution to bed-making and you may wish to make provisions for friends staying overnight – say,

bunk beds or a day bed that can also be used for seating during the day. Hammocks strung across the beams in a loft ceiling are a fun idea for the teenager with frequent guests.

An ideal study area would be located in the vicinity of a good source of natural light and would have a number of electrical sockets positioned nearby. Space for a work surface, a bookcase and housing for computer equipment should be allowed for. A flexible storage unit is also a good idea for accommodating a television and audio equipment.

The provision of personal bathing facilities within the room itself will free more bathroom time for the rest of the family. Most teenagers seem to prefer a shower to a bath and, as this is more economical and takes up less space, the idea could be encouraged. A cubicle might be housed within a wall of deep cupboards or in a small room annexe.

Sometimes it seems as though teenagers think of little else apart from their clothes, so a dressing space will be an important area of the room. A walk-in closet is ideal: it provides lots of space and can be shut out of view at will. Alternatively large cupboards with masses of hanging space and a full-length mirror could be provided. A system of wire baskets within a metal framework works well for the quick 'filing' of items of clothing within a cupboard, and a rail on castors behind a curtain makes a cheap wardrobe substitute.

Decoration ideas are soon outgrown, so a flexible scheme is likely to be the most successful. Plain walls of an oil-based paint will provide a good background on to which posters and so on can be attached (and replaced when no longer in favour) and non-themed soft-furnishing fabrics will give the room decor longevity. A carpet with thick underlay will help to prevent noise pollution.

*Bright primary colours add a punch to this fun teenager's
room in cool grey.*

# HOW THE ROOM MIGHT LOOK

### THE PLAN

Flexibility is the key to this teenager's den. All furniture is free-standing and, when outgrown, the sturdy DIY climbing-frame structure can be redesigned and repositioned with little effort. The desk, providing ample space for two to work, sits neatly beneath a storage deck that can easily be converted to a spare bed when required. Additional storage is provided in the two cupboards, and an audio system is to be found in a low unit beside a sofa.

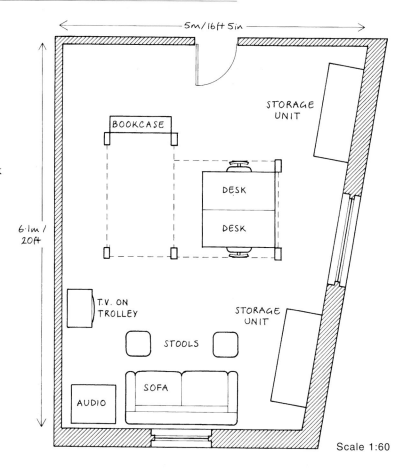

### DESIGN DECISIONS

1 **Scheme** Bright primary colours are used to enliven the essentially neutral backdrop. Black unit fronts and bed covers punctuate the scheme.

2 **Walls** Paint of the palest grey gives this room a clean, uncluttered look and forms a good background for pictures and posters. The teenager is unlikely to tire of this plain treatment and can change the look with the minimum of cost and effort by simply swapping pictures.

3 **Flooring** Polished floorboards provide a flooring that is practical without appearing utilitarian, and forms a natural link with the climbing frame. A grey carpet, continued from the landing, gives the central area a softer feel.

4 **Climbing frame** Constructed from pine, this is an adaptable structure to provide amusement and accommodation for two teenagers – with a possible space for a third to stay over. The frame also helps to enclose the study area.

5 **Storage cupboards** Positioned to either side of the window and in the same style as the desks, these units are cleverly divided into display shelves, large pull-out drawers and a hanging cupboard – addressing all the needs of the teenager.

6 **Desks** With ample workspace for two, a pair of desks with lockable cupboards provide the centrepiece for this perfect study area. A generous waste-bin beneath asks to be filled!

**7 Window treatment** Venetian fine blinds, sitting within window reveals, create a tailored look and allow the occupants easy control of the amount of natural light entering the room.

**8 Lighting** Practical and fun, the various fittings have been chosen to amuse and to target light where needed. The fittings are free-standing and can easily be repositioned should the furniture arrangement change.

**9 Coloured boxes** These robust containers are roomy and good-looking. Out of the way on top of the cupboards, they provide extra long-term storage space.

**10 Door furniture and light switches** These are white and modern in design to co-ordinate with this contemporary interior.

# WORKROOMS

The world has evolved considerably since the days when the only workrooms within the home were considered to be 'his study' or 'his workshop'. It was uncertain just how much work was undertaken in these rooms, but their attractions appeared to increase as domestic pressures mounted!

Today the spheres of work, study and leisure frequently merge. Many more women have taken up employment in recent years and family commitments mean that, in many cases, the home has become the most suitable location for work. Technology too has played its part, enabling information to be swapped from remote locations and rendering commuting to the city office an obsolete practice for many. Technology has also meant that domestic chores are reduced, thus freeing many more hours for leisure pursuits.

The rewards of combining work and leisure in the home are numerous and, by now, well recognized. A work package that includes spending the day in close proximity to loved ones, the elimination of wasted travel time and the possibility of working in an altogether more pleasant environment is indeed attractive.

It is not necessary, nor is it always practical, to devote a large space or considerable budget to providing a work area – it may even be self-defeating if the income gained through employment is eroded by the cost of providing facilities and if the space sacrificed detracts from family life. Perhaps just an old door supported by two second-hand filing cabinets (which will double up as a dressing table, see page 162) in the spare room are all that is needed. It is really just a question of priorities. However, one thing we are sure of is that a room that is properly equipped, well located and appropriately decorated is more conducive to work than one that has to serve other purposes as well.

It is not long since out-buildings were thought of as a liability rather than the asset they are now considered to be. These form ideal locations for workrooms, but if they are in short supply, room must be found for a workspace within the home itself. For preference and convenience this should be a dedicated space – possibly a converted basement or loft? Or perhaps an extension could be constructed or a teenager's abandoned bedroom refurbished? A room dedicated to work will allow for peace and privacy and will mean that work and equipment can be left out until next required. It also allows you to decorate the room in a workmanlike fashion to encourage concentration.

If, however, it is not possible to dedicate a whole room to work, much thought needs to be applied towards ensuring that any multi-purpose room does not compromise both work and leisure activities and that the two functions do not become confused. To divide a room into distinct play and work zones, a piece of useful furniture (such as a bookcase) could be placed to form a screen, or perhaps the two areas could be defined by a change in floor level.

Although you are primarily creating a workroom, do not neglect to provide for some relaxation. Without the natural punctuations of a day in a busy city office, time can seem to drag. When these moments arrive, it is often better to switch off completely for a short period and then return to your work refreshed. An easy chair, music, hot/cold drinks, reading matter – these will all help to provide a contrast to the main activity.

*Bookshelves and a desk make good use of this understairs space and natural light is enhanced by the inclusion of a mirror.*

*Dressing table conversion to desk.*

One of the great advantages of a home workroom is that you can tailor it exactly to your own requirements, and, in doing so, can express your own personal style. This style need not necessarily be too businesslike, but may reflect in some way the activity you are involved with or simply your personal preferences. Attention too can be given to such pleasurable aspects as how your room is scented and to background sounds. Think of a beautifully decorated space, smelling perhaps of hyacinths. Beyond the window daffodils are billowing in the breeze and in the background can be heard a string quartet. Who needs a city office now?!

When planning a workroom, it is tempting to plunge in straight away with wonderful ideas for businesslike colour schemes and so on, but there are many more fundamental things to consider first.

Here is a checklist of questions to prompt your ideas:

- Do you need to be in close contact with any particular rooms in your home or is a remote location preferable?

- Is separate access desirable?

- What activities are going to take place within the space?

- What equipment will these activities require?

- What services (for example, telephone, running water, heating, ventilation) are needed?

- How will you illuminate the various activities (using both natural and artificial light)?

- What are the storage requirements?

Other points to consider are:

- facilities for guests (seating, cloakroom, car parking and so on);

- soundproofing (either to exclude or contain noise);

- space and equipment for guest workers (for example, book keepers, temporary secretaries);

- security (locks, safes, alarms and so on);

- safety (for instance, non-slip floors, fire prevention).

## DECORATIONS

The style you adopt for your workroom will very much depend upon the dimensions of the space and your personal preferences. Whatever these might be, your activity is likely to entail the need for a certain amount of equipment, a good expanse of work or floor surface and lots of storage, so it is recommended that your room has a certain sparseness about it to enable all these things to be accommodated without creating a cluttered feeling. If the room is to be used for professional purposes, try to avoid creating too domestic a style or you may find that your work is not taken seriously.

## STORAGE

Try to plan storage right from the start rather than let it evolve haphazardly. By all means reuse existing furniture, but wherever possible custom-make and build in for a more streamlined, organized, efficient appearance.

## LIGHTING

Although sited in a workspace, lighting does not have to be utilitarian so long as it fulfils its purpose. Concentrate on providing a good overall level of illumination and ensuring that specific tasks are in good glare-free light coming from the correct direction.

*Unlined ecru silk-taffeta curtains, slotted on to a clear acrylic pole, demonstrate David Hicks' innovative approach to window dressing in this smart study area.*

# Home Office

The great technology revolution of the latter part of the twentieth century has impacted upon our lives in no less a way than the industrial revolution on the lives of the people in the mid-nineteenth century. All the commuting, the monolithic head office, the secretaries, the separation from home and family – these embedded life threads are gradually being consigned to the history books. Our concerns for quality of air, of work time and of family life have ensured their demise.

The home office, for many, provides the perfect solution. It permits you to work variable hours to suit your lifestyle and that of your family in agreeable surroundings and ensures that little time is wasted on travel.

Your home working area can adopt many guises depending upon the type of work undertaken and the space available. Whatever the set-up, your office should offer you the easiest possible method of working. With the working week averaging some forty hours, it is clearly worth spending some time on planning the space where it is going to take place.

Distractions in the home can come from many directions – interruptions from family members, demands created by other activities happening in the same space, callers at the door and so on. For your office to be productive in these circumstances, you will need to isolate yourself to some extent from what is going on around you. This may involve housing the office in a separate building, attaching locks to the door, installing separate telephone lines or even building in some form of soundproofing.

The professional home office should reek of efficiency. Not only will this impress the visiting bank manager, business colleagues, representatives and clients, but it will also help you make the transition from domestic to work mode so much more easily. This atmosphere can best be engendered by creating

*Natural light floods into this businesslike loft office space.*

a dedicated work area which is furnished to match and which is not used for any other purpose. The ideal office has its own entrance and cloakroom nearby. Coffee-making facilities and comfortable seating for guests are an added bonus.

Decorations should generally tend towards the more serious colours (neutrals and deeps being particularly suitable) and distracting patterns used with caution. Many suitable floorings are available and selection will most probably be determined by budget. Cord carpets are reasonably priced; they are hard-wearing and will not be easily damaged by chair castors (less hard-wearing floorings can be protected by clear plastic mats positioned beneath desk chairs). Soft furnishings are best kept restrained – simple clean lines and discreet trims to give a tailored finish. Should funds be limited, a basic cloth such as ticking, made up with trims of petersham ribbon, could be used to great effect.

Lighting needs to be well targeted and care should be taken to ensure that glare is not caused by the reflection of light fittings on a computer screen. Remember also to light storage areas and bookshelves. To make best use of any available daylight, site desks directly in front of windows (ensuring that these are screened in some way if the view beyond is likely to cause a distraction).

It may be tempting, in this domestic environment, to incorporate residential furnishings. These will certainly make the office appear more homely, but for comfort and efficiency, purpose-made office furniture is recommended. A computer stand on castors to house monitor, keyboard, printer, paper and so on is ideal and will accommodate all these items at the right height. Your chair is equally, if not more, important. This should be well made, ergonomically designed and adjustable so that your sitting position is not injurious to your posture.

Nothing detracts more from the appearance of an office than for every surface to be spilling over with paperwork, files and samples. Far from it promoting an image of endeavour, it demonstrates that the owner is disorganized and consequently inefficient. This problem can be overcome by the provision of sufficient, conveniently placed and well-designed storage space. Storage units can, of course, be in the form of free-standing cupboards and shelves, but look much neater and more streamlined if built in. Should the room already contain fitted wardrobes, the interiors of these could be converted: the rails could be replaced with suitable partitioning or, if the room is to be reused as a bedroom in the future, perhaps a free-standing framework could be incorporated into the wardrobe.

It may be that you are not professionally employed, yet still need some sort of management centre to run your personal life and an active household efficiently. This office could well be based upon nothing more than a telephone and a file, and finding a suitable location should not cause a problem. The bay window of a bedroom, the space in the hallway under the stairs, a desk in the library, a recess in the dining room, a cupboard in a rarely used guest room – these may all be capable of housing a mini office.

Much can be done to disguise work and storage elements in a multi-functional room. Files can be bound in attractive wallpaper, a trestle table can be draped with a full-length cloth that co-ordinates with your room scheme and which conceals beneath it your work paraphernalia, and pinboards can be made of attractive material trellised with some pretty ribbons.

As an alternative to making your work accessories good to look at, you might consider concealing your whole work area within a cupboard, behind a screen or masked from view behind a curtain or blind.

# HOW THE ROOM MIGHT LOOK

## THE PLAN

Loft space has been converted to create a spacious room for business activities. The structural contours provide architectural interest and roof lights allow natural light to flood in. The furnishings have been cunningly arranged so as not to waste space where headroom is limited. To one side desks are lined up under the natural light and opposite a relaxed seating/sleeping area is arranged. Bookshelves are contained within a triangular recess and at the opposite end of the room an area is partitioned off for storage of equipment, files and stationery.

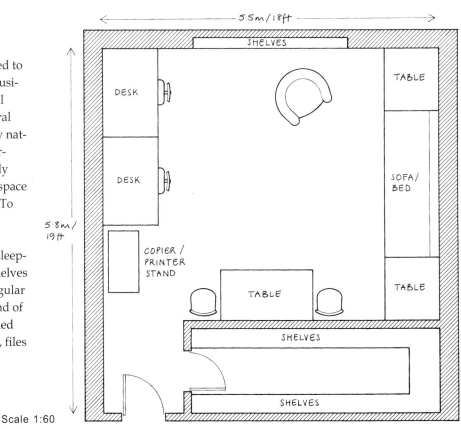

Scale 1:60

## DESIGN DECISIONS

1 **Scheme** White walls and beige flooring combine to form the background to modern black furnishings in this loft space: a very businesslike scheme, relieved only by a scattering of brightly coloured chintz cushions.

2 **Desks** These are of a good size and have additional pull-out surfaces. Faced with laminate, they are tough and easily cleaned.

3 **Bookshelves** A case of a storage problem becoming a decorative feature: the triangular shape of the recess adds interest to a featureless wall.

4 **Sofa** In the seating area, a day bed has been formed by placing a foam mattress on a solid base. A bolster and numerous other cushions give the bed its day-time disguise.

5 **Lighting** Large black Anglepoise lamps are of an appropriate style to go with the scheme and to direct light exactly where needed. Table lamps would be a suitable choice in a more domestic style of office. Natural light from dormer windows and a skylight floods the room.

6 **Flooring** A low-pile corded carpet is suitably robust to stand up to chair casters and heavy usage.

# Studio/Workshop

The dream of most creative people, a studio is a wonderful space in which to indulge the imagination, a peaceful oasis where artistic endeavours are nurtured. Whatever your passion – dance or découpage, photography or physiotherapy, cake-making or calligraphy – a dedicated, well-equipped studio provides the ideal environment for its expression.

Choosing the right location for your studio/workshop is critical if home and work are to operate harmoniously side by side. As with the other work areas discussed in this book, a certain amount of separation from the rest of the home and its activities may be desirable – except, of course, where there is a need to be within view or earshot of children or an elderly family member. As well as the hazard of home life impinging upon this creative space, there is the reverse problem of the studio perhaps causing a problem for the rest of the household. Your pastime/work may involve unsociable elements such as noise and mess that will require some form of isolation if they are not to upset other household members.

When thinking of creating a workshop space, it is a great idea first to make a list of all the activities your work involves, because from that list will evolve all else that you are likely to need (see the introductory section to this chapter, page 162).

The availability of services may well determine where your studio or workshop is best located. Here are some of the facilities you might require:

- **Power points**  For tools, audio equipment, heating, cooking, lighting, refrigeration and so on. As always, it is wise to think ahead and build in more sockets than you currently require, remembering to site these where most convenient (possibly at worktop height).

- **Water**  For photographic work, pottery, painting, cooking, cleaning up and so on. Consider whether you need a hot water supply as well as cold. Mixer taps with a single spout that can be swung to one side over a large sink will allow you to run water to the desired temperature and to manoeuvre a bucket in and out of the sink easily.

- **Gas**  For firing, heating, welding and so on. If a mains supply is not available, it may be worthwhile considering a tank supply.

- **Ventilation**  To eliminate any noxious fumes/smells and to maintain a suitable temperature in which to work. This can be provided by an open window or fan system (either manually or automatically operated).

- **Lighting**  For all your tasks and for overall conditions – think carefully about what sort of lighting would best suit your purposes. It is always advisable to include some free-standing lighting that can be directed at will – for instance, an Anglepoise lamp. Fluorescent fittings provide good overall shadowless lighting, but be careful with your selection of bulbs if you have a need to recreate daylight conditions (for colour rendition purposes and so on).

- **Security**  Door locks to keep your studio equipment and work safe, and to exclude minors from dangerous areas. You may require a safe for storing precious materials and an alarm system to reinforce your security. Always keep poisonous substances under lock and key. Where there is a fire hazard, smoke alarms should be installed and emergency fire-fighting equipment kept close at hand.

*Red and white combine to provide a bright and cheerful workroom on a budget.*

The clever planning of storage facilities within your workshop will be vital to its success. If you apply the same principles as used in planning kitchen storage, you will be on the right track. Plan chests, filing cupboards and similar units are best designed to your own specification and, wherever possible, built in and out of the way. A distinction should be made between those items you may be using on a daily basis and those used less frequently. You may choose to store often-used tools on a wall-mounted racking system where they can be easily reached, while those that are rarely required can be housed within less accessible units.

The position, size and height of work surfaces should also be carefully thought out. The availability of natural light will probably determine the best site for your working zone and it is important to remember that, for your comfort and health, your seating arrangement should be ergonomically determined.

When it comes to deciding upon finishes for the various surfaces within your studio, consider first the practicalities. What will stand up to the 'abuse' you are likely to inflict? A painted cement floor (which can easily be repainted when badly damaged) is suit-able for heavy-duty wear and areas where high temperatures are involved. A sheet-vinyl or ceramic-tile flooring may be the answer for messy but less damaging activities. For 'dry' activities, cork or vinyl tiles (which, when worn out, can be individually replaced) may be the most suitable floor covering. If you are working with textiles, a hard floor will be easier than a soft one to keep clean. A wooden flooring may prove the most apt for a room used for physical activities, but do take care with slipperiness and splinters. Whatever your selection, think also about the acoustics of the room (soft finishes help to cushion sound), and remember that, where mess is concerned, a threshold mat will help prevent dirt permeating your home. Walls with a gloss-paint finish are generally considered fairly robust, and can be repainted when badly scarred.

Your second consideration should be the aesthetics. For most situations a plain paint wall surface may provide the best answer. It will form an ideal blank canvas against which your activities can take place and can act as a display surface to which items can be attached with removable masking tape or adhesive pads. A picture rail might also prove useful.

# HOW THE ROOM MIGHT LOOK

### THE PLAN

Eked out of a larger workshop space, this inviting corner caters for the multi-purpose craftsperson. Storage and workspace are the priorities in this studio converted on a budget.

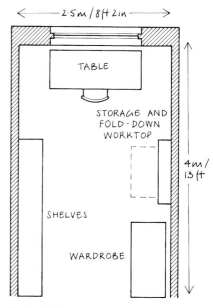

Scale 1:60

## DESIGN DECISIONS

**1 Scheme** White gloss paint has been used to good effect visually to enlarge this restricted space. Red introduces a sense of fun to the straightforward two-colour scheme.

**2 Flooring** Sheet vinyl in white with a red diagonal stripe reflects the light, is a dream to clean and is inexpensive.

**3 Shelving** Of the most basic kind, these shelves are deep and well supported. Notice how the upper shelf has an upstand at its edge to prevent rolls of paper from falling off. Hooks on the wall below allow vacuum cleaner, iron and so on to be neatly stowed.

**4 Worktable and chair** Positioned in maximum natural light, the table, with its tubular construction, is adjustable in height. The chair, in matching style, neatly folds up when not in use.

**5 Wall unit** Simply and cheaply constructed, this ingenious unit opens out to provide an additional work surface and space for tools (see picture, left).

**6 Wardrobe** This second-hand buy has been painted to match the scheme and provides useful storage for dressmaking activities.

**7 Window treatment** A single curtain with eyelets, simply slotted on a wire, is the answer to prettying up this room and providing privacy after dark.

**8 Lighting** Two pendant lights with large reflective coolie shades come from an existing ceiling point and are redirected over work areas. A clip-on spot light provides directional lighting over the worktable.

# Library

What luxury – a room dedicated to quiet contemplation, to academic pursuits, to pure pleasure! Even in these days of information technology, the book remains our vital link with history and other worlds, and whereas books are considered our 'friends', it is rare indeed to hear of anyone having a similar relationship with a personal computer. Although a library may be considered a workroom where serious research, study and perhaps writing are carried out, the title 'library' also conjures up a picture of an altogether more pleasurable space: warm and welcoming, a comfortable cocoon in which to while away the hours.

Your choice of colour scheme can do much to contribute to this feeling of cosseting. The selection of traditional, deep, jewel colours – ruby, sapphire and emerald – or warm earth tones – terracotta, sand, clay and volcanic rock – will give your room an intimate feeling (remember that dark warm colours advance: see page 34) as well as suggesting security and tradition. Lining the walls, the books themselves may well provide the starting point to inspire your scheme. By echoing the colours of the book spines you will give your room a cohesive feel and you will create the illusion that the books are part of the structure of your room. The books themselves will provide plenty of interest, so you may opt to forgo strong patterns that may fight for your attention and distract from the 'stars' of the room. Instead you may like to concentrate on incorporating an interesting variety of textures. Imagine your shiny book spines against a background of dark green felt walls; rough natural seagrass flooring is underfoot, green-and-red plaid, heavy linen curtains grace the window and worn, glossy, red leather chairs stand in an inviting group. The picture is completed by a log fire blazing brightly in the grate.

Lighting can so easily enhance or spoil this wonderful ambience that you have gone to such trouble to create. The central pendant light is to be avoided –

it will flatten all the textures and you will lose all feeling of intimacy. Instead choose several individual lights positioned in the lower portion of the room – table lamps, desk lamps, standard lamps – all these fittings will create pools of light that will impart a warm feeling. It is also important for the shelves to be well lit so that books can be located, removed and examined on the spot. Ceiling-fixed recessed wall washers (see page 28) will bathe the shelves in light or, as an alternative, you might consider library lights fixed to the uprights of the shelving units themselves. Strip lights behind baffles, fixed within the bookcase, will highlight attractive books but are to be avoided if the bookcase is antique as the routing of wiring is likely to cause damage.

Of the furnishings in your library, a comfortable chair is paramount. This could be upholstered in either fabric or leather and needs to provide arm rests at a good height for reading comfortably. A high-backed chair (such as a wing chair) is wonderful for resting the head and for shielding the occupant from draughts. Positioned near a window, it will have the benefits of good natural light for reading and perhaps a pleasant view for idle moments. A foot rest will ensure perfect relaxation. It is also useful to include a desk and a more upright chair (possibly on castors) in your furniture arrangement. Other items that might be added include library steps to reach high-up books, a side table by your favourite chair to hold a lamp and possibly a drink, a coffee table to display decorative books and a magazine rack for current periodicals.

There are numerous methods of storing books and much will depend upon the layout and size of your room. By locating shelves around the perimeter of the room (not forgetting the dead area above the

*Well-placed light fittings ensure that reading and writing are carried out in comfort in this cosy library.*

doorways) you will maximize the space, but in a larger room bookcases can be utilized to divide the space into different zones for varying activities. When planning storage, remember that books come in all shapes and sizes, so allow for some extra-deep/tall spaces. For a more decorative look include ornaments on some shelves.

What style or theme could you choose for your library? Most popular is the 'gentlemen's club' look – lots of antique or reproduction furniture, club fend-ers before an open fire, leather upholstery with brass nailing, heavy velvet curtains and rich dark colours. Victorian style (see page 192) includes many of these elements and would be a most suitable theme, especially if your house is of the period. But there is no reason why a more modern style could not be adopted for this room. Lighter colours, streamlined shelving and modern light fittings could give your library a totally different yet no less attractive appearance.

# HOW THE ROOM MIGHT LOOK

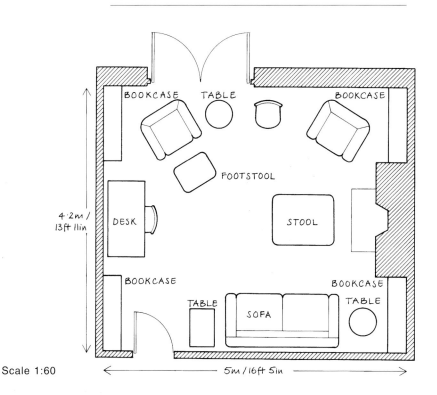

Scale 1:60

4·2m / 13ft 11in

5m / 16ft 5in

## THE PLAN

Symmetry prevails in this relaxing library with bookcases flanking both the fireplace and the desk opposite. The summer reader's favourite spot is near to the French doors with a view of the garden. In winter the fireplace draws occupants to its side. A sofa offers additional seating.

## DESIGN DECISIONS

1 **Scheme** Painted faux tortoiseshell walls form the background to this rich scheme. The same treatment extends over the ceiling and appears on woodwork to give the room a cohesive intimate look. Red upholstery introduces some warmth and the light beige flooring lifts the mood.

**2 Flooring** A plain beige, cut-pile carpet, fitted to close cover, ensures a hushed environment. A pretty floral needlepoint rug helps to break up the expanse of beige.

**4 Bookshelves** By having the same finish as the walls these bookcases appear to be part of the structure of the room and are far less intrusive than if they had been painted in a contrast.

**3 Upholstery** Comfort is the name of the game here. An upright chair at the desk ensures good support while writing and near the window a wing chair is just the shape to encourage a nap. A small footstool adds to the reader's comfort. In front of the fire (out of view) is a larger stool with a flat top to accommodate decorative books and the occasional tea tray. A small sofa along one wall offers extra seating and converts to a bed for the occasional guest.

**5 Window treatment** Full-length and luxuriously heavy, these curtains are sure to keep draughts at bay. The positioning of the curtain pole, high up above the French doors, contributes to a feeling of elegance.

**6 Lighting** Ceiling-fixed downlighters with gold baffles produce strong but warm pools of light, while table lamps and a swing-arm standard lamp pay deference to the traditional theme of the room. Pleated silk shades give out a soft diffused light.

# Part III

# STYLE

A stylish room doesn't just happen – it is carefully researched, planned and assembled. This section of the book is designed to trigger your imagination and to demonstrate just how easily a particular style can be interpreted, even on the slimmest of budgets.

Designer dictatorships are a thing of the past and no longer do we hang on every word emitted from the lips of style gurus. As for sources of inspiration, in modern times, exhibitions, historical documents, holiday brochures and theatre hoardings are just as likely to inspire a style as the latest editions of interior design magazines. The late twentieth century has seen a revolution in thinking on home decoration and, just as in the world of clothes fashion, there is now a new feeling of freedom.

Style, however, should not be confused with fashion in interiors. Although a certain way of doing things, the use of a particular group of colours or the inclusion of a specific material may become popular, these are no indicators of style. This year we may be mad about voile, verdigris and Venetian blinds, but including them in our scheme does not qualify us for membership of the good decorating club. What *will* earn us a place, is the skill we employ in selecting one item and rejecting another.

One of the most frequently made mistakes is to attempt too much in a room, resulting in a very confused message. The temptation to include a favourite but inappropriate element is sometimes just too hard to resist, even though its inclusion may dilute the look. But be strong! Remember that a perfect room is one from which *nothing* could be removed without lessening its aesthetic appeal.

Your starting point for choosing a particular style, be it modern or historical, domestic or imported, is likely to be the architecture of your home. In most cases this can be determined fairly easily and quickly, but it is certainly of benefit to live in a house, if this is at all possible, for several months before settling on a particular style or proceeding with major structural changes. 'Listen to the architecture' is the best advice that can be given.

# PERIOD PIECES

More than practically any other outward manifestation, house styles can be seen to reflect the world in which they were created. Examined carefully, they will reveal much about the economic state of the people, their aspirations, major scientific developments and even the movement of populations. It is perhaps this fact, together with the amazing standard of craftsmanship and artistry that was displayed so many years ago, that explains our fascination with traditional styles.

Researching a particular style can be a stimulating process in itself. It can involve visits to museums, libraries, historical homes and even trips abroad. A book, play or film might prompt interest in a specific era and involvement with a local historical society could provide valuable background information on the style of your choice.

The words 'authentic' and 'pure' are often bandied about fairly indiscriminately when describing historical styles. But just as perfectly matched colours can result in a rather boring scheme, so, by being fanatical about a particular period or style, you may be in danger of creating an interior that is totally predictable and rather lacking in character. Feel free, then, to be creative and, every now and then, to interject an element of surprise or an item from outside the period perimeters. Colours, too, can be liberally interpreted as they were in the past when paints would have been mixed by individual decorators. The hues featured in the following chapters are intended merely to suggest the flavour of the period and provide you with a starting point for your scheme.

Historically, rooms were very much allowed to evolve over the years rather than all the contents being put in place at one specific time and kept as a shrine to their year of birth. Your own modern home may feature an Art Deco wall light, a dressing table in the style of Mackintosh and a chair inspired by the popular designs of the 1950s. So long as the items have a design affinity, there is no reason why they should not be grouped together. For this reason no attempt has been made in this section for the book to lay down any definitive laws. Rather, the styles are merely hinted at and gaps left for you to fill in as you please.

Few styles are entirely new – most borrow from an earlier age, the fashion of furnishings often generated by an influx of ideas from abroad and motifs stolen from a previous incarnation. Take Gothic style, for instance. This was first seen in the Middle Ages only to be revived again in the mid-eighteenth century. In Victorian times, it once again became the people's favourite – a phenomenon comparable on a smaller time scale to clothes fashions, when hemlines and shoulder pads vie for our attention in turn every decade or so.

Each of the following chapters describes a particular style. Some of the background events that brought the style into prominence are recounted and a general description of the look is given. This is followed by photographs showing the ways in which the style could be interpreted in different rooms in your home and details of the furnishings that might be employed. Finally, under 'Putting on the Style', several colour suggestions are made and there are hints on how you might like to introduce the style in your own rooms – all with minimum effort and without spending a fortune.

*Brilliant Chinese-yellow stippled walls create a stunning background for eclectic furnishings in this drawing room in the traditional English country house style.*

# Tudor and Jacobean Style

It's hard to think that such a simple thing as the placement of the home fire against a wall instead of in the accepted position at the centre of the main room could totally revolutionize the way in which houses were constructed, how people lived and how they decorated dwellings, but that's exactly what happened in the sixteenth century. Until this time the fire – such a life essential, providing heat, light and a means of cooking – was generally centrally placed for practical reasons. The houses of the time in the main consisted of one single hall-like room in which most domestic functions took place. At the centre of the activities was the all-important fire, the smoke from which was gradually drawn through a hole in the roof. This precluded a dwelling having a second storey and also meant that any attempts at decoration were soon defeated by the effects of smoke.

Once the position of the fireplace had been moved there was a blossoming of interest in the home and its comforts. Two-storey buildings could now be erected, which allowed for additional rooms to be allocated quite separate functions. The amount and categories of furniture increased, more textiles appeared – carpets (placed on walls and tables initially), upholstery and wall hangings, and there was an eruption of surface decoration.

The other factor that considerably helped this new-found interest was the spread of the use of small glass window panes (known as quarries) at previously open window spaces. Slightly dull and certainly misshapen, these blown pieces kept the elements at bay and meant that window openings could now be enlarged, thus allowing more light into the interior – an added spur to decorating not unlike the first spring sunshine that prods us into spring cleaning. The proliferation of solid floors (replacing compacted earth and loose rushes) and timber wall panelling in many cases also made the home into an altogether more comfortable and controllable space.

It is impossible to put an exact date on these developments. Much depended upon location (urban or rural, north or south), closeness to the court and those who travelled internationally, availability of local materials, the skill of artisans and economic factors. This all meant that one home might have a style of decoration a hundred years behind another of the same age, and, rather like an old oriental rug, it should be appreciated for its local quirks as much as for its mainstream style. With these vast differences the desire among wealthier people to identify with the *cognoscenti* by adopting the latest fashions in interior styles must have been fierce.

English modes of decoration were very much determined by what was happening further south. As the classically influenced styles emerging from Italy gradually filtered north, they brought with them an increased appreciation of scale and proportion. On the way they were subjected to interpretation by the great skills and patronage of the French (in particular, the court). Also having an effect on English native styles of the time were the many displaced peoples arriving from Europe – principally the Low Countries and Germany – bringing with them their own heritage and creative skills. These various factors amalgamated to produce what we now describe as Tudor and Jacobean style.

*Modern convenience is provided by radiators and fitted carpets that do not distract the eye from the period features in this North of England manor house.*

# MATERIAL MATTERS

### WALLS

Whitewashed plaster between wooden structural beams was the most common wall finish. Timber panelling of oak was also a strongly featured finish in the houses of wealthier people. This would have been in a lighter tone of wood than we might expect, the darkening with which we are familiar having occurred through age or staining. Other cheaper woods were also used and these were often painted in colours or finished to imitate finer woods or other rich materials. The most commonly seen division of panels was in squares or rectangles. Additional decoration might also be applied in the form of painting or carving (especially in the popular linenfold design). Later in the period the joins of panel sections were often concealed behind carved pilasters. Wallpapers, made in panels for adhering to fabric before being attached to walls, were produced during the sixteenth century, but these were only to be seen in a minority of houses. Ceilings in the larger houses, later on, tended to be highly decorated with plasterwork, the designs for which were often geometric in nature. Heraldic and floral motifs featured and strapwork was often to be seen.

### FLOORING

Compacted earth strewn with loose rushes gradually lost out in favour of rush matting. Wooden floorboards in oak, elm or imported fir and of varying widths – generally of more generous proportions than their present-day equivalents – began to be seen in wealthier households. In the latter part of the period these might be covered with carpets from the Orient, Turkey or continental Europe, or perhaps even home-produced examples. Flagstones were also a widely used floor surface.

## FURNISHINGS

The most notable feature of furniture during this period was the number of new items coming into use. The canopied four-poster bed was still the most important piece (mattresses were now filled with feathers instead of straw), but newly introduced were such pieces as chests on stands, presses (tall cupboards for clothing or foodstuffs) and bookcases. Oak was still the popular choice of wood for those who could afford it. For others, cheaper softwoods might be used and these were usually painted to disguise their humble origins. Furniture was often turned and quite bulbous in nature with a highly carved surface. Upholstery started to appear and house interiors became altogether more comfortable thanks to the use of cloths such as brocade, silk damask, woollen cloth and velvet. Textile window treatments were rarely seen (where they existed, they would consist of just one curtain, on a pole and swagged to one side), wooden shutters being more usual.

## LIGHTING AND ACCESSORIES

Interiors were lit by either rush lights or tallow candles plus, of course, the light emanating from an open fire. Unlike our modern, odourless, smooth-burning candles, the tallow variety, being manufactured from animal fats, would have performed erratically and given off smells and smoke. Accessorizing as we know it – employing items purely for their decorative value – was less prevalent. However, pewter serving ware and bold candlesticks, functional as well as attractive, would often be on display.

RIGHT *A stunning strap-work ceiling, modern reproduction wallpaper and oriental carpets form a fitting background for the magnificent four-poster bed in a West of England hotel.*

OPPOSITE *Pale oak panelling, typical of the period, is decorated with luxurious textile wall hangings.*

# PUTTING ON THE STYLE

Because of its reliance upon architectural features and spaces, this style may not seem an obvious one to interpret in any place other than a building of the period. However, to dismiss it so lightly could be a mistake. Be prepared to be charmed by the elegance of its simplicity, by the grace of its curves and by the honesty of materials and natural colours. It is the perfect solution for a large hallway, impressively proportioned dining room or ample bedroom (especially if you possess a grand antique or reproduction four-poster bed to form your centrepiece). A large open fireplace is a marvellous starting point that will necessitate little more to evoke this romantic theme.

◆ Paint walls a slightly greyish, creamy-white to represent aged whitewashed plaster. Decorate with faded watercolour stencilled motifs from the period if this appeals. Alternatively, attach reproduction panels made of resin/foam in a design of the period.

◆ Wood planking, stone flags and terracotta tiles would all be ideal floorings. However, to give a floor an instant Tudor feeling, lay chunky medieval-style rush matting or one of the other natural floorings now widely available.

◆ Wooden shutters at the windows give an authentic look, but for a more homely appearance drape a single curtain of heavy brocade or velvet from a handsomely proportioned, wooden pole and swag to one side.

◆ Hang simple-design wrought-iron chandeliers or wall sconces and fill your room with candle-light. Another idea would be to convert a large blue-and-white jar into an electrified table lamp with a parchment shade. A similar conversion to an ecclesiastical brass candlestick would also produce an appropriate result.

◆ To accessorize, scatter pewter drinking vessels and plates, wooden bowls and basic eating implements around the room. World trade shops may be a good source of imported items with the right basic feel.

◆ Large blue-and-white oriental ginger jars and vases, grouped together atop a chest or table, will provide some colour for your scheme.

◆ Modern-day crewelwork fabric made in India is widely available and would make most suitable bed, window or door drapes. Textiles featuring flamestitch designs are particularly appropriate, as are velvets, brocades and leather.

◆ Portraits of the period and naïve paintings of domestic animals are now being reproduced by photographic means and finished in oil at a very reasonable cost. These will distract the eye from any lack of period architectural details and will fill your walls with interest.

◆ Some most attractive machine-made tapestries are currently being manufactured by the metre. Backed with batons, these make ideal wall hangings. Tapestry borders are also being produced and look wonderful when used as an edging to natural floor coverings.

◆ Trimmings are an all-important element of the style. Tassels and tasselled fringes in particular are appropriate and provide a suitable finish for upholstery.

◆ A large rush log-basket beside the fireplace will help to conjure up the period.

## COLOUR CUES

To bring colour to what might otherwise be a rather neutral setting, introduce furnishings of rich jewel colours – deep blue, green and red. A rich, deep, timber brown is useful for creating faux wood finishes and touches of gold will enliven your rooms. Whitewash was the most common finish for wall plaster: represent this by using a slightly creamy, off-white emulsion to give an aged look. As an alternative you might consider a pale, terracotta colour wash.

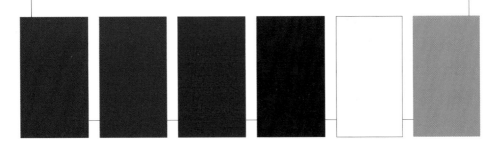

# Georgian Style

Considered by many to be the epitome of all that is desirable for the interior (and, incidentally, the exterior too), the Georgian period has a great influence on how we arrange our homes today and is, in fact, the basis for the currently popular English country house style. A combination of perfect proportions, symmetry and harmony is hard to resist for long.

Covering a period of about a hundred years from George I's accession to the throne in 1714, Georgian style represents the sum of several highly diverse, imported styles, the homogenization of which produced a high point in English decoration. This style in turn was re-exported, influencing, in particular, the newly established colonies in North America.

At the start of the period, rococo was all the rage in France and to some extent in the rest of Europe. With its rampant, florid, asymmetrical lines featuring such motifs as scrolls, shells, flowers and ribbons – in fact, anything which could be represented by a curve – it had many admirers, not least the French court, the font of fashion in Europe.

In England, however, there were other forces at work. The Grand Tour, undertaken by many a well-heeled gentleman to enrich his cultural knowledge of the world, meant that continental ideas, especially those espoused in Italy – a 'must stop' on the trek – were given an airing back home. The Earl of Burlington was one who made the trip. An architect, he was much influenced by the work of Andrea Palladio in Italy, and upon his return to England did much to popularize this classical style of architecture.

The clash of these two very different styles could have meant an awful compromise. Instead the best of both was retained and the result was magnificent. The straight lines, symmetry and control of the Palladian style served to restrain the more excessive fluidity and glitz of the rococo interpretation. In turn the French delicacy and freedom of line lifted the rather constrained classical style.

To these two important influences were added two more, Gothick (the 'k' denotes the revival period) and chinoiserie. Every age draws upon the past and this was no exception and, with the increased availability of furnishings from the east, oriental taste also crept into the currency of English decoration.

One outstanding feature of the period was that, through the genius of people such as Robert Adam and William Kent, the designs of interiors were, for the first time, indelibly linked with those of the exterior. Classical pediments, plinths and pilasters all found their way indoors to become common interior embellishments.

Overseas trade and increased wealth led to a demand for a more sophisticated lifestyle. Rudimentary plumbing (running cold water at ground level and basic waste disposal) became available, as did better heating and illumination in the homes of the nobility and merchant class. Lower down the social strata it was a very different story, a fact that can be used to great advantage when planning a Georgian-style interior today. It is not necessary to inherit a grand country mansion together with a substantial budget before considering the adoption of Georgian style. All you need are rooms of pleasing proportions and a knowledge of the materials and styles adopted by the average household of the day. A modern-day natural floor covering, such as jute over a quarry-tiled floor, will serve every bit as well as a precious Aubusson carpet on ancient wood.

As with the interior styles of other ages, it was the development of materials and skills which greatly influenced the changes in interior fashion. The use of hardwoods (mahogany in particular) and the refinement of glass production meant that early 'heavy' designs gave way to more delicate styles.

Rooms were dominated, as ever, by practical considerations. The need to keep warm and to introduce as much light as possible meant that considerable thought was given to fireplaces and windows. Mirrors were also an important feature, reflecting and increasing what natural light was available and, at night, candlelight. Practical though these elements were, it did not mean that they had to have a utilitarian appearance. Fireplaces were surrounded by the grandest of treatments in fine marble, mirrors framed with intricately carved, gilt mouldings and windows dressed either with beautifully panelled shutters or curtains hanging from delicately worked, wooden pelmets. In addition, doors (often double) were fielded, ceilings moulded and walls frequently panelled.

Not only was this a golden age of architecture and decoration but furniture making too was at its height. The designs of Thomas Chippendale, George Hepplewhite and Thomas Sheraton are legendary and constantly revived. No wonder, then, that elements of Georgian style have endured and are as popular today as ever.

*A surprisingly bright but entirely appropriate yellow has been used on the walls of this Georgian dining room.*

# MATERIAL MATTERS

## WALLS

Walls were a very important part of the Georgian interior and much attention was paid to their treatment. Classically, the wall area would have been divided into three sections: the dado/wainscoting, incorporating the skirting/base board, dado panel and rail (which would be at a height of approximately 75 cm/2ft 6in); the field or mid-wall section; and the top section made up of frieze and cornice. Early in the period these panels would most probably have been made of oak and finished with a simple wax polish. Later, with the introduction of softwoods, the panelling may have been painted, albeit in rather drab colours, or given a faux wood finish. Hangings of precious textiles and tapestries were fashionable and fabric walling as we know it also popular (except in the dining room, where food smells might be trapped). Fabrics such as silk and wool damask were attached to walls above dado height by means of wooden battens and finished with a gilt fillet. Costly wallpapers (including flock types and patterns with oriental themes) in sheets rather than rolls were highly prized and most frequently attached to a canvas backing before being hung, thus enabling them to be removed when the owners departed.

## FLOORING

Exposed bare wooden planks or parquet, simply scrubbed and waxed (and, for cosiness, topped with an oriental or area rug) are typical Georgian treatments. For an alternative covering, a painted and varnished floor cloth made of canvas might be incorporated into the scheme. For halls and the grander areas of a house, stone or marble flooring, possibly in a classical pattern, was considered most appropriate.

## FURNISHINGS

Close co-ordination between all the soft furnishings within a room would have been evident, each item echoing the material and style of others. Popular fabrics of the day were velvet, brocade, damask, silk, chintz and tapestry. Oriental themes influenced many of the fabrics and toile de jouy might well have depicted scenes from Chinese life. Embroidered textiles were also very popular.

## LIGHTING AND ACCESSORIES

The main source of light, apart from the fire, would have been candles. These were housed in candlesticks, candelabra, wall sconces and lanterns made of wood, glass, brass or silver. Many candlesticks were based on classical designs, while those for the candelabra were mainly rococo in feel. Mirrors in gilt frames featured strongly, as did lacquerwork screens, porcelain ware and fans from the Orient. Paintings (often hung from a visible fabric bow) were a popular form of wall decoration and sometimes prints were applied directly on to the wall. Silhouettes and silverware were also favoured. Items were usually displayed in a symmetrical pattern.

*The panelling of this North London home typifies the way in which wall surfaces of the period were divided and painted.*

*The frieze and fireplace of this Scottish drawing room demonstrate classical influences on Georgian interiors.*

# PUTTING ON THE STYLE

The perfect foundation for interpreting English country house style, the Georgian idiom will sit quite happily in houses of any period. Choose early Georgian style for a highly decorated look and late Georgian for a purer classical look. Perfect for imprinting on a grand drawing room, the style is equally well suited to entrance halls and bedrooms.

◆ The wall space of a room can be divided into three in Georgian style (see 'Walls', page 188) by the use of inexpensive and easily applied polystyrene mouldings. If you are unsure as to how to divide the walls, work out an arrangement using squared graph paper. The ready availability of historical paints should make the selection of a suitable finish problem-free (see 'Colour Cues' opposite). Avoid paints with a gloss finish. Alternatively panelling can be given a faux wood finish.

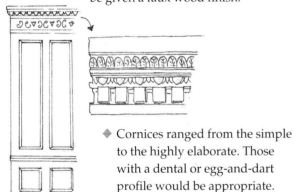

◆ Cornices ranged from the simple to the highly elaborate. Those with a dental or egg-and-dart profile would be appropriate. Select one made of polystyrene for cheapness and ease of installation.

◆ Many wallpapers of the day, expensive at the time, are now being faithfully reproduced and at a reasonable price. To give your room that genuine period feel, run borders of gilt fillet around the perimeters.

◆ Print rooms were popular during this period. Create your own from readily available prints, borders, ribbons and swags pasted directly on to the walls.

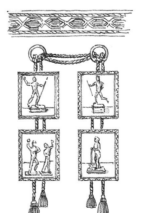

◆ Stone or marble flooring can be costly. Instead lay a vinyl or linoleum flooring depicting a faux marble design and laid out to a geometrical pattern. In a kitchen a quarry-tiled flooring would be appropriate.

◆ Finding furniture of the period should present few problems, though funding such purchases may. There are, however, many Victorian and modern reproduction items available at a fraction of the cost of the originals. Do not try to fill your room with furnishings – these were much more sparse in the Georgian interior than we are accustomed to in modern times.

◆ Upholstery covered with loose covers in fabrics such as ticking would not be out of place in a Georgian interior.

◆ Add a modern wing chair (the style has changed little) covered in damask for comfortable seating in your Georgian room. A squab cushion tied with bows to a cane-seated chair will serve as additional seating.

◆ By placing furniture around the room against the walls and drawing it up only when you wish to use it, you will be imitating the typical Georgian layout.

◆ The use of blinds – either roller or festoon – at the windows would be perfectly in keeping with the period, especially if hung from a carved and gilded wooden cornice.

A swag-and-tail pelmet, with or without curtains, might be attempted by the skilled curtain-maker or more modest curtains could be made up from muslin swagged to one side.

◆ Although electricity was not widely available until the twentieth century, it is possible to suggest the period by selecting modern light fittings with candle features. Wall sconces and candelabra are particularly suitable. Candlesticks of the period can be used to accessorize the interior.

◆ Mirrors are easily introduced and are typical of the period. These should preferably have carved gilt frames (in classical or rococo style) and be placed around the room, especially above a fireplace. The positioning of a pier glass (extra-tall mirror) between two windows will give the room a strong Georgian flavour.

◆ Adam-style plaster plaques – either oval or round – placed symmetrically around the room or along a corridor will help reinforce the style.

◆ Collect silhouettes in their typical black frames and display these in a symmetrical pattern.

# COLOUR CUES

The lack of colour technology in the early eighteenth century meant that the majority of tints had a natural earthy look about them and the description 'drab' is aptly earned. Colours such as pea green, grey, stone and off-white were in most common usage, as were biscuit, dusty pink and eau de nil. Panelling would typically have been painted in one of these sombre colours or given a faux wood treatment to imitate a more expensive wood. Paints generally had a lead base and were applied to interior and exterior as much for protection as for decoration. Unlike today, when one colour costs the same as another, a brighter shade then may well have cost up to four times as much as a dull one and so was used with great discretion. Later in the century, as dye production improved, brighter colours such as Chinese yellow, sky blue and pink came into use. Gilding was utilized extensively to enliven the grander interior.

# Victorian Style

With wealth and security inevitably come a profusion of styles and an irresistible temptation to go over the top: a broad statement, but one borne out by history. In the twentieth century we have to look back no further than to the 1980s to see evidence of this. If we retreat even further – to the mid-nineteenth century – we find perhaps an even finer example.

Victoria was on the British throne, her empire was churning along quite nicely and the rewards of the industrial revolution were being appreciated by a rapidly growing middle class. In the 'workshop of the world', as England was then known, fortunes were being made through trade with the colonies. Add to this newly found wealth and security, a monarch with strong feelings about home and family, and you have all the background ingredients of Victorian style.

With all attention on the home, it was obvious that this was where an individual's status could best be demonstrated to the world at large. The message was loud and clear: 'I have arrived, I have substance and I espouse family values' (sounds familiar?). A great surge in building and urban development ensued, much of which constitutes the English housing stock of today.

The penchant for classical styles was declining, but without any strong, new, directional fashion surfacing, the only way to look was back and to reviving previously popular interior themes (this too has its parallel in the 1980s when shabby-chic country-house eclecticism became all the rage). Gothic, Elizabethan, oriental, Scottish baronial, Egyptian and rococo – these were among the many styles that the Victorians mixed somewhat indiscriminately. When interpreting Victorian style today, you have the choice of jumbling these various furnishing styles within one room or perhaps of concentrating on just one theme in each individual space.

Industrialization had arrived and furniture was produced *en masse* (but, alas, not always to the highest standard). At least this meant that furnishings cost less and were therefore available to a wider public and in greater abundance. It should be no surprise, then, that house dwellers of the time overdosed on exuberance. The Victorian home is typified by the cluttering of furnishings, layer upon layer. Why stop at one pair of curtains at a window when these can be accompanied by blinds and net drapes too? Every imaginable item was draped, trimmed and bedecked; every inch of floor space crammed with furniture and every table spilt over with memorabilia. While the dictates of today's decorators may be 'Less is more' or 'If in doubt, leave it out', the byword of their Victorian equivalents was 'More is marvellous'!

Although at the beginning of this long-enduring period (1837–1901) schemes tended to be relatively light in feel, by the turn of the century they had become altogether more sombre. Window treatments were designed to restrict light, the decorator's palette took on deeper tones, furnishings became bulkier and dark woodwork dominated. Artificial lighting, despite the arrival of oil lamps followed by gas lamps, did little to brighten interiors. This all sounds rather dull until you remember that the Victorians would dress their rooms according to the season. Come spring, many of the heavier elements would be replaced or covered by lighter-weight materials in paler colours; then the winter scheme would be re-imposed in the autumn. We adopt this arrangement for our personal clothing, so why not for our rooms?

In Victorian times there was a preciseness that we perhaps lack today with our flexible casual lifestyles. Each room had its definitive purpose and style of decoration. Libraries, drawing rooms and dining rooms tended towards the sumptuous, while upstairs was generally given a lighter, more feminine touch.

*The floor tiles in this Victorian hallway have been cunningly designed to reflect the pattern featured in the glazing panels of the entrance door.*

# MATERIAL MATTERS

## WALLS

From about 1860 walls were often divided horizontally into three somewhat after the Georgian fashion, only now there was perhaps a greater co-ordination in the finish to the three sections, for the Victorians were very aware of the relationship between colours and patterns and their proportions within a room. The popularity of wallpapers increased as mass production got under way. Flock papers, especially red for dining rooms (they must have harboured food and tobacco smoke odours considerably), were in demand, as were Gothic-inspired patterned papers popularized by Pugin (through his use of them in the Houses of Parliament). Papers with trailing botanical themes were also common. Paint too was used for walls and ceilings, but frequently this would be brushed on to relief or textured papers, and stencilled patterns were often applied to friezes and dados. White was rarely used for ceilings, cream and drab colours being the preferred choice. Woodwork (deep skirting/base boards, doors and so on) was most usually stained or grained to give the appearance of mahogany.

## FLOORING

Hardwood floors were still popular. While many of these exhibited intricate designs, other, less elaborate ones would be covered either by oriental rugs or by carpets depicting bold floral patterns. Carpets were often bordered and most frequently laid in a square or rectangle with a margin of floor visible around the room. The floor surrounding the carpet would then either be dark-stained or perhaps covered with felt or oil cloth. Marble was popular, and tiles (ceramic and earthenware) and linoleum were the preferred choices for more utilitarian areas – encaustic tiles in geometric patterns

being especially favoured for hallways. Many of these floorings survive today and replacement tiles are still being made to old designs.

## FURNISHINGS

Furnishings were characterized by elaborate multi-layered treatments. Curtains, often hung from brass or wooden poles and pelmets, were generally softly draped. Later in the period stiff pelmets became more popular and these sometimes extended down the outside of the frame to form a lambrequin. Lace curtains and roller blinds to give added privacy and to filter dust were often used in conjunction with the main treatment. Elsewhere, drapery was used at doorways, on upholstery and even over mantelpieces. In all cases, trimming details were strongly featured. Upholstery tended to be on a grand scale, overstuffed and deeply buttoned. Fabrics were equally plush – velvet, lace, damask, satin and chintz all added to the feeling of lushness. Mahogany was a favourite wood for furniture, which was now often sold in suites.

## LIGHTING AND ACCESSORIES

Candles and oil lamps were somewhat superseded by gas lamps in the second half of the nineteenth century and electricity was introduced in the 1880s. Glass was a popular material for shades and many reproduction models are still available today. Crystal fittings, especially suspended from a central ceiling rose, featured in more formal areas, as did brass, bronze and copper fittings. The Victorians had a mania for collecting and loved nothing more than to cover every surface with memorabilia. Walls were littered with paintings and prints, and cabinets brimmed with figurines, boxes and souvenirs of every description.

ABOVE *Lincrusta paper below the high dado rail is accompanied by a reproduction Victorian patterned paper above to set off handsome period bathroom fittings.*

OPPOSITE *A claret bullion fringe edging to the swags-and-tails window treatment and mantelpiece drapery echoes the rich upholstery colour.*

# PUTTING ON THE STYLE

A decision to adopt Victorian style in your home offers the most wonderful opportunity for decorating. The abundance of Victorian properties and the profusion of artefacts from the period make decorating in this fertile style an easy and enjoyable task. Moreover, you have so many different themes from which to choose. If a cluttered, busy interior is not to your taste, simply embody the period by bringing together single items of furniture and decorative objects and placing them sparingly against a background of typical colours (see 'Colour Cues' opposite). This is a particularly apt style of decoration for studies, dining rooms, hallways and conservatories.

◆ Plaster architectural details are a strong feature of Victorian design. Buy reproductions made from original moulds and surface-mount ceiling roses, corbels/brackets (supporting a shelf, decorative item or arch), picture and dado rails and cornices (particularly with acanthus-leaf and Gothic decorations). A narrow shelf, supported by brackets, could be added at picture-rail height for displaying china of the period.

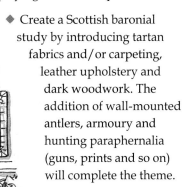

◆ Create a Scottish baronial study by introducing tartan fabrics and/or carpeting, leather upholstery and dark woodwork. The addition of wall-mounted antlers, armoury and hunting paraphernalia (guns, prints and so on) will complete the theme.

◆ You might consider exchanging your fitted carpet for one that leaves a margin around it. Alternatively oriental rugs laid over an existing carpet or hard flooring will reflect the look. On the stairs a runner carpet, held in place by brass stair rods, would be perfectly in keeping. The margin of exposed wood should then be stained.

◆ A harlequin (mixed) set of balloon-back chairs could be fun to assemble and will look far more interesting than a matching set in your dining room.

◆ Many a Victorian afternoon was whiled away partaking of tea. Reflect this by including in your living room a small round tea table with a chenille undercloth topped by one of lace to provide a useful surface for the display of period china and silverware.

◆ Victorian rooms were full of drapes. Trimmed velvet pelmets over mantelpieces, tasselled shawls draped across the backs of upholstered furniture, velvet portières at the doors – these will all help to evoke the period.

◆ Lace was widely used by the Victorians. Add a layer to your window dressing, place anti-macassars on chair headrests and edge shelves with lengths of lace trimming. A lace 'skirt' can be made for a plain lampshade from shallow lace café-curtaining by threading ribbon through the ready-made slots and tying this in a bow so that your new lace shade rests over the original one.

◆ Light your rooms with reference to whichever date within the Victorian era is your preference. Candles are wonderful for giving rooms that desirable soft glow and electrified versions of oil and paraffin lamps are widely available. A magnificent crystal chandelier will look splendid in your dining or drawing room and a lantern of the period is perfect for a hallway. The use of tinted (especially peach) bulbs will increase the period feel.

◆ Displays of pictures, hung from a picture rail in the traditional manner, should virtually obliterate your wall covering. Look out especially for portraits in oils, prints depicting hunting, rural scenes or romantic themes, watercolour landscapes and silhouettes in black frames.

◆ Compiling collections from the period can provide many a happy hour at antique fairs and car boot/garage sales. Look out for: papier-mâché trays, shell frames, tortoiseshell boxes, ivory fans, dome-top display cases containing natural subjects, blackamoors, majolica ware, coloured glass and ceramic figurines.

◆ The craft of découpage is enjoying a revival. Apply motifs of the period (perhaps taken from

old cards and calendars) to a traditional screen (or a new one constructed from MDF).

◆ Place potted plants, particularly ferns and palms, at random. Mounted on a Victorian plant stand, such an arrangement will instantly conjure up the period mood.

# COLOUR CUES

We generally tend to think of Victorian colours as being somewhat deep and gloomy, but with the invention of aniline dyes towards the end of the nineteenth century came colours that were much brighter and more intense than we imagine. Perhaps they are recalled as dull because they were originally viewed in poor lighting conditions. If we are to give our homes a Victorian look in modern bright conditions, we need to use slightly 'dirtier' versions of the original hues. The richer deeper tones were generally reserved for the dining room, drawing room and study, while the paler ones were more popular for bedrooms.

# Art Nouveau Style

Springing out of the Arts and Crafts movement, Art Nouveau style came to the fore in the last decade of the nineteenth century. Industrialization was taking a hold at an increasing rate and there was a great fear that, in the process of mechanization, individuality and respect for the work of the artisan would be lost. The Arts and Crafts movement sought to redress the balance and to stress the value of natural forms, the integrity of the hand-crafted article and the honesty of materials.

Viewed in retrospect, Art Nouveau style slots happily into the traditional idiom, but at the time it must have been seen in a very different light. By the 1890s Victorian decoration was reaching what can only be described as a stage of excess. Rooms were dark, heavily draped, overembellished and filled beyond reason. The New Art ideas of flooding rooms with light, of presenting materials in their natural state and of clearing away the clutter must have seemed quite revolutionary at that time, to be attempted only by the brave. Interestingly enough, after the excesses of the late twentieth century, Art Nouveau is once again looking fresh and appropriate.

Unlike many previous fashions, Art Nouveau borrowed little from historical styles. Medieval and Celtic influences are there, but merely hinted at. The rest was the creation of such designers as Charles Rennie Mackintosh in Scotland; Voysey and Morris in England; Gustav Stickley, Frank Lloyd Wright and L. C. Tiffany in America; Georges de Feure in France; and Josef Hoffmann in Austria. Other countries notable for embracing the style were Italy, Spain, Germany and Belgium.

Two distinct threads can be identified within the style. On the one hand there is the essential fluid, curvilinear nature of the designs depicting natural forms, and on the other, strongly disciplined, geometric forms with the emphasis on vertical lines as exemplified by the furniture and architecture of Mackintosh and the Glasgow School. It is the combination of these paradoxical aspects that creates such a stimulating style.

Few extravagant or exotic materials were used in the Nouveau interior. Oak, formerly the material of country craftsmen, was taken to town and used for furniture, panelling and floors. Window treatments tended towards the mean and walls were most often painted white or a shade of off-white. Faux finishes were seen as pretentious and were banished, being so totally at odds with the belief in the honesty of materials.

The style is typified by the depiction of natural subjects – in particular, striated images of flowers and foliage. Flowers such as lilies, roses and irises were strongly featured, as were twining stems with tendrils enveloping whatever they were emblazoned upon. These rounded forms contrasted sharply with the vertically exaggerated shapes promoted by Mackintosh.

Although there was originally an intention for Art Nouveau to be reflected in the exterior as well as the interior of buildings, most people opted for doing little more than importing the motifs and interior furnishings suggested by the style. Stained-glass windows were introduced and many fireplace surrounds designed in the Nouveau style. Stair balustrades also often featured the florid forms. Liberty, the London store, did much to promote the idiom, producing and selling furniture, wallpaper, textiles and accessories that reflected the movement's image.

*A wonderful example of the Mackintosh style, relying as it does upon a magical mix of curvilinear and geometric shapes and a neutral palette.*

# MATERIAL MATTERS

## SURFACES

There was a general movement towards making rooms lighter and altogether less cluttered. This was reflected in the newly popular, paler paint colours for walls that were in strong contrast to the previously fashionable, darker shades and were seen as fresh and airy by comparison. To provide interest, a paper or painted frieze might have been added at the ceiling line and borders above the skirting/base board were not unusual. Architectural embellishments were few. Dados diminished in popularity, but a picture rail or plate rack at approximately eye level might have been featured. Pilasters and panelling were also sometimes applied, especially if they could be employed to emphasize the vertical. Wallpapers, mostly depicting botanical themes, continued to be favoured, particularly now that their cost was much reduced as a result of machine-manufacture. Plain window and door glazing now gave way to more decorative treatments. Stained glass featuring geometric patterns or representations of botanical subjects was popular. The latter part of the nineteenth century saw a decline in the fashion for large area rugs. These were often removed in favour of wood floors, both board and parquet, which were frequently covered with faded oriental carpets.

## FURNISHINGS

Plush curtain treatments and deeply buttoned upholstery were eschewed by the followers of the New Art. In their stead simpler furnishings were in evidence. Attention was directed to the windows themselves rather than to how they were dressed. Pelmets, if they were used, were now flat and of simple design, otherwise lengths of fabric would be simply gathered and suspended from a plain wooden pole. With the emphasis on vertical lines, the curtains were frequently full length and rarely caught in a tie-back. Furniture designs were pared down to a more basic form and were usually constructed from oak or satinwood for a lighter look than the traditional mahogany. These items would have a simple wax finish and the grain was much in evidence. Cutouts, often in the form of a heart, inlaid work and simple carving were the principal embellishments to be seen. Other items of furniture, in the Mackintosh manner, were highly stylized, and chairs with their exaggerated ladder-backs were often painted black.

## LIGHTING AND ACCESSORIES

Probably the first item that springs to mind when Art Nouveau is mentioned is the Tiffany lamp. Its skilled American creator, L. C. Tiffany, who also designed whole houses (appropriately enough, for someone whose middle name was Comfort), produced some of the loveliest coloured and leaded glass lamps to be seen. Although electricity became available during this period (to those who could afford it), in general the appearance of light fittings varied little from those fittings previously designed for gas. Far fewer accessories were displayed, the emphasis being on objects made from silver, copper, ceramic, glass, bronze and pewter.

LEFT *A highly decorated bedroom suite is all that is needed to anchor this room firmly in the late nineteenth century.*

OPPOSITE *Stylized roses and vertical lines are the chief components of the wall decoration in this room in Scotland designed by Charles Rennie Mackintosh.*

# PUTTING ON THE STYLE

Art Nouveau style is a perfect one to imprint upon the house of more modest proportions, especially if it was constructed around the turn of the century. With few architectural features to worry about, a flavour of the style can be achieved by simply assembling artefacts of the period and placing them judiciously against a fairly bland but well-lit background.

◆ Should your room be embellished with classical or even Victorian features, these are best obliterated by removal or by painting in the same colour as their background so that they visually disappear. A dado rail might be left in a hallway, but elsewhere this could be repositioned at eye level or replaced with a plate rack at the same height.

◆ A fireplace can be very evocative of the style and could form the centrepiece of an Art Nouveau room. Look for models made of cast iron, wood, brickwork or copper with the tell-tale stylized floral and geometric designs depicted on ceramic tiles, in metal relief or formed from coloured glass mosaic. Trawl architectural salvage companies for a suitable example.

◆ Strip away your fitted carpet and hope to reveal a timber floor. Whether planks or parquet, this, simply waxed and covered with oriental rugs, will summon up the right feel for the period. A painted stencil border would also be in keeping.

◆ Since the style is only around a hundred years old, numerous examples of Art Nouveau furniture survive and can even be bought from so-called 'junk' shops for little cost. Many modern furniture makers have rediscovered the look and are interpreting it anew. These items, though not for the purist, will look fine in a room of the period.

◆ If your budget will run to it, insert stained, leaded glass panes of Nouveau designs in windows (and doors) where there was previously a plain sheet.

◆ Curtains, if any, should be relatively insignificant. Made of a plain fabric or from a typical Nouveau design material, these are best hung from either a wooden pole or a track with a flat, simply shaped pelmet in front. You might also think of painting designs on a plain silk or canvas material.

◆ Accessories are the greatest fun to collect and to position to great effect under good lighting in your room. Remember that you need many fewer than in a typical Victorian interior. Masterpieces are priceless, but humbler artefacts can be found at fairs and auctions for a fraction of the cost. Look out for mirrors, picture frames, lamps, figurines and items made from beaten metalwork.

◆ Fortunately, although few original examples remain and those that do tend to be expensive, lighting of the period is currently considered fashionable and so reproduction models are widely available.

◆ Give plain lampshades the Nouveau treatment by painting on designs typical of the period.

◆ To give your bathroom or kitchen a feel of the period, install Art Nouveau-style ceramic tiles or paint suitable designs on your existing plain ones using ceramic paints.

## COLOUR CUES

Art Nouveau reflects an altogether lighter palette than that of Victorian style. You may not find shades of white an exciting prospect, but when these are used as a background for exquisite artefacts from the period, their purpose becomes clear and it can be a relief to have got away from the dominating backgrounds that were previously in vogue. Other prettier pastel shades became popular too, such as salmon pink, grey-green and lilac. Black was also featured, notably as the colour for Mackintosh-style furniture, and white was generally used for structural woodwork.

# Art Deco Style

Think of a 1930s Hollywood movie or an elderly cruise liner and you have Art Deco style in a nutshell. And anyone who has visited Miami in Florida, USA, cannot fail to appreciate this chic, streamlined, sugar-coated style. First fashionable between 1920 and 1940 and named after the 1925 Exposition des Arts Décoratifs in Paris, Deco is currently undergoing revived popularity – with good reason. The lifestyles and homes of the latter part of the twentieth century form an ideal backdrop for this style with its clean lines, ethnic elements and lack of interior architectural ornamentation. Perhaps it was a reaction to all the clutter and dark colours of the Victorian period or simply a desire to escape from the ugliness of the events of the First World War, but without doubt, in contrast to what went before, Art Deco demonstrated great optimism, clarity and modernism.

The style featured aerodynamic rounded forms together with vivid colours that, in common with all fashionable styles, reflected what was happening in the world at the time. Technological advances in England and abroad (many connected with the concept of speed) were an obsession. A particularly strong feature is the ziggurat or stepped profile taken from the outline of ancient pyramids. Archaeological discoveries in Egypt, the popularity of African safaris, increased trade with the East and the vogue for all things Latin American combined to produce a rich mix of exotica – just the tonic your home may be waiting for!

A style as famous for the introduction of the coffee table (as we know it) as of the cocktail cabinet (which we may prefer to forget), Art Deco has much more to offer. The introduction of new materials and the growing use of mechanization were exploited to the full by the designers of the day, enabling new stylistic forms to evolve. Artists, too, were of great influence and the Cubist movement provided favourite motifs for both fabric and carpet patterns.

Unlike the Victorians, who used automation to recreate essentially traditional styles of furnishings, there was now a greater understanding of the strengths of this type of manufacture, and methods of production began to determine new styles. Highly decorated surfaces gave way to uninterrupted expanses and arching forms. At a stroke the work of the Arts and Crafts movement was struck a deathly blow. There was no way these designs could have been hand-crafted and materials such as chrome, lacquer and mirror provided surfaces that were as far removed from nature as could be imagined.

Introducing Art Deco into your home today should present few problems. Open any lighting manufacturer's brochure and you will see how popular the style is. Modern furniture designers borrow heavily from the period and antique fair stalls groan under the weight of Deco artefacts. Because of Deco's current popularity, you may well find that original items are hard to locate or beyond your budget, but faithful reproductions can in many cases be easily found and at a fraction of the cost.

Fitted furniture, so essential to our modern lives, is a strong feature of Deco style. When interpreting the style today, simply ensure that the modern equivalent is streamlined (rounded corners help the illusion) and lacking moulding or intricate hardware.

*Abstract forms, highly polished surfaces and curved contours all typify the Art Deco theme in this stylish room.*

# MATERIAL MATTERS

## WALLS

The most popular wall treatment of the time was paint, often in shades of cream, beige and brown. In many cases this was left unadorned; in others, border frame lines and corner motifs would be stencilled in (see the photograph below). On occasions, broken-paint techniques were used and walls were ragged, stippled or marbled. Wallpapers were less favoured among the *cognoscenti* of the day, though some were available. Embossed papers, together with those featuring geometric patterns (particularly the chevron), were produced, as were papers with botanical themes.

## FLOORING

Linoleum was in its heyday. Far from being boring, this was often formed into exciting geometric patterns (for instance, checkerboard) with two or three different colourways or left plain with just a border created from linoleum of a contrasting colour. In the more formal areas of the house, wall-to-wall carpeting as we know it today was rarely used. More popular were pale wooden floors (either strip or parquet) often adorned with area rugs featuring Greek key or Cubist patterns.

## FURNISHINGS

The post-war yearning for a return to glamour meant that luxurious materials were once more in demand. Figured moquette (with either cut or uncut pile), satin, velvet, leather and even animal skins were fashionable. Despite this desire for glamour, window treatments on the whole were not a strong feature of the Deco interior. Curtains were generally of simple design and floor length. These would sometimes be headed by a flat pelmet with a geometric outline which might be reinforced by a binding. Fabrics for curtains tended to remain plain, but upholstery and other items featured strong patterns based upon such motifs as shells, Aztec prints, sunbursts and fans. Furniture was predominantly rounded in form and constructed in pale wood. Chrome, lacquer, glass and mirror all added to the overall glossiness of the look.

## LIGHTING AND ACCESSORIES

Although electricity was still considered a luxury by many, lighting was an important constituent of interior decoration in the 1920s and 1930s. The design of fittings veered away from the intricacies of Victorian and Edwardian styles, and opaque glass and chrome became popular. Shapes were often streamlined, the half-bowl or fan-shaped wall uplighter being typical. Other fittings included figurines holding globes and shades with deep fringes.

Because of the very plainness of the Art Deco interior, accessories took on an important role. Here, just as with the fabrics of the time, luxury was the name of the game. Artisans set to work on ivory, lacquer, bronze, mother-of-pearl, snakeskin and tortoiseshell. Glass was also to the fore and highlighted the talents of René Lalique. It is possibly through the use of accessories such as these that the style of the Art Deco interior will be most easily and effectively evoked in the modern home.

ABOVE *This more comfortable face of Art Deco style exhibits a stencilled wall decoration that might easily be copied.*

OPPOSITE *Black defines the contours of this stylish Deco kitchen with its ziggurat-profile unit handles and checkerboard flooring.*

# PUTTING ON THE STYLE

Perfect for incorporating into modern homes as well as those of the period, Art Deco style will give your home a clean modern look. Many furnishings of today echo this period and so completing your scheme from modern resources should prove unproblematic. Architectural details are few and the style can be conjured up by the judicious use of slick materials and art objects. It is particularly suitable for interpretation in the bathroom, kitchen and connecting areas.

◆ If an original wooden floor lies beneath the current cover, this can be revealed and refinished (including bleaching if it is too dark) to bring back its original glory. For a greater feeling of comfort, scatter area rugs of abstract design. Linoleum, cut to your own pattern, is an inexpensive alternative.

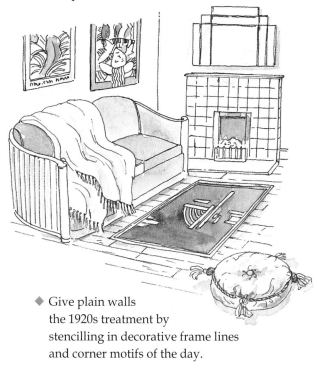

◆ Give plain walls the 1920s treatment by stencilling in decorative frame lines and corner motifs of the day.

◆ Architectural details are best removed or simplified. A basic modern coved cornice is in keeping, as is the three-step style. A skirting with a similar profile can be easily formed from planks of differing widths.

◆ Windows will take on the right look if furnished with either a wide-slatted Venetian blind or a length of fabric casually draped over a pole. Alternatively, a simple wooden pelmet, possibly with outline trim, can be formed to conceal the curtain headings.

◆ A deep fringe added to a lampshade will give it a period feel.

◆ Mirrors should be frameless and either round or ziggurat (stepped) in shape. They may also be coloured (especially rose-tinted).

◆ Reproduction posters from the period are widely available. Enclose them in frames of black moulding to give definition.

◆ Genuine or reproduction accessories bought from junk sales or specialist dealers will do much to imprint the style on your room. Typical examples emanate from the designs of Lalique (glass) or Clarice Cliff (colourful pottery). Subjects commonly featured are birds (flamingos are typical), animals (especially black panthers), botanical themes (particularly lilies and palm trees) and dancing human figures. Fans are also strongly featured.

◆ Furniture will instantly adopt a 1920s feel if covered with a draped shawl (preferably fringed).

◆ Cushions covered with velvet (and trimmed with the inevitable tassel), placed on the floor, will not only evoke the style, but will also help with additional seating problems.

◆ Add tassels to anything.

◆ If a cocktail cabinet is not to your taste, simply deck your sideboard with cocktail glasses and decanters of the day.

◆ A display of large palms will produce the right atmosphere. Add a floor-standing uplighter to the rear of the plants and you will endow a room with instant drama.

## COLOUR CUES

Cream, beige and brown may have been the predominant shades in humbler homes, but the decorating palette of the time encompassed many other more brilliant hues. The arrival of Diaghilev's Russian Ballet in 1909, with its exhilarating costumes and resplendent sets, had an enormous impact on popular taste for many years. Vibrant orange and strong yellow, lime green and intense blue became acceptable. Bright lavender and deep purple also gained favour. Reflective and metallic finishes (such as mirror, lacquer and chrome) served to intensify these colours, while black gave the style definition and a certain seriousness. To interpret the style now, a slightly aged version of these colours is suggested. Different shades of eau-de-nil combine well, as do cream and beige when accented with orange, terracotta and green.

# Future Living

For those who fear that, in the not too distant future, we may be required to live in hideous alien constructions, the lack of historical precedent for radical change may be a comforting thought. To know that our last refuge from the world, like a well worn-in pair of shoes, will continue to be predictable and familiar engenders a feeling of security.

Recent statistics reveal that nearly 50 per cent of the housing stock in England was built more than fifty years ago. The same figures also disclose that some 20 per cent was built in excess of a hundred years ago. This seems hardly credible when the incompatibility of the lifestyles of then and now are contrasted. How many homes, for example, were designed with the push-chair/baby carriage in mind and what percentage have a bathroom per bedroom? Where are the houses that include a home office and how many have gas and electrical meters that can be read from outside the building? Where is your garage located – sensibly next to your house or more remotely? Because we love our historic homes, we tend to mend and make do, extend and partition – but is this really the answer to modern living?

What do we really need for our homes to provide in modern life? First of all, we want variety – we want developers to recognize that, families apart, students, the handicapped, the elderly and divorced people also want homes of their own. We are cost- and time-conscious and need thermal-efficient houses that make few demands of us. We want to live in houses which have a style that is every bit as individual as we are. We need to be able to work, learn, rest and play in the vicinity so that we can avoid environmentally costly journeys. We also have a deep-seated need to rekindle the concept of community to give us a sense of belonging and to help reduce crime.

The crux of the problem is that what we want comes at a price – a price that we may or may not be willing or able to pay. The individual home is more costly to create than its mass-produced cousin. Our desire to live in a green-field environment may be fulfilled at the expense of someone else's landscape, and hasn't that idea of building communities by providing employment, education, shopping and entertainment facilities on the doorstep been tried before?

Four hundred years ago houses were built of brick, the internal space was divided into a fixed pattern of rooms and many had open fireplaces. When compared with the houses of today, it may seem that little has changed – except our lifestyles. True, there have been some advances. We have flush WCs that demand a waterfall for disposal. Instead of using open fires we heat our draughty houses by filling our rooms with plumbing and we light our rooms using resource-wasting electricity. And what do we do when we really want to make ourselves feel comfortable? We light an open fire, cook a meal on a Victorian-style range and illuminate our dining room with candlelight. Add to this our obsession to get close to nature by building Victorian-style conservatories and we have an indication of just how forward-looking we are not.

The bankruptcy of ideas is currently also manifest in our choice of styles. The fashion for historical paints and ancient images is witnessed everywhere. Period adds greatly to the price of a property, and a past desired over a future. Spanking-new houses are even being sold on the strength of offering 'Tudor' beams or 'Georgian' porticoes. All this retrospection is in spite of the availability of superior materials and the development of improved construction methods.

So just how should we be catering for the needs of the twenty-first century? We appear, if rather belatedly,

*An exercise in space, light and rounded forms that banishes conventional thoughts on rectangular rooms.*

to have finally accepted that our houses are no longer served by an army of helpers, and so the traditional upstairs/downstairs division between servants and owners is no longer required. The kitchen is now located in the central area of the house and is more of a food-processing room than a traditional kitchen. Children are rarely banished to the loft; instead, they are more likely to occupy a family room in an open-plan area off the kitchen. Our newly informal lifestyles render drawing rooms and dining rooms somewhat obsolete. Instead, what is wanted is a large space where various activities can take place.

Technological developments in the areas of processing and communicating information have enabled the career-minded to function without the necessity of attending an office on a daily basis and the housekeeper has little need to visit the bank or even a shopping centre regularly. These facts radically alter the priorities in a home – not just in the requirement for office space but also for space for those other activities that used to happen near the place of work. Visits to health clubs, hairdressers and beauty salons, centres of entertainment, libraries, shopping centres, restaurants and so on may be eschewed in favour of in-house facilities.

All these indications lead logically to the conclusion that there is a need for an open studio-style space in the home rather than individual rooms. This would ideally be large and perhaps divided roughly, by means of movable walls, into zones of activity. It could then function as a playroom, gym, library, cinema, workshop or office and the layout changed as new demands arise. This is not as radical a solution as it sounds. The idea in fact has its roots in ancient history and signals a return to the old idea of the hall house, a concept that was current for many centuries but utterly alien to our more recent ancestors, the Victorians, who felt that it was necessary to have a room for every function.

*Familiar features remind us of the past while providing a multi-functional space for modern living.*

With so much of our lives now being played out in the public arena, another concept from the past (and still popular in many continental areas) that we might borrow and adapt is the house with an inner central courtyard and cloister. An alternative to the conservatory, this enclosed garden blurs the dividing line that separates us from our environment and provides a space where the pleasures of nature can be enjoyed in quiet privacy.

Technology will undoubtedly have applications in many areas of the home. At one time it was thought that robots would replace the human helper, but now it seems that other controls will come to our assistance. Remote automatic programming will relieve us of many routine chores. Already cookers, videos, heating systems and so on can be set this way – why not other items such as humidity control and ventila-

tion, as in plant nurseries? Internal room-to-room communication seems an obvious development, and imagine pressing a button at a distance to lock/unlock your front door in much the same way as you can presently secure a car. The house could also be safeguarded in the same way last thing at night. The provision of eco-friendly sources of power is a priority and solar panels could well become part of every home and have an influence on architectural styles.

Our current reaction to a change in lifestyle or number of household members is to create an extension, build fixed partitions or demolish walls. These are not sensible solutions in the twenty-first century.

In the commercial world it has been realized that needs are continually evolving and a system of 'flexible' walls has been devised for office use – screens that can be moved as requirements arise. Could the domestic sector not also adopt this logical solution?

When it comes to spotting trends in interior decoration, there are many 'experts' who are skilled at predicting what lies around the corner, but few are bold enough to venture beyond the immediate future. What is evident, though, is that, after all the recent design dictatorships and the overembellishment of houses, we are increasingly seeking a more ordered, individual background against which to play out the game of life: a simpler form of decoration that requires little effort to assemble and less to maintain, and that values clean lines and space above clutter and ostentation.

This new minimalist style will also be the perfect answer to the 'quick-fix' transient lifestyle that so many of us now lead. A simplified approach to deco-rating will allow us to move home effortlessly, our few well-chosen furnishings transported with ease and the plainness of their design adapting well to a variety of architectural styles.

No need, then, to be knowledgeable about historical styles or to have the skills necessary to create complex schemes – and just think of the time saved by not having to shop endlessly for accessories. In this new, simpler world, home decoration will be accessible to all and the customizing of houses a sure way to assert individuality in a mass-production-mad age. We have learned how to use paint on walls, and this might be extended to the creation of our own wallpapers, the addition of three-dimensional wall details and even the design of personalized fabrics. Who knows, perhaps we will see a revival of the Arts and Crafts movement – twenty-first-century style!

*Traditional room layouts are called into question in this home with its alternative space arrangement.*

# INTERNATIONAL FLAVOUR

In the modern world it seems that there are two sorts of people – those for whom the homogenization of national identities is something to mourn and those who embrace the trend and feel that their culture is enriched by the inclusion of foreign influences. You may well be inclined to stick with a style of expression in your home that has evolved from a familiar culture, one that is indelibly linked with the past and which is tied to local materials, skills and conditions. If however, you decide to take a more global perspective, there is the possibility of going on an exciting journey of discovery, of learning about foreign customs and images and experiencing the sights, sounds and smells of far-away places.

On the following pages you will find a number of different styles – some exotic, others humble – to tempt your taste buds. Your own choice of an individual style may stem from having lived in another country, a fascination with a particular people or perhaps simply a desire to bring an alternative palette of rich or pallid colours into your home, together with the sunshine or coolness they represent.

One of the attractions of adopting an international style of decorating is that it is not necessary to spend a fortune to achieve a successful result. Rather than making major purchases of large items of furniture, you could introduce your chosen idiom by doing nothing more than creating a fairly bland background against which a collection of souvenirs might be displayed. Then, if you wished to take a particular theme further, surface treatments such as floor matting, stencils or wall tiles might be adopted to reinforce the cultural association.

*The bed in this orientally inspired bedroom appears to 'float' on a sea of marble, providing an illusion of coolness and calm.*

Before selecting your 'flavour', think carefully about the area it will occupy. Is the size and shape of the room suitable and does it possess any architectural details which conflict with your chosen idiom? The dimensions of the space may be difficult to adjust, but embellishments such as dado rails, skirting/base boards and picture rails can, with little effort, be removed or at least disguised. Tented ceilings and fabric walls (which might be achieved for minimal cost if a cloth such as muslin is used) are useful devices for temporarily hiding details and fabric throws over furniture will transform items of upholstery in an instant. Much can also be done by way of window treatments. A lambrequin formed from medium-density fibreboard, or simply made shutters, could disguise window features and impart a whole other look to your room.

As well as using colours to suggest a particular style, do not forget the vital role played by textures. The gloss of oriental lacquer, the roughness of coir matting and the sheen of chintz are all examples of qualities that can be introduced to evoke a specific style.

To complete your far away fantasy, summon up a fragrance of the country that gave birth to your chosen style. We have all experienced the dramatic reminder a particular odour can induce: the delicate scent of frangipani that prompts thoughts of a long-ago African safari, the smell of incense which transports us to a Thai temple and the perfume of lily-of-the-valley which plants us firmly in the drawing room of an English country house. Candles, room essences and incense sticks can all be employed to take us on the journey of a lifetime.

# Global Style

Holidays abroad may never be the same again. Adopt the global style in your home and your days of boredom on the beach will be swapped for early-morning trawls through local markets, exciting expeditions to souks and fascinating hours whiled away in artisans' workshops. In short, your vacations will take on a whole new meaning and may even inspire trips further afield to seek yet more exotic finds.

It is not necessary to go to Disneyland to discover that it's a small world. The late twentieth century has seen the concept of the global village reflected in so many aspects of our lives. Just as the meals we eat may feature sun-dried tomatoes from Italy, coconut milk from the Caribbean and seaweed from Japan, so this trend is echoed in the furnishing of our homes, and the opportunity to decorate with the rich mix of sunshine, colour and crafts from many lands becomes irresistible.

There is nothing new in ethnic style. Throughout history, fashions in decoration have been greatly influenced by the importation of foreign elements. The popularity of the French rococo style in the early eighteenth century, the fad for chinoiserie in Regency times and the importation of Greek motifs in the early nineteenth century are all examples.

Inspiration is all around – we have the world to trawl for ideas. We only have to think of the colours of an oriental carpet, the patterns of West African textiles and the shapes of continental pots to realize what a rich palette we have to draw on. Materials, too, play a large part in ethnic decoration. Terracotta, rattan, native woods, tin, bamboo, papier-mâché and woven textiles of every description all contribute, as do patterns of paisley, ikat and batik.

Remarkably, mixing items from different ethnic sources does not present a problem. It may seem strange, but the colours, textures and patterns emerging from these remote locations have unexpected parallels. Perhaps it is the reliance upon natural colour pigments, basic shapes and forms and crude implements that produces this pleasing amalgam of disparate cultures.

An added bonus for decorators of global style is one of cost. Based, as this style is, on the more native elements of the various cultures from which it derives, items that are hand-made, often in local workshops and of locally sourced natural materials, are unlikely to claim too large a portion of the decorating budget. Neither should the provision of a suitable background for all these treasures. The expensive skills of a professional are not what is required here, but rather the inspiration of the creative amateur who will naturally render the style in all its naïveté.

Recycling is an essential element of ethnic decoration. The conversion, for the price of a tin of paint, of everyday objects is part and parcel of the tribal tradition. What better use for that discarded baked-bean can than for it to be painted a brilliant colour only to reappear as a plant pot?

There is not even a requirement to move out of your own environment in order to gather goodies for this colourful style. Nowadays 'trading posts' are to be found in or near most major cities. Imported in bulk, items are gathered from the four corners of the world, and it is the importer who has the burden of excess baggage. Other treasures may be picked up at charity shops, antique fairs and rug auctions. A visit to an anthropological museum may yield yet more contributions.

*A scheme that defies the belief that conservatories have to have a garden theme. Here ethnic elements conspire to transport the occupier to faraway places.*

# MATERIAL MATTERS

## WALLS

Rough plaster, brick or stone walls speak for themselves and can be left unadorned – or painted white or some brilliant colour – to provide the perfect background for displays. Plain walls decorated with ethnically inspired patterns are also typical. For a focal point why not feature stunningly patterned ceramic tiles from such countries as Morocco or Portugal?

## FLOORING

This is *not* the world of fitted carpets – think instead of peasant dwellings; of uneven floors of stone slabs, terracotta tiles and wooden planking. For comfort, these cold finishes may be warmed up by the addition of a tribal knotted carpet, woven mat or rag rug. Natural materials such as sisal, seagrass, jute or coir also provide suitably unsophisticated floor coverings.

## FURNISHINGS

Colourful hand-crafted textiles of all descriptions may hang on walls, be used for upholstery or loose covers or be made into curtains. Draped fabric may also form room dividers instead of conventional doors. These fabric lengths fill the room with exotic patterns and colours in stark contrast to the rough hard finishes that surround them. Furniture is simply designed and made from whatever materials are available locally – indigenous woods and metals being favourite choices. Windows are frequently dressed with shutters or fretwork screens instead of curtains. Alternatively, blinds of split cane or other natural material may be seen.

## LIGHTING AND ACCESSORIES

Candles are a must – housed in sticks of every description, wall sconces, lanterns and simple candelabra, made of recycled tin, iron, terracotta or brass. Accessories form a large part of the decoration. Many items, such as baskets, bowls, jars and cooking implements, have an everyday practical purpose, being used in the kitchen, for transporting goods or for working the land. Other objects may have more specialized purposes and may include armoury and items of apparel: daggers, swords, shields, spears, jewellery, robes and other garments are frequently displayed. Also to be seen are ceremonial items: musical instruments, head-dresses, masks and so on. The theme common to all these items is the material from which they are made – inevitably natural, distressed and unrefined.

RIGHT *Brilliant indigo blue is used to striking effect to set off a neutral sofa covered with multi-coloured cushions.*

OPPOSITE *Cacti 'sculptures' are reflected in the light fittings of this 'desert' setting and red earth walls complete the association.*

# PUTTING ON THE STYLE

Global style is one of the easiest to interpret, requiring few skills and the slimmest of budgets. The global home will be colourful and fun to assemble. Perfect for the student bed-sit, it is just as much at home in a formal living room as in a kitchen, and in fact the style interprets well throughout the house.

◆ To rid your room of those unwanted classical details, swathe the ceiling (and walls if you wish) in fabric to create your own tribal tent. You will need large amounts, so opt for a basic cloth such as muslin.

◆ Give walls an aged rough plaster look by randomly applying a skim coat of plaster, or create a textured look with a colour wash.

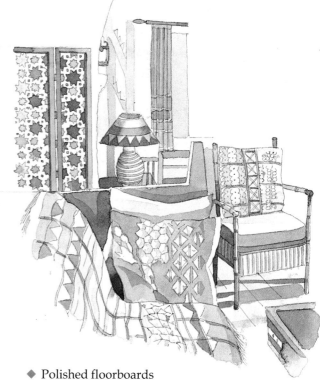

◆ Decorate plain walls with stencilled tribal patterns. No need to take too much care – the more hand-crafted they appear, the better.

◆ Polished floorboards can be stripped and scrubbed for a natural look.

◆ Natural floor coverings of sisal, jute, coir and seagrass are widely available and are an excellent accompaniment to your tribal treasures.

◆ For furniture on a budget, go for rattan, wicker or bamboo. For seating comfort add tie-on cushions covered in a crewelwork or embroidered textile.

◆ A fretwork screen can easily be made of MDF panels – widely available and many having an eastern profile. Place an uplighter behind for added drama.

◆ An old carved Indian door on supports makes an excellent coffee-table top. Cover with sheet glass to provide a flat surface.

◆ Simple curtains at the windows or room entrance can be made from lengths of fabric, bedspreads, saris or shawls suspended from rings on a wooden pole.

- A ceiling-hung metal lantern will light your room appropriately.

- Give a large mirror the flavour of the East by making a cutout frame with an oriental profile. This can be constructed from stiff card, ply or polystyrene, then painted or covered with a suitable fabric.

- Cushions (for floor, sofa or bed) covered in mirrored fabric will add sparkle to your room.

- A plain-covered sofa can be transported to foreign parts with the help of a tribal rug draped over back and seat.

- Ceramic plates depicting local patterns or scenes can be found almost everywhere. Display these in groups on walls.

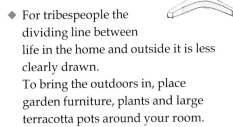

- To accessorize your room, display necklaces and other items of jewellery on clear acrylic shop-fitting stands. Driftwood, shells, fallen fir-cones and travel agency posters are free – gather and group them for impact.

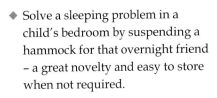

- For tribespeople the dividing line between life in the home and outside it is less clearly drawn. To bring the outdoors in, place garden furniture, plants and large terracotta pots around your room.

- Solve a sleeping problem in a child's bedroom by suspending a hammock for that overnight friend – a great novelty and easy to store when not required.

- Suspend a mosquito net over a bed for a safari sensation.

## COLOUR CUES

Mediterranean blue, tribal-rug red, monk orange, lime green, canary yellow, baked-earth brown and plaster white are the colours to use: a magical mix of rich earth hues combined with shocking brights that stand up in sunlight. For once we can forget such cautions as 'Blue and green should never be seen'. Global style gives us the excuse to employ as much bad taste as our imagination will allow us. It is perfect for injecting character into a bland structure and for creating excitement and warmth in a climate lacking either.

# American Colonial Style

No pale imitation of fashionable European images, American Colonial style, although inevitably influenced by the influx of peoples of European stock, was very much a product of local materials, skills and conditions. Starting with the arrival of settlers in the early seventeenth century, the period extends to the Declaration of Independence in the late eighteenth century. It tracks the evolution of ethnically diverse peoples, some wealthy, others arriving penniless and without possessions, who developed over the years into a homogenous sophisticated society with its own unique character and individual style.

Out of necessity, early dwellings were basic and 'country' in feel. They also incorporated many features adopted from local crafts and the folk culture of the indigenous people. Towards the end of the period, with greater wealth, increased trading with the rest of the world and the availability of pattern books from Europe, the style made a shift towards the popular fashions of Europe and yet still interpreted these in a uniquely American way.

The timing of the settlement of America was fortunate indeed from a stylistic viewpoint. Europe overflowed with creative activity, culminating, in the latter part of the period, in what became known in England as Georgian style, elements of which were happily taken on board by the settlers who localized the designs for their own purposes.

*Deep terracotta paintwork and polished floorboards give this colonial kitchen a homely air.*

Wood was perhaps the most readily available material to the builders of the New World. This is evidenced by its generous use, especially in the weather-boarding of house exteriors and for shutters, both internal and external. Dwellings, in the main, were of wooden construction (though this varied from area to area), and wood was used almost exclusively for heating and cooking purposes. The interior decoration of houses also benefited from its availability: floors and walls were often decked out in the material. In the early days there would have been no skirting/base boards, but structural timbers would often have been left exposed and the fireplace wall might well have been covered with wooden boarding. Later, a wainscoted dado was a familiar sight, and in the very best of houses full-height wall panelling was to be seen. Unless the finest wood had been used, panelling would almost invariably have been painted with a flat or grained finish.

Furniture either arrived with the settlers from Europe or was made locally out of whatever woods were available. The finest pieces were made of mahogany (imported), walnut, chestnut or cherry wood (all locally produced), while the more rudimentary pieces would have been made from maple, oak, birch or ash. Of particular interest is that, even in these very early days, the concept of built-in furniture was already being developed in the more well-appointed homes. Shelves with a cupboard below were a popular means of storage within an alcove.

In interpreting the style today we can choose to reflect the elegant grandeur of the well-established home, or the rusticity of the simpler homestead. The proportions of the space you have available to you, existing furniture and your own personal taste will no doubt dictate which is more appropriate to adopt for your home.

## MATERIAL MATTERS

### WALLS

Walls were generally painted (see 'Colour Cues' on page 227) and woodwork was often depicted in brighter/deeper tones. Sometimes plain walls would be decorated with stencilled Americana motifs. Full-height panelling was rarely seen outside the most elegant of houses but a wainscoted dado was a more common sight. Wallpapers (frequently depicting oriental motifs and sometimes having a flock finish) were available, but these too were very expensive and considered suitable only for the more elevated households.

### FLOORING

Simple scrubbed pine planking was a common flooring in modest homes, while parquet would be seen in grander residences. Sometimes the flooring would be embellished with American folk motifs and at other times plain floors would be covered with painted floor cloths. Carpets (orientals and other imported weaves) were expensive and seen only in the most prestigious homes. Simpler abodes would make do with rag rugs.

*Bright turquoise walls provide a stimulating setting for a dinner for six.*

*In a simpler style, country furnishings complement this Colonial room with its emphasis on natural wood.*

## SOFT FURNISHINGS

Window dressing for the modest home would be a fairly simple matter. A typical treatment would be tab-headed curtains made of a basic cloth, such as ticking, muslin or a simple check fabric, slotted on to a wooden pole. Sometimes there would be no curtains at all – just shutters. A grander house might have festoon blinds or curtains made of imported satin, silk, taffeta, damask or brocade and given an imposing treatment such as swags and tails.

## LIGHTING AND ACCESSORIES

In the early part of the period, lighting was fairly rudimentary. The main sources of light would have been an open fire and candles in holders. Wall sconces were also used, but these too would have been of modest design and sometimes incorporated a reflective back-plate to intensify the available light. Chandeliers are often shown as being typical of the period; however, these were not so widely used. In a grand house they might have been made of brass and of Dutch inspiration. Lower down the scale, iron and wood would have been more common materials. Accessories mainly consisted of dishes, bowls, vases and candlesticks in pewter, earthenware and wood. In smarter homes, imported items of silver and fine china would be found and mirrors were popular.

# PUTTING ON THE STYLE

Homespun or grand, this style will flex in either direction. Perfect for the dedicated needle-person, Colonial style will result in a home that is both elegant and at the same time homely. Suitable for every room, it is perhaps best demonstrated in kitchens, bedrooms and living rooms.

◆ To decorate the walls of a Colonial kitchen, paint with flat paint and hang early kitchen utensils for decoration.

◆ For an elegant room, either a wainscoted dado or full-height panelling can be achieved by applying mouldings (of either wood or polystyrene).

◆ Rag rugs can be bought (or made) and scattered on a wooden floor to add a feeling of warmth to the home.

◆ If trying to evoke the grander style, your seating arrangements could include a camel-back sofa and chairs after the designs of Chippendale. A

wing chair would also be suitable for inclusion (although modern versions of this chair have altered little, for the authentic Colonial look try to find one as near as possible to that shown in the drawing opposite).

◆ For the simple look, choose country Chippedale-style chairs (preferably antique or at least old). Alternatively Dutch, French, English or German country-style chairs can be painted and decorated with hearts and flowers or other Americana motifs. A Windsor chair is typical of the period: try to find one that has an all-spindle back.

◆ Simple curtains made with tab headings slotted on to a wooden pole will provide a typical window treatment of the time.

◆ Wooden shutters are now widely available. Fixed to either the interior or exterior of your home, these will impart a Colonial flavour.

◆ The fireplace is an important feature. A surround in wood with simple classic lines and possibly without a sill would be perfectly in keeping for the mid-range house. The inclusion of andirons would complete the picture.

- A cast-iron wood-burning stove in a living room or kitchen will not only evoke the period but will also provide heating.

- A tall-case clock of the period would provide a fine example of Colonial decoration.

- Pewter was a popular material for drinking vessels, platters and candlesticks. These are widely available at antique fairs and may be used to accessorize your rooms.

- In a bedroom, a patchwork quilt based on traditional designs and draped on the bed will add the correct Colonial period feeling. A four-poster treatment with drapes in toile de jouy would also be appropriate.

- Hand-worked needlepoint cushions and seat covers, especially if depicting a flamestitch or folk pattern, will give your room a Colonial homespun look.

- The skilled needleperson might like to work samplers in the traditional manner. Framed, they will provide typical wall decoration.

## COLOUR CUES

Colours similar to those available in Europe at the time were widely used as well as some surprisingly bright hues. Generally, walls and ceilings would have been painted in matt white, while woodwork was given greater prominence by being painted in deeper, richer tones. Panelling, with the exception of that made of fine mahogany, would have been painted over in a range of colours. As well as plain finishes, paint was often grained or marbled. The science of paint-making was still in its infancy, so it is not necessary, when trying to replicate colours of the period, to be too concerned as to the exactness of shades.

# Gustavian Style

What makes this style so marvellous is the exciting fusion of country rustic with classic grandeur. Well-worn floorboards contrast with elaborately carved mirrors, farmhouse chairs with chandeliers. It is almost as if a once-elevated family had since hit upon hard times – traces of the past, now worn and faded, hinted at in a wall clock here or a delicately painted panel there, now all seeming somehow to belong together, linked by a common distressed and bleached rendering.

This Swedish style should not be confused with the modern streamlined Scandinavian style so approved of throughout the Western world in the 1950s and 1960s. That essentially city style, with its horizontally inclined, tapering furniture and hard-edged fabrics, was a very different animal, unrelated to this gentler simpler version that revels in its age and limited palette.

Gustavian style came to prominence in the eighteenth century and was named after the monarch, King Gustave. Taking inspiration from neo-classicism and other popular themes then so fashionable in France, the Swedish chose to interpret the idiom in a gentler, less ostentatious manner. While France and, in turn, the rest of Europe, indulged in an orgy of marble, gilt, silk and other finery, and artisans toiled from morning till night to produce beautifully carved furniture, exquisitely woven carpets and stunning paintings, the Swedes pared down the look and produced a style of decoration that was altogether more accessible.

Wood features strongly, as might be expected in a country so richly endowed with the material. Some surfaces are left bare, but many are painted in colours of ice – surprising, perhaps, in a land deprived of the sun for so much of the year. But the life of the wood is, in many cases, allowed to show through, the surface merely having been washed with colour or distressed with age.

It might seem as if this mode of decoration could render a room cold and bland, and, as such, appropriate only for warmer climes, but in fact it introduces brightness and lightness to the home. Imagine how your room might appear on a sunny day after snow has fallen outside and you will have a picture of how it will benefit, with everything gleaming and not in the least bit gloomy. And although many of the colours associated with the style are from the chillier side of the spectrum, others, such as pale ochre and barely pink, bring a hint of warm sunshine into rooms.

One of the style's most endearing characteristics is its unpretentiousness. True, you may well find fine items of great value in the Gustavian interior, but these are never displayed to impress. No single item is allowed to shout at you; each one is placed merely to serve the purpose for which it was intended and to be part of the whole scheme of things. It is the same story with accessories, which are few and well spaced, air being valued and allowed to circulate between objects.

*Swedish style in the grand manner – gilt-framed upholstery is arranged before a highly decorated stove.*

# MATERIAL MATTERS

## SURFACES

If the look were to be summarized in one word, that word would be 'bleached'. It is almost as though a room has been submerged beneath the ocean for some years and then left out on the beach to be weathered by the elements like some old ship's timber. Pale floors of lime-washed wooden boards identify the style. Walls also are pale, usually painted a cool pastel colour (particularly aqua) and sometimes divided into panels by the use of a lighter or darker shade. Embellishment might take the form of swags of flowers or vases of swirling floral images – painted or stencilled but always keeping to the limited palette. Blue-and-white tiles might be seen in a bathroom or kitchen and oriental themes are in evidence.

## FURNISHINGS

Furniture constructed from blond wood (typically beech) and finished with wax polish, lime-wash or paint, is illustrative of the style. Furnishings tend to be in either solid country style or a pared-down version of classical taste and often strongly influenced by French Empire styles (such as the chairs shown in the photograph on page 229). The wood grain may be seen, either through a thin wash or layers of distressed paint. Upholstery is straightforward, without buttoning or elaborate trim. Sofas with an exposed wooden

*What could be fresher or prettier than this coolly decorated dining room with its simple window treatments and painted dining chairs?*

*Simple muslin drapes above the bed and at the window soften this delightful Swedish interior and lend it a certain delicacy.*

frame, lyre-back chairs and tripod tea tables are all items characteristic of the period. Fabrics are basic and often cotton-based, checks, stripes and floral designs predominating and often printed in one or two colours on white. Blue features strongly, but green and red are also fitting. Window treatments are likely to be of simplistic design, hanging from wooden poles and made from one of the basic cotton fabrics mentioned above or finer materials such as muslin or voile.

## LIGHTING AND ACCESSORIES

The look is characterized by the sparseness of accessories – English country house style this isn't. Fresh flowers, glassware and bowls of fruit give the right impression. Lighting is provided by continental-style chandeliers, either city-grand or country-plain and bearing candles. Wall sconces in similar styles, and candles lodged in storm lamps and candlesticks of wood, ceramic, pewter or silver are also featured.

# PUTTING ON THE STYLE

Gustavian style belongs to the eighteenth century, yet is bang up to date. You can choose to emphasize either its grander elements if your room possesses suitable proportions, or the more rural features if your home is of a more modest scale. Regardless of climate or orientation, the Gustavian room will always be bright and welcoming. It is a fabulous style for the bedroom, where the pastel palette creates an atmosphere of calm, and is equally suitable for a fresh pretty breakfast room.

◆ If you have painting skills, why not attempt to embellish your walls with painted sections of panelling garnished with flower motifs, all in cool colours? A stencilled border would not look out of place. Should your skills lie in other directions, try creating panels with a background of wallpaper in one colour and cut strips of a slightly different shade to form the framework. Remember to mitre the corners for a professional look.

◆ Wooden tongue-and-groove walling is easy to fix and goes well with the country feeling. Form a dado with it or take it up to ceiling height. A finish of bleached wood or pale paint would be appropriate.

◆ Wooden chairs, purchased from junk shops or auctions for a pittance, can be stripped down. Once the bare wood is exposed, they can be bleached, lime-washed or painted a pale colour or shade of white.

◆ If you already have some high-back dining chairs, rather than spoil the existing finish simply cover them with slip-covers made from canvas or other inexpensive fabric.

◆ To add comfort to wooden upright chairs, make tie-on cushions with short (say, 15cm/6in) pleated skirts.

◆ A dressing table can be created by covering an oblong table (made from MDF for cheapness) with an old, white, embroidered linen table cloth. Topped with a mirror and candlesticks, this will look perfectly in keeping with the style.

◆ On a limited budget, transform a sofa by enclosing it in an off-white decorator's dust sheet. Ensure that the fabric is well tucked down into the seat corners and finish with some pretty cushions of varying textures and colours.

◆ Should you be lucky enough to have shutters at your windows, do nothing other than perhaps ensure that they are of a light shade of wood or paint them in a pale colour.

◆ For an alternative window treatment, make very simple, unlined curtains of a plain or check fabric and hang them from a wooden pole (make sure that the wood of the pole co-ordinates with other wood in the room). Sheers of muslin, lace or voile would also complement your room.

◆ Buy a mirror with a carved frame and paint it off-white. Rub down the surface and reveal the surface below (gilt, paint or raw wood) to give it a distressed look.

◆ The secret of accessorizing the Swedish interior is to practise restraint. Tempting though it might be to enliven the fairly plain background with numerous objects, this should be resisted. Instead limit your selection to a few well-chosen items with a natural theme or to accessories that exhibit interesting textures. You might consider glassware and mirrors, ostrich eggs, shells, twigs, fir cones, beach pebbles and bowls of fruit.

◆ Collect blue-and-white ceramic plates and display these, grouped together symmetrcally, on a wall or arranged on the shelves of a dresser.

◆ For a finishing touch, fill your room with flowers. A large arrangement of lilies in an anodized bucket, or bunches of blossoms and twigs in a stone garden urn, would look spectacular. On a dining table, aged earthenware plant pots filled with well-anchored candles and a selection of fresh-cut herbs will not only enhance the look of the table but will also light it subtly and fill the room with sweet scent.

## COLOUR CUES

Think of verdigris, ice creams, lilies, milk and slubby unbleached silk and you have your palette. Nowadays, paint manufacturers are keen to pro-mote 'hints of' – white paint with a touch of another colour. These less-than-white shades are perfect for a Swedish interior. The addition of discreet touches of aged silver or gold will allow your room to glint at night. Lighting has a big effect on colour rendering and in this case it should be warm and natural – candlelight is perfect.

# Classic English Country House Style

Taking its inspiration from late eighteenth-century designs, the English country house style is constantly being revisited. Originating in southern Europe and popularized by Palladio, the classical idiom was adopted by the English with great enthusiasm, leaving the rest of the continent to divert to other, more elaborate, gilt-laden styles.

What so attracted the English to this elegant but highly restrained way of interior decorating? Perhaps it was their love of order, or perhaps it was just that all those disciplined lines on such a grand scale contrasted so well with the small, undulating English landscape. Whatever the reason, the classical theme has become indelibly identified with English interior design and is constantly being reinterpreted by skilled exponents such as the firm of Colefax and Fowler, and designers John Stephanidis and Nina Campbell among others.

Symmetry, balance and proportion are key elements of the look. Attention, in the first instance, should be given to correcting any room shape distortions, ill-matched details or asymmetrically positioned features. For instance, a fireplace might be repositioned centrally or a second niche created to balance an existing one.

At the very core of the style are the architectural details, such features as cornices, dado rails, skirtings/base boards, panels, niches, friezes and architraves. Once in place, these details will endow a house with a genuine feel of the period and the rooms will require little more than dressing.

As with every other style that has travelled, elements of local taste and conditions have had their influence along the way. The Anglicization of the style has resulted in a much more informal, softer rendering of the classical theme. Furniture is arranged more casually, colours are soft and muted and floral motifs blur the edges.

There is much more to creating classic English country house style than simply gathering together a number of related historical components. It is about adopting a whole new attitude to decorating. If possible, all thoughts of precisely matched patterns and colours should be set aside and everything learnt about sticking scrupulously to a particular period disregarded. The essence of the style is that the contents should appear to have been lovingly collected over the years – favourite pieces handed down through the generations and added to, layer upon layer. This is not an easy task when the interior has to be created instantly and in modern times. Even more difficult to overcome is the decorator's constant urge to co-ordinate the ingredients: this goes against the very nature of English decorating. It is those slightly quirky, discordant features that make the style unique and stop it from becoming too predictable or serious.

Lest you be tempted to imagine that this style requires no special skills of assembly, do not be deceived. Eclectic the room certainly is, but it is also highly engineered, the balance of space, colours and patterns being meticulously planned. The clever bit, after all the careful planning, is in making the room look totally unselfconscious – not unlike the well-dressed woman.

A Georgian country mansion may be thought of as an ideal backdrop for the style, but if your home is modern and of more modest proportions this should not be seen as a barrier to creating a classically inspired home. Indeed, the style may even lend to the smaller room a highly desired sense of grandeur.

*A grand drawing room in the English tradition,*
*its floor a patchwork of oriental carpets.*

# MATERIAL MATTERS

## SURFACES

Fine-quality materials showing their age are in evidence, perhaps best summed up in the term 'shabby chic'. Wood, either in the form of planks or parquet, provides a typical flooring and an aged patina is preferred to a new wood look. Other natural materials such as marble, bricks and stone flags are used to provide alternative hard floors. Raw matting materials, such as jute, coir, seagrass and sisal would not be out of place and, in a utility area, linoleum might be seen. Soft floor finishes are provided by area rugs (oriental, needlepoint and Aubusson are examples) and fitted carpets. Walls might typically be painted and panels picked out in several shades of the same colour or outlined in white. Wallpapers, often with oriental or floral themes, are featured and decorative paint effects – dragging, stippling, sponging, *trompe l'oeil* and so on – are also evocative of the style.

## FURNISHINGS

Soft furnishings, rather than merely forming a dressing for rooms, are central to the classical English interior. Grand windows, for instance, demand grand treatments and beds impress when elaborately draped. Fine furniture too deserves the very best quality upholstery, exquisite fabrics and tasteful trimmings. Textiles such as velvet, silk, tapestry, chintz, wool and linen are much in evidence. Oriental themes and floral motifs are to be seen everywhere. The style was conceived at a time when furniture-making was at its height, with such exponents as Chippendale, Sheraton and Hepplewhite producing the finest examples. These styles might be typical of the period, but furniture from other ages is also acceptable in the eclectic mix that is classic English country house style.

RIGHT *Chintz of the palest pink lines an attractive half-tester bed treatment against walls of grey edged with green.*

OPPOSITE *An important room in the English country house, the bootroom reflects the pursuits and pastimes of the household.*

## LIGHTING AND ACCESSORIES

To match this understated aged room style, the lighting is warm and easy-on-the-eye. Decorative table lamps based on such items as ceramic ginger jars, metal tea caddies and bronze or brass classical columns are typical. Shades are mostly of pleated silk, chosen for the way in which they diffuse the light. These might be accompanied by chandeliers, wall sconces, desk lamps, picture lights, candle lamps and lanterns, all creating soft pools of light that are so instantly welcoming. Accessories form an extremely important ingredient of the English country house interior and, in particular, collections of books, porcelain, framed photographs, memorabilia and paintings are often to be seen displayed in groups. China plates will frequently be hung on walls and books left around in piles. Fresh and dried flowers dotted around the room and housed in a variety of vessels (copper jugs, glass drinking goblets, celery vases and so on) complete the picture.

# PUTTING ON THE STYLE

Install English country house style in your home and you will never be out of fashion. It is a style that, like good wine, will evolve and improve over the years as fabrics fade and furnishings take on that enviable distressed look. Its universality will also ensure that it never looks out of place, even if re-created in a modern apartment or Docklands warehouse. It is a perfect style for the well-proportioned drawing room and is equally at home in an ample hallway.

◆ Foam (much easier to handle than reinforced plaster) architectural details are widely available and simple to fix. A pediment might be fitted over a doorway or perhaps a rail installed at dado height. If adding a cornice, take care not to choose one that is too shallow: remember that, when seen from an angle and at a distance, its dimensions visually shrink.

◆ Modern flush doors can be given a period look by applying moulding to form panels. Try out your measurements in a scaled drawing first.

◆ An open fireplace is an important element of the look. Original surrounds are costly, but cast reproductions in plaster or reconstituted stone are more reasonable. Mounted above the mantel, a gilt mirror will complete the ensemble.

◆ A swags-and-tails curtain treatment or festoon blind will dress windows with suitable grandeur. Should your windows have less-than-generous proportions, fit the curtains well outside the glazed area and allow them to drop to the floor for a more elegant result.

◆ 'Piranese' prints depicting views of ancient Rome and designs for classically inspired furnishings (urns in particular) will instantly identify the theme.

◆ Loose covers made for sofas and arm chairs will give upholstery a suitable country air.

◆ Trawl museum shops for classically inspired ornaments. Plaster busts are especially suitable.

- Masses of mismatched cushions are often to be seen littering sofas. Collect remnants of antique textiles, tapestry and carpets to make your own covers and finish with faded trimmings.

- On a tight budget? Then why not take photocopies from a book of architectural prints, wash them with a weak solution of tea to give them the appearance of age and mount them in frames bought cheaply at auction.

- Garden statuary frequently follows classical lines. Import stone figures and urns from the exterior and highlight with focused lighting for dramatic effect.

- Should your fabrics appear too crisp and new, soak them in tea for that suffering-from-exposure look.

- Start your own collections. Cranberry glass, miniatures, leather-bound volumes of poetry, oriental porcelain plates and other suitable items can all be found at antique shops and fairs. Having a particular category in mind can make shopping a whole lot more exciting.

- In a bedroom, panels of seamed fabric hung from a half-moon corona that is fixed with brackets high on the wall above a bed will transform the room with minimal effort.

- Fill your room with flowers arranged in a variety of traditional vases. If you can so organize it, a dog lying on a rug before an open fire will complete the picture!

## COLOUR CUES

Although many colours, when originally installed, were quite vivid, our interpretation of them today is of more faded hues. Many tints take their inspiration from nature – rose pink, leaf green and buttercup yellow, for instance – while others might have been prompted by the pale blue of oriental china, the beige of stone and the ever-popular eau de nil. If interpreting the style in more brilliant light (say, in Australia or California), it is a good idea to choose more vivid colours that will stand up to the bleaching effect of the sun.

# Oriental Style

Admiration for all things eastern is not a new obsession. Over the years, Europe has returned again and again to the style that brings with it all the mystery, artistry and exotica of the Orient to warm and enliven our lives.

In the eighteenth century, chinoiserie, as the style was known, was much in demand. With the opening up of the trade routes came a taste for new and unaccustomed delights. Fine china, lacquerwork, gorgeous silks and beautifully worked carpets were the chief benefits for the home. At first a prerogative of the court and the aristocracy, but gradually filtering down the social scale via the merchant class, this style was enthusiastically received, adapted and adopted.

Even though home-grown interior design in Europe was probably at its zenith, so exciting was this new style that it was readily taken on by artisans who reinterpreted their familiar European designs with one eye on the Orient. In some cases this must have been disastrous, but history is kind and all that remains today are the finest examples of East meets West. Classic among these must be the work of Thomas Chippendale. Through his ingenuity he was able to merge two very different idioms, producing the familiar Chinese Chippendale style still so popular today.

Historical references apart, oriental style, as it is adopted in modern homes, can be roughly broken down into three differing interpretations: South-east Asian Decorative, Oriental Ethnic and Japanese Minimalist.

South-east Asian Decorative style combines brilliant pure colours with gold – shocking blue and iridescent pink being particular favourites. All kinds of imagery, fabulous fabrics, parasols, kites, lanterns, and wood carving of a standard long since diminished in Europe, are featured. The music is of the 'tinkly' kind and the smells are those of incense: sweet and alluring.

The second category, Oriental Ethnic, summons up a much more earthy look. The colours are those of nature and exciting textures abound. It is a simpler style, without ostentation. Furniture is handcrafted – carved or turned teak, bamboo, rattan and cane being particularly in evidence. Accessories are predominantly of the utensil or ritual variety. Fabrics are dyed the natural way and reflect the colours of the earth and vegetation. The smells are those of the warm earth mixed with exotic spices.

The last grouping, Japanese Minimalism, provides an image of serene peace, clarity and order. Colours are neutral and wood is strongly featured. Everything is pared down to its bare essential state. 'Less is more', and everything in this interior is justified, all superfluous matter having been jettisoned. The straight lines of the architecture are relieved by the elegant curves of fine china bowls, bamboo leaves and sweeping calligraphy. Embellishments are few and well ordered and accessories vary from large-scale pots and plates to precious small items of ivory and jade.

The key to interpreting any of these variations is to start with a fairly bland, naturalistic background and to build up your theme gradually, layer by layer.

*Clever lighting within the cornice gives this oriental-style room an airy feeling, while recessed downlighters highlight the exquisite table.*

# MATERIAL MATTERS

## SURFACES

Interior walls frequently tend not to be the solid structures with which we are familiar in the West. More typical are screens. These may be movable and designed with dominant horizontals as in the Japanese tradition or carved into a fretwork of swirling flowers or strong geometrics. Painted folding screens are also a feature and black lacquer a favourite finish. Grass-cloth wall coverings give a luxurious feel to a room and precious panels of hand-painted oriental wallpaper make a stunning statement in a formal dining room. Apart from these examples, walls tend not to feature strongly beyond forming a background for the room's contents – plain soft-white-painted walls are a safe alternative. Floors tend to be of natural materials: wood, of course, but also terracotta tiles, natural matting (such as jute, sisal or coir) and oriental carpets.

## FURNISHINGS

On the whole, oriental rooms tend to be much more sparsely furnished than their counterparts in the West, an economy to be admired as much from a spacial standpoint as a fiscal one. Teak, a wood strongly associated with the East, is used both as a building material and for constructing furniture. Cane, rattan, ebony, bamboo and lacquerwork are also featured. Seating comes in a variety of guises, but mostly it hugs the ground. A traditional Japanese futon bed based on a low slatted frame and with a roll-up mattress is a useful item that can also serve for seating during the day. Wooden shutters are a typical window treatment and mosquito nets a suitable bed or window dressing. Silk, as a furnishing and fashion material is closely associated with the Orient, and toile de jouy, with its depiction of daily life, an excellent material for summoning up eastern images. Fine embroidery is executed widely and batik a speciality of southern Asia.

## LIGHTING AND ACCESSORIES

The most evocative light fitting is probably the lantern. It is seen throughout the East in various guises and can be made of any number of materials, including paper. Particularly attractive are stone 'temples' which can enclose candles to light a garden at night. Few accessories are used, and these are generally hand-crafted and delicate. Precious stones and ivory are much in evidence.

ABOVE *A simple wooden framework encloses twin beds in this Japanese-inspired bedroom.*

OPPOSITE *Beautifully crafted pots in an aesthetically pleasing arrangement set the mood in this oriental interior.*

# PUTTING ON THE STYLE

In its purest form this exotic style provides a tranquil background to a busy life and, with its minimalist methods, offers a highly fashionable style. Collecting can provide a wonderful excuse to visit some of the most beautiful parts of the world or even prompt a trip to a local Chinatown.

- A flooring of jute, sisal or coir makes an excellent background for oriental artefacts. Either fit the material to close cover or make up as an area rug on a wooden floor.

- An old, hand-carved fretwork door makes an interesting and practical coffee table when supported on four sturdy brown jars and covered with a sheet of glass.

- A folding fretwork screen, fixed to the wall, forms a highly decorative bed head.

- Pinoleum and cane blinds are a solution to window dressing. Their natural construction and tailored finish make them a perfect choice.

- Large metal tea caddies and ceramic ginger jars, when converted, make excellent table lamps. Any lanterns with an oriental feel to them would also be suitable. If you are on a tight budget, a large round paper lantern can be purchased for very little money.

- A ceiling fan (perhaps one that incorporates a light) is very evocative of the East and will be especially welcome on hot summer days.

- Typical oriental blue-and-white china in the form of plates, jars, bowls and vases is widely available. For impact buy big and group closely together on top of a piece of furniture in the eighteenth-century manner.

- Garden centres sell all manner of garden pots imported from the East. Bring these indoors and arrange differing sizes and shapes together. A tall one might even be used as an umbrella stand.

◆ The most beautiful kites in the world come from the Orient. Created from fabric or paper in all shapes and sizes, these make a colourful statement when attached to a wall or hung from a ceiling – an especially suitable form of decoration for a child's bedroom or playroom.

◆ A collection of coolie hats takes on a highly decorative quality if hung on a wall in a group. Focused lighting will bring their textures to life.

◆ The kimono is a beautiful garment. Displayed on a wall (say, above a stairway) and supported by a bamboo pole through the arms, this can bring colour to an otherwise dead area.

◆ A mosquito net with ring support, available from some chain stores or holiday resorts, can be used as a delicate and inexpensive drape for a bed. Simply fix it to a hook attached to the ceiling above the bed.

◆ Orchids and bird-of-paradise flowers have the necessary delicacy and sculptural profile to qualify for this theme. Blossoms also are characteristic. Whatever blooms are selected, they should be arranged carefully with great dedication and artistry.

# COLOUR CUES

Think of the colours of saffron, cinnamon and paprika. Mix these hues with the blue of Chinese porcelain and the green of jade and celadon stoneware. Hint at the bright red and gold of Thai temples and the vivid orange of monks' robes. This will give you the basis for a palette that reflects all the richness of the Orient.

# American Shaker Style

It is easy to see why this simple but elegant style is currently undergoing a revival. The clean lines, the honest use of natural materials, the lack of ornamentation – all are values much appreciated in today's world. Many of us have realized that the ostentation of previous decades serves only to crowd and complicate our already busy lives and we now hanker after a purer, plainer backdrop to our daily activities. Amazingly, while over-the-top, cluttered Victorian style was at its most popular in England, Shaker style in all its simplicity was thriving simultaneously a mere few thousand miles away.

The Shaker movement was introduced into America by an Englishwoman, Ann Lee, who gathered together like-minded people who could not find an accommodation for their beliefs within the Quaker community in Europe. They set off for the New World in the latter part of the eighteenth century, searching for an environment where they could practise communal life based upon humility, simplicity and, above all, honesty in everything. Initially they settled in New England but, as the number of followers increased, they gradually moved further west, establishing communities as they went. Despite the vast distances between settlements, all exhibited a remarkable uniformity of lifestyle and the movement does not appear to have suffered from dilution as it spread. The style is therefore easily identified and interpreted.

Despite the restrictions imposed by the unavailability of certain materials locally and by the lack of funds, Shaker buildings and furnishings were, though humble, always elegant, exquisitely designed and beautifully crafted. Their furniture was made of the finest timber and was worked by the most skilled of craftsmen. Quality and simplicity were their bywords and wood (principally from the maple tree) the material most easily accessed.

In order to adopt this classic rural style today, a total rethink of decorating approach is necessary. Any indulgence in embellishment for its own sake should be resisted. All thoughts of ornamentation and pattern need to be restrained and any items which are considered solely for their decorative qualities discarded in favour of more functional pieces. The quotation 'Beauty rests with utility' sums up the Shaker approach.

For the Shakers a sense of order was paramount. Everything had its purpose and everything its place. Storage was therefore a speciality. Much of this was built in and what loose items remained in a room (chairs, baskets, shoes and so on) were hung tidily on peg rails which ran around the circumference of nearly every room at approximately picture-rail height. These timber rails would be built into the wall, their surface lying flush with the surface of the plaster, and wooden pegs would be fixed at intervals of approximately 20–30cm/8–12in.

The reliance on wood as a building and furnishing material was almost total. In most cases it was left unadorned, but on occasions when it was painted this was more likely to be done with a type of wash rather than with opaque colour, so that the wood grain could still show through – demonstrating, yet again, honesty in all things.

*Demonstrating that Shaker style need not be neat and neutral,
this brilliant-blue bedroom declares its colours.*

# MATERIAL MATTERS

## SURFACES

Walls were most often plain-painted, underscoring the austerity of the look. Soft white was perhaps the most typical non-colour seen in interiors, but other pastels were also called upon. Woodwork – window frames and shutters, skirting/base boards, doors, peg rails and sometimes dados – were usually bereft of anything but the simplest of mouldings and might have been painted in a darker shade of the wall colour. Cornices were rarely a feature of the Shaker home. The most usual flooring to be seen was simply treated wood planking, sometimes covered with home-made rag rugs.

## FURNISHINGS

Because of the lack of diverting decorations on walls and floors in the Shaker home, great reliance for interest was placed upon beautifully crafted pieces of furniture. In nearly every case, furniture was both delicate and, at the same time, extremely strong. Many designs were based upon items of furniture brought with the members from the Old World – the ladder-back chair, with either a cane or fabric tape seat and sometimes on rockers, epitomizes the style.

Fitted storage units were also a feature of Shaker interiors and, once again, these were efficiently designed and made to exacting standards. Soft furnishings did not play a large part in the decoration of homes, comfort not being high on the agenda. At windows, in preference to curtains, shutters would most often be used to provide privacy and to shut out exterior elements.

## LIGHTING AND ACCESSORIES

In line with Shakers' beliefs, few accessories would have adorned their homes. The exception might have been simple wooden boxes, usually round or oval in shape, left plain and seen stacked one upon another. Baskets lined with fabric and other purposeful items might also have been displayed. The main source of artificial light was candles. These would generally be placed in simple candlesticks of wood or metal. Bent and pierced tinware was a popular material and was used to make lanterns and different styles of candle-holders. Ironware also featured in the Shaker home – items such as hooks, coat hangers and rails were made of this material and would frequently incorporate a heart-shaped motif.

RIGHT *Simple purposeful items are true to Shaker ideals in this Massachusetts kitchen.*

OPPOSITE *A plain plank flooring, tongue-and-groove dado and practical peg rail all point to this bathroom's Shaker origins.*

# PUTTING ON THE STYLE

Economical to install and simplistic in finish, this is a style that even the most modest of DIY decorators could interpret successfully. Shaker style is perfect for the Georgian home with its small-paned windows and comfortable proportions, but would not be out of place in any building of simple structure. The essence of the style relies upon clean lines, craftsmanship and a sense of order: look for these qualities when selecting pieces to introduce to your Shaker room and you will not go far wrong.

◆ For walls, an oil-based paint with a flat or soft sheen finish in a suitable colour (see 'Colour Cues' opposite) will provide an apt background for your furnishings. Alternatively, a gentle wash of pale terracotta will bestow on your room a 'new plaster' look. Woodwork in a deeper tone than that chosen for the walls will give the room definition.

◆ A wood plank floor is typical of the period. For a softer feel, make your own rag rugs from fabric remnants and place these around the room.

◆ Furniture is the most important ingredient. Original pieces can be hard to find these days and are expensive to buy. However, reproduction items are widely available and reasonable in price. Non-Shaker furniture will not look out of place so long as it follows the same clean lines as the genuine pieces.

◆ In a bedroom, a wooden bed frame in a country style or a four-post framework in tapering timber would both be suitable. Beds are best left undraped, but a cover of patchwork quilting can be added to emphasize the American folk theme. A chest in classic Shaker style at the foot of the bed could provide an ideal resting place for a folded spread.

◆ An old metal stove in the style of the period will add interest and, if in working condition, will warm your room in the traditional way.

◆ Although, strictly speaking, bare windows are more typical, a soft treatment would not look inappropriate if kept simple. A plain roller blind would have the right feel, as would simply gathered curtains of a basic cloth such as plaid cotton, ticking, canvas or gingham.

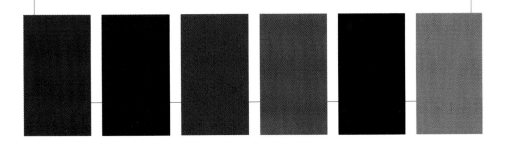

◆ Lots and lots of candlesticks, especially of a characteristic plain design from the period and made of wood or metal, will give your room the correct feel. Also appropriate for lighting the room are metal chandeliers and wall sconces of the simplest design.

◆ Make a simple peg rail from narrow planks of wood and surface-fix at about eye level around the room. Wooden pegs for preference (alternatively, metal hooks) should be inserted at intervals of approximately 20–30cm/8–12in.

◆ A simple and cheap way to store items such as books and cutlery is simply to wrap them in gingham or similar fabric squares. Shoe boxes can be covered with canvas or plaid fabric to hold other small items and drawstring bags constructed to accommodate toys, laundry and so on. Baskets could also be put to good use.

◆ Although accessories are limited in a true Shaker interior, typical boxes, coloured with wood stain in a variety of hues and stacked one upon another in graded sizes, will set off an otherwise rather monastic interior. Items such as home-made dolls, simple picture frames, utensils and agricultural tools might also be displayed.

◆ Although not within the true Shaker tradition, naïve paintings of domestic animals and pretty embroidered samplers in plain frames might be hung on the walls to add interest to this austere interior.

## COLOUR CUES

Deep natural colours made from earth pigments predominate, terracotta being the colour most associated with the exterior of Shaker buildings. The cost of pure white paint prohibited its frequent use, but subtle variations of off-white were common. Interior woodwork was most often painted a deep slate blue or darker shade of the wall colour and bedsteads were frequently painted green. Ochre, plum and beige were popular wall colours.

# INDEX

Page numbers in *italic* refer to the illustrations

# PHOTOGRAPHIC ACKNOWLEDGEMENTS

*The publishers have made every effort to contact copyright holders whose pictures are included in this book; however, omissions may inadvertently have occurred, and they will be pleased to hear from any copyright holder whose work is not properly acknowledged.*

**Camera Press Ltd** 12, 89, 136, 149, 153, 157, 169-70, 212, 218, 230, 243, 247, Appeltoffl 68, 231, Avotakk 207, J. & I. Kurtz 213, Schneider 145, Symons 75; **Robert Harding Picture Library** Brook 100, Michael Jenner 189, Jonathan Pilkington 65, Walter Rawlings 249, Adam Woolfitt 183; **Robert Harding Sindycation** Henry Bourne/ Homes and Gardens 116, Simon Brown/Country Homes and Interiors 41, Marie Clare 83, Brian Harrison/Country Homes and Interiors 173, 181-2, Homes and Gardens 85, 161, Mark Luscombe-Whyte/Homes and Gardens 141, James Merrell/Homes and Gardens 173, Hugh Palmer/Country Homes and Interiors 60, Peter Reuter/Country Homes and Interiors 37, Trevor Richards/Homes and Gardens 237, Schulenburg/Homes and Gardens 97, 107, 217, Country Homes and Interiors (Designer: Stephen Ryan) 133, Brad Simmons 146, 223, 225, **Interior Archive** Tim Beddowns 236; James Mortimer 33, 38, Schulenburg 25, 11, 199, 229, 235, 241-2; **Jane Nelson Associates** 77; John Spragg (Designer: David Hicks) 7-8, 19, 21, 28-9, 35, 46, 73, 81, 93, 98, 106, 112, 115, 129, 163, 176; **Times Syndication** Jeremy Young 143; **Elizabeth Whiting Associates** 2, 53, 57, 123, 125, 139, 164, 179, 187-8, 193-5, 200, 205-6, 211, 214, 219, 224, 248; **Henry Wilson** (Designer: Stephen Ryan) 31, 42, 109, 121.

Sketches on pages 110, 111, 122, 134, 135 from designs by Stephen Ryan.

# MEASUREMENT CONVERSION CHART

### Inches

### Metres and millimetres

| Feet \ Inches | 0 | 1 | 2 | 3 | 4 | 5 | 6 | 7 | 8 | 9 | 10 | 11 |
|---|---|---|---|---|---|---|---|---|---|---|---|---|
| 0 |  | 25 | 51 | 76 | 102 | 127 | 152 | 178 | 203 | 229 | 254 | 279 |
| 1 | 305 | 330 | 356 | 381 | 406 | 432 | 457 | 483 | 508 | 533 | 559 | 584 |
| 2 | 610 | 635 | 660 | 686 | 711 | 737 | 762 | 787 | 813 | 838 | 864 | 889 |
| 3 | 914 | 940 | 965 | 991 | 1.016 | 1.041 | 1.067 | 1.092 | 1.118 | 1.143 | 1.168 | 1.194 |
| 4 | 1.219 | 1.245 | 1.270 | 1.295 | 1.321 | 1.346 | 1.372 | 1.397 | 1.422 | 1.448 | 1.473 | 1.499 |
| 5 | 1.524 | 1.549 | 1.575 | 1.600 | 1.626 | 1.651 | 1.676 | 1.702 | 1.727 | 1.753 | 1.778 | 1.803 |
| 6 | 1.829 | 1.854 | 1.880 | 1.905 | 1.930 | 1.956 | 1.981 | 2.007 | 2.032 | 2.057 | 2.083 | 2.108 |
| 7 | 2.134 | 2.159 | 2.184 | 2.210 | 2.235 | 2.261 | 2.286 | 2.311 | 2.337 | 2.362 | 2.388 | 2.413 |
| 8 | 2.438 | 2.464 | 2.489 | 2.515 | 2.540 | 2.565 | 2.591 | 2.616 | 2.642 | 2.667 | 2.692 | 2.718 |
| 9 | 2.743 | 2.769 | 2.794 | 2.819 | 2.845 | 2.870 | 2.896 | 2.921 | 2.946 | 2.972 | 2.997 | 3.023 |
| 10 | 3.048 | 3.073 | 3.098 | 3.124 | 3.150 | 3.175 | 3.200 | 3.226 | 3.251 | 3.277 | 3.302 | 3.327 |
| 11 | 3.353 | 3.378 | 3.404 | 3.429 | 3.454 | 3.480 | 3.505 | 3.531 | 3.556 | 3.581 | 3.607 | 3.632 |
| 12 | 3.658 | 3.683 | 3.708 | 3.734 | 3.759 | 3.785 | 3.810 | 3.835 | 3.861 | 3.886 | 3.912 | 3.937 |
| 13 | 3.962 | 3.988 | 4.013 | 4.039 | 4.064 | 4.089 | 4.115 | 4.140 | 4.166 | 4.191 | 4.216 | 4.242 |
| 14 | 4.267 | 4.293 | 4.318 | 4.343 | 4.369 | 4.394 | 4.420 | 4.445 | 4.470 | 4.496 | 4.521 | 4.547 |
| 15 | 4.572 | 4.597 | 4.623 | 4.648 | 4.674 | 4.699 | 4.724 | 4.750 | 4.775 | 4.801 | 4.826 | 4.851 |
| 16 | 4.877 | 4.902 | 4.928 | 4.953 | 4.978 | 5.004 | 5.029 | 5.055 | 5.080 | 5.105 | 5.131 | 5.156 |
| 17 | 5.182 | 5.207 | 5.232 | 5.258 | 5.283 | 5.309 | 5.334 | 5.359 | 5.385 | 5.410 | 5.436 | 5.461 |
| 18 | 5.486 | 5.512 | 5.537 | 5.563 | 5.588 | 5.613 | 5.639 | 5.664 | 5.690 | 5.715 | 5.740 | 5.766 |
| 19 | 5.791 | 5.817 | 5.842 | 5.867 | 5.893 | 5.918 | 5.944 | 5.969 | 5.994 | 6.020 | 6.045 | 6.071 |
| 20 | 6.096 | 6.121 | 6.147 | 6.172 | 6.198 | 6.223 | 6.248 | 6.274 | 6.299 | 6.325 | 6.350 | 6.375 |
| 21 | 6.401 | 6.426 | 6.452 | 6.477 | 6.502 | 6.528 | 6.553 | 6.579 | 6.604 | 6.629 | 6.655 | 6.680 |
| 22 | 6.706 | 6.731 | 6.756 | 6.782 | 6.807 | 6.833 | 6.858 | 6.883 | 6.909 | 6.934 | 6.960 | 6.985 |
| 23 | 7.010 | 7.036 | 7.061 | 7.087 | 7.112 | 7.137 | 7.163 | 7.188 | 7.214 | 7.239 | 7.264 | 7.290 |
| 24 | 7.315 | 7.341 | 7.366 | 7.391 | 7.417 | 7.442 | 7.468 | 7.493 | 7.518 | 7.544 | 7.569 | 7.595 |
| 25 | 7.620 | 7.645 | 7.671 | 7.696 | 7.722 | 7.747 | 7.772 | 7.798 | 7.823 | 7.849 | 7.874 | 7.899 |
| 26 | 7.925 | 7.950 | 7.976 | 8.001 | 8.026 | 8.052 | 8.077 | 8.103 | 8.128 | 8.153 | 8.179 | 8.204 |
| 27 | 8.230 | 8.255 | 8.280 | 8.306 | 8.331 | 8.357 | 8.382 | 8.407 | 8.433 | 8.458 | 8.484 | 8.509 |
| 28 | 8.534 | 8.560 | 8.585 | 8.611 | 8.636 | 8.661 | 8.687 | 8.712 | 8.738 | 8.763 | 8.788 | 8.814 |
| 29 | 8.839 | 8.865 | 8.890 | 8.915 | 8.941 | 8.966 | 8.992 | 9.017 | 9.042 | 9.068 | 9.093 | 9.119 |
| 30 | 9.144 |  |  |  |  |  |  |  |  |  |  |  |